MY
70 YEARS
OF SPURS

NORMAN
GILLER

MY
70 YEARS
OF SPURS

A Long Walk Down
White Hart Lane

A Norman Giller Books Publication
In association with Pitch Publishing

First published by Pitch Publishing, 2021

Pitch Publishing
A2 Yeoman Gate
Yeoman Way
Worthing
Sussex
BN13 3QZ
www.pitchpublishing.co.uk
info@pitchpublishing.co.uk

ISBN 978 1 78531 889 4

Typesetting and origination by Pitch Publishing
Printed and bound in the UK by TJ Books, Cornwall

Contents

In memory of 'Sir' Bill Nicholson,

The heart and soul of Spurs

ACKNOWLEDGEMENTS

I THANK Steve Perryman for his fee-free introduction, and pledge that a share of any profits will go to the Tottenham Tribute Trust who quietly help many of our old heroes. Thanks, too, to omniscient Tottenham disciple David Guthrie for his fact-checking, to number-one son, Michael, for his in-depth knowledge, and to Spurs Odyssey webmaster Paul H. Smith and *BackPass* editor Mike Berry for their support. Bowing the knee, relatively speaking, to brother and sister Paul and Jane Camillin of Pitch Publishing for their positive and productive work in surreal times, Duncan Olner for making me suitably jacketed; also thanks to diligent editor Gareth Davis, proofreader Nigel Matheson, and layout artist Graham Hales.

I could not have been so accurate with my reminiscences without the statistical facts and figures over the decades from Tottenham loyalists Les Yates, Andy Porter and John Fennelly, plus the extraordinary My Football Facts website pioneered by Paul Yarden. Thanks also for the encouragement from Voice of Spurs, Paul Coyte and my friends Mike Leigh and Theo Delaney at The Spurs Show.

I have repeated many of the stats and facts from a previous book of mine, *The Managing Game*, and for that diligent research I am again indebted to that fount of all Spurs knowledge, David Guthrie.

Across the years I have been furnished with photographs for my private collection by late, great Fleet Street cameramen Monte Fresco, Norman 'Speedy' Quicke and Bob Stiggins, combined with the up-to-date pictures from the exceptional agencies, Getty Images, Colorsport and Alamy.

Both the publishers and I acknowledge that this book, *My 70 Years of Spurs*, does not have official recognition from Tottenham Hotspur Football Club. The views expressed are entirely those of the author, and I accept that all historic facts about Spurs are the intellectual property of the club. Thank you, Spurs, for allowing me to share my memories. It's been a long and winding White Hart memory Lane. COYS!

INTRODUCTION
STEVE PERRYMAN MBE

Captained Tottenham in back-to-back FA Cup Final triumphs and played a club record 854 games for Spurs

I HAVE known Norman Giller for more than 50 years, and clearly remember the first time we were introduced by legendary manager Bill Nicholson. It was at the then Tottenham training ground at Cheshunt, and Norman was there in his role as chief football reporter for the *Daily Express*. I was 17 and about to play my first game for the Spurs first-team, and Bill said to Norman, 'I'd like you to meet Steve Perryman, a diamond of a prospect.'

Bill famously never threw around compliments, and he later told Norman that he had said it to boost my confidence, knowing he was throwing me in at the deep end. It certainly worked because I felt like a giant when I made my debut, little realising I would go on to play a club record 854 games in the famous Lilywhite shirt.

Norman was there for many of my games, sitting in the press box and reporting on what were golden years, including the winning of two back-to-back FA Cup Finals at Wembley – both after replays. I had to work hard for my winners' medals!

When I want to know the history of Spurs, Norman is the man I turn to. He is a walking record book on the club's past, and no wonder. He first saw Tottenham play in the Push and Run championship season of 1950/51, the little matter of 70 years ago! He started reporting on them professionally in 1958, the year that Bill Nick became manager, kicking off with that famous 10-4 victory over Everton. Throughout Bill's 16 years as Spurs boss, Norman was closer to him than most and got many great interviews, several of which are featured in this revealing book.

Norman was even closer to the one and only Jimmy Greaves, and together they have produced 20 books. Jim would undoubtedly have been providing this introduction but for the savage stroke that hit him in 2015, shortly after Norman and I had helped him celebrate his 75th birthday at a dinner organised by our mutual mate, Terry Baker.

I was very happy to deputise for Greavsie, particularly when Norman told me that he will be sharing any profits from this book with the Tottenham Tribute Trust that quietly helps those old Tottenham pros who missed the gravy train of the Premier League days. The Trust pays medical and care bills without song or dance. It just gets the job done.

Virtually every manager since the 1950s has been interviewed by Norman, and he uses this inside information to make this fascinating book authoritative, informative and entertaining. Seventy years of watching Spurs. Wow! Enjoy.

KICK-OFF
by Norman Giller

THE YEARS between the two photographs on pages 14 and 15 have been filled with me watching the rollercoaster fortunes of a Tottenham Hotspur Football Club that have demanded a faith, loyalty and love – yes, love – that you would not find outside the strongest of marriages.

I am not a boastful type (he boasted), but I know I am the only person walking this earth who could write this book. For a start you need to be firstly, 80-plus (check), secondly, to have watched the Push and Run side that was the first Tottenham championship team (check), thirdly, reported from the original White Hart Lane press box *and* the new stately, state-of-the-art 'media centre' (check).

I have supported Spurs since the 1950/51 Push and Run season and have reported from the press box on their trials, tribulations and triumphs since 1958, the year that 'Sir' Bill Nicholson took the reins as manager. We became good friends, as have many of the main characters in the following pages, so hopefully the book carries an authority that will crush those critics who would claim I am not a true supporter.

The fact is I have never put my hand in my pocket to watch Spurs play, so that – many will consider – disqualifies me from calling myself a Lilywhite supporter. But I like to think I have made up for it by continually making donations to the Tottenham Tribute Trust from the proceeds of my Tottenham-themed books. The Trust, quietly without fuss or fanfare, helps our old heroes who are now paying the often-painful price of all the efforts they made on the pitch to entertain and excite us. I will be sharing any profits from these memoirs with the Trust, so my conscience is clear about calling myself a Spurs supporter.

Throughout my Fleet Street reporting years I had to hide my unswerving support for Spurs because in a press box you have to at least give the impression of being neutral. Now, as I enjoy the last of the summer wine, I can come out of the closet and for several years I have had a home and a voice on the highly respected Spurs Odyssey website, run by Tottenham disciple Paul H. Smith.

So that I do not wander, I have disciplined myself to sharing my 70 years of Tottenham memories through the processional order of the managers who have been holding the reins, starting from the original 'one of our own', Edmonton-born Arthur Rowe, back in the 1950s. I am retelling many of the tales I have told previously, and my regular readers (okay, reader) of my 114 books to date might feel they are reading familiar passages. There is no way I can rewrite history.

I come right up to date with a chronicle of the surreal 2020/21 season that just happened to be the 120th anniversary of Tottenham's 1901 FA Cup triumph, the centenary of the 1921 FA Cup win, the platinum celebration

of the 1951 Push and Run title, the diamond jubilee of the 1961 Double year, the ruby anniversary of Ricky's 'Goal of the Century' in the 1981 FA Cup Final, and, of course, the pearl anniversary of the last time Spurs won the FA Cup in 1991.

It's been quite a journey and I invite you now to make yourself comfortable as you accompany me on my first date with Spurs. It was love at first flight.

1

Love at First Flight

IT WAS 70 years ago that I first clapped eyes on Tottenham Hotspur, and it was love at first flight – witnessing goalkeeper legend Ted Ditchburn diving across his goal as if in imitation of Superman. Come with me back to Saturday, 2 September 1950. The place: The Valley; the match: Charlton Athletic versus Tottenham Hotspur. There I was – a skinny as a pipe cleaner ten-year-old primary schoolboy in my older brother's hand-me-down short trousers – trembling with excitement and anticipation of my first view of First Division football. I had been taken south of the Thames from my East End home by my uncle, Roy Robinson, who was expecting to convert me to his religion of worshipping Charlton.

The classic opening words to *The Go Between* by novelist L.P. (Leslie) Hartley are captured perfectly by the whirling world of football, 'The past is a foreign country ... they do things differently there.' It was a different game then, not just another country but another planet. Ration book times, London still being rebuilt after the Second World War blitz, footballers earning £11 a week, going to and from the ground in their Demob suits, like the rest of us by bus and speaking a language that would be foreign to today's players.

There were wing-halves, inside-forwards, shoulder-charging and barging of goalkeepers, tackling from behind, two points for a win, no floodlights, no yellow and red cards, no TV cameras (certainly no VAR), a leather and laced, panelled ball that was like a pudding on heavy, mud-heap pitches that made every step a challenge.

This trip to The Valley of dreams cost my uncle three shillings (15p), two bob for him and a shilling for me to stand on the vast, concrete terracing behind the goal at the Floyd Road end of the sprawling stadium. There were 61,480 mostly standing spectators shoehorned into the ground, and I could not see a thing through the heaving wall of fans towering above me.

No problem. Dock worker Uncle Roy picked me up as if I was a packing case and handed me high to the man in front, and I was carried – the stench of Weights and Woodbines cigarette smoke in my nostrils – on a willing relay of raised hands above hundreds of heads, most adorned with flat caps, and down to a cramped standing place against the fence, right behind the goal being defended by Tottenham.

I will not pretend that 70 years on I can remember the exact details of the match, but what has remained with me is the sense of excitement and the sheer ecstasy of feeling as if I was involved in the action. Yes, a spectator but I kicked every ball, scored goals that were missed and made every save. All these years later that sense of involvement in every game has never left me. I have been the Ron Burgess, the Len Duquemin, the Greavsie, the Glenn Hoddle, the Ledley

King, the Harry Kane of spectators. If only they would play the game the way I see it, my team would never lose.

Uncle Roy had been teaching me chants, 'Come on, you Robins'; 'Get in there, you Addicks.' He wanted me to wear a red and white rosette as big as my head, but instinct made me declare myself too shy to pin it to my jacket. Little did he know that I had been nobbled before he got to me by another uncle, Eddie Baldwin of Edmonton, who was my godfather.

He and Aunt Emmy, Dad's youngest sister, were Spurs through and through, and followed them home and away. The home bit was easy. They lived within the crowd's roar of White Hart Lane. They had been filling my head and my imagination with stories of the great Tottenham teams, and telling me how they had waltzed away with the Second Division title in 1949/50 with what was known as Push and Run football. The cynics sneered that it was playground football that would be exposed in the top echelon of the First Division.

Now here I was immediately behind the goal at The Valley watching Arthur Rowe's Spurs chase and chastise Charlton with their push-and-run tactics that were simple yet sophisticated, predictable yet played to perfection. They followed the Arthur Rowe commandments, 'When not in possession get into position … make it simple, make it quick … keep the ball on the ground … the three As, accuracy, accuracy, accuracy.'

At right-back, Alf 'The General' Ramsey was showing the poise and polish that made him a regular in the England team. Ahead of him, gingery-haired right-half Billy (that's what they called him then) Nicholson was full of energy and urgency, making the team tick with his unselfish running and tigerish tackling.

Striding across the pitch like a colossus, skipper Ronnie Burgess, as tough as if hewn from a Welsh mountain but able to intersperse delicate skill with his startling strength (no wonder Bill Nick later described him to me as the greatest player ever to pull on a Spurs shirt). Burgess would prompt the attack, and then in the blink of an eye be back at the heart of the defence helping out alongside immense centre-half Harry Clarke.

Imperious in the centre of the pitch was the thick-thighed emperor of the team, Eddie Baily, the 'Cheeky Chappie' of the dressing room who could land a ball on a sixpence from 40 yards. He was the schemer in chief, providing a conveyor belt of telling passes for twin centre-forwards Len 'The Duke' Duquemin and Londoner Les Bennett. The Duke was a Channel Islander, the nearest thing to a 'foreigner' on the Spurs books.

Tottenham's alternative route to goal was down the wings, with flying Sonny Walters and tricky Les Medley turning defences inside out with their stunning running. Their crosses, usually to the far post, were met high and mightily by the Duke or Bennett, both of whom could head the ball as hard as I could kick it.

Incredibly, 15 or so years later, I would be regularly interviewing Alf, Bill Nick, Ron Burgess and Eddie Baily in my role as chief football reporter for the *Daily Express*. Seeing them through my schoolboy eyes they were like giants, but one player stood above them all.

In about the tenth minute of the match, Charlton's powerhouse centre-forward Charlie Vaughan shook off a challenge from Harry Clarke and unleashed a thunderbolt shot from the edge of the Tottenham penalty area. From my best view in the ground, I could see that the ball was going to fly into the top-right corner of the net. Fifty thousand of the 62,000 crowd – Charlton fans – roared in anticipation of a goal and hundreds of wooden rattles produced an ear-shattering background effect like a snarl of snare drums.

Then out of nowhere appeared somebody doing his Superman impression. Was it a bird, was it a plane? No, it was the flying form of goalkeeper Ted Ditchburn, not touching the ball away like most goalkeepers would have tried to do. My schoolboy eyes looked on in amazement as he caught the ball while at full stretch and in mid-air.

It was a stunning, astonishing save that silenced everybody but the knot of 12,000 travelling Tottenham fans at the other end of the ground, who switched from cheering to choruses of the club theme song, 'McNamara's Band'.

From that moment on I was a Tottenham disciple. Yes, it was love at first flight.

Throughout a long football reporting career I had to stick to press box neutrality, and it was not until surrendering newspaper work for full-time authorship that I was able to come out of the closet as a Spurs supporter.

And I can trace the start of my love affair to that magical moment when Ted Ditchburn appeared to defy gravity and make a save that has lived on in my memory. Thank goodness there were no television action replays to taint or tarnish the picture in my head. It still sits there, and is occasionally brought out from the vaults of my memory and admired, without anybody being able to produce proof that perhaps, just perhaps, I have exaggerated the lightning shaft of genius that turned me into a lover of all things Lilywhite.

For the record, Tottenham forced a 1-1 draw thanks to an Alf Ramsey penalty and they pushed and ran their way to the league championship.

And a ten-year-old boy in his brother's hand-me-down short trousers went home to the East End converted to the Tottenham way of playing football.

I was off on my 70-year journey. Please take every step with me in the company of the managers who have called the shots.

2

ARTHUR ROWE
Professor of Push and Run

Born: Tottenham, 1 September 1906
Died: Norbury, London, 5 November 1993
Appointed: 1 May 1949
Resigned: 1 July 1955
Games managed: 293
Won: 135
Drawn: 59
Lost: 89
Goals scored: 517
Goals conceded: 387
Win percentage: 47.70

WHEN THE Tottenham players reported back for league duty at White Hart Lane after the Second World War they found themselves under the management of a man who had been a legend – with Arsenal. Enter Joe Hulme, whose flying right-wing exploits in the Herbert Chapman era had made him a hero at Highbury. Hulme steered Spurs to the 1948 FA Cup semi-final, where they were beaten at Villa

Park by a Stanley Matthews-inspired Blackpool. He felt quite at home at the Lane, because for nearly seven years since the outbreak of war Arsenal had shared the ground with Tottenham while Highbury was requisitioned as an Air Raid Precaution Centre.

But Joe was never totally accepted by the old enemy, and when he moved on in 1949 to a distinguished career in journalism it was a Spurs-through-and-through-man – Arthur Rowe – who took over as manager.

I now dip into previous Tottenham history journeys of mine to give Arthur Rowe the platform he deserves in my 70-year odyssey. I caught up with Arthur in my *Daily Express* reporting days when he was 'curator' of the short-lived PFA-supported Football Hall of Fame in Oxford Street in the early 1970s (a venture that quickly died because of lack of public interest before being revived in Manchester).

A gentle, kindly man, Arthur was easy to talk to and we had many long conversations about his career in the game in general and his management of Spurs in particular.

He revealed that the art of push and run football – the signature style of Spurs – was born against the walls of north London. Tottenham-born Arthur, the chief architect of the meticulous method, remembered playing with a tennis ball against the wall as an Edmonton schoolboy and suddenly thought to himself, 'That's how easy and simple the game should be!'

I caught Arthur in reflective mood 20 years after he had entered the land of football legend by steering Spurs to back-to-back Second and First Division titles. Speaking quietly, with a discernible Cockney accent, he told me:

(My philosophy was that the easier you made the game the easier it was to play it. So I used to tell the players to push the ball to a team-mate and then run into space to take the instant return pass. It was making the most of the "wall pass" or the "one-two". Make it simple, make it quick. It was easier said than done, of course, but I got together a squad of players with the football intelligence to make it work. We used to operate in triangles, with Eddie Baily, Ronnie Burgess and Les Medley particularly brilliant at the concept out on the left. It was amazing to watch as they took defenders out of the game with simple, straightforward passes and then getting into position to receive the return. Over on the right Alf Ramsey, Billy Nicholson and Sonny Walters were equally adept at keeping possession while making progress with simple passes. It was very similar to the style I introduced while coaching in Hungary before the war.)

Arthur, as modest and likeable a man as you could wish to meet, was never one to want to take credit for his own genius. He would always stress that the real father of Push and Run was his old Tottenham mentor Peter McWilliam, who had been a noted tactician in two spells in charge at White Hart Lane.

McWilliam was building Tottenham's 1921 FA Cup-winning team when Arthur joined Spurs as a schoolboy. The Scot had been an idol on Tyneside in his playing days and was nicknamed 'Peter the Great' by the Geordie fans. He brought his play-it-on-the-floor footballing philosophy into management and helped launch Arthur's playing career with the Spurs nursery team, Gravesend and Northfleet. He carried on the Spurs tradition – started by fellow Scot John Cameron in the Edwardian days – of encouraging football that was smooth, stylish and sophisticated, and played along the ground. 'It's a game of fit'ba not heed ba',' he was fond of saying in his strong Scottish burr as he watched contemptuously the teams who played the hump-it-high-and-long game, a crude version of what is known today as route one. He wanted the kick-and-rush method rooted and booted out, and laid the foundations to the style that became known as Push-and-Run. His methods not only brought winning results but also had a huge influence on the thoughts and deeds of two future Tottenham legends under his spell, Arthur Rowe and Bill Nicholson.

Rowe developed into a thinking man's centre-half for Tottenham throughout the 1930s until a knee injury forced his retirement after an international career confined to one England cap. He travelled through Europe as a full-time coach and was on the verge of accepting the Hungarian team manager's job when war was declared. There is a school of thought that it was his ideas passed on to young Hungarian players that was the foundation for the Magical Magyars of the 1950s, who buried 'the Old Masters' of England under an avalanche of 13 goals in two mesmeric matches.

His son, Graham, who lives in Los Angeles where he operated as a financial adviser, made perfectly pertinent points about his father's impact on football in a 2006 letter to the sports section of the esteemed *Financial Times*. I tracked down Graham in California, and I am grateful for his permission to publish his letter here:

Sir, In his piece "Magyars mourn their lost magic", Jonathan Wilson states, "Half a century ago Hungary were not merely the best in the world but possibly the best team there has ever been."

'I disagree with his assessment of the Hungarian soccer team. The great Hungarian team of 1953 played the same fast, short-passing game that humiliated England and was played by Tottenham Hotspur from 1949 to 1953. During that reign they won the then Second Division championship, followed by the First Division title, and followed that by being runners-up to Manchester United and FA Cup semi-finalists.

In 1952 they toured North America playing an attractive style of football called "push and run", a fluid, fast-moving style that entertained capacity crowds wherever they played. That Spurs team was managed by my father, Arthur Rowe, who had won championships while in charge of Chelmsford City, a Southern League club, from 1946 to 1949.

After a stellar career as a Tottenham player in the 1930s, my father took a coaching position in Budapest, Hungary, before returning to England in 1939 to join the army.

In Budapest were sown the seeds of the "push and run" approach, which for the next 13 years, incubated and ultimately manifested itself in that great Hungarian team. But it was a style that was first played by the glorious Spurs team of 1949–53.

In an *FT* article of July 1 1998, Peter Aspden wrote of "the beautiful version of the game, invented by the Hungarian side of the 1950s". The Hungarians did not "invent" the beautiful version of the game. If anyone "invented" it, it was my father.

On my wall at home there is a photograph of my father with Ferenc Puskas, the peerless member of the Hungarian team of the 1950s, and my thoughts turn to what kind of a game might have been played between those two great teams. What a feast it would have been. Graham A. Rowe, Los Angeles.

Yes, what a feast. It would have been a banquet of football at its purest and best; definitely the Beautiful Game.

* * *

On his war-forced return to England from Hungary, Arthur became an army physical training instructor and then manager of non-league Chelmsford, making him ideally placed to take over at White Hart Lane as successor to the far from popular ex-Gunner Joe Hulme in 1949.

His first major signing was Southampton right-back Alf Ramsey, a player he knew shared his keep-it-simple principles. Nicknamed 'The General' because of his fanaticism for talking football tactics, Ramsey took the secrets of simple football with him into management, and there was something of the Push and Run style about the Ipswich side he steered to the 1962 league championship and the England team he led to the World Cup in 1966.

Spurs waltzed away with the Second Division title in Rowe's first full season in charge, but sceptics said their 'playground push and run' tactics would be exposed in the First Division. Wrong!

They powered to the top of the table, eventually taking the championship with 60 points, four ahead of Manchester United and the highest total since Arsenal's record 66 20 years earlier, all of course in the two-points-for-a-win era. It was their attack, led aggressively by Channel Islander Len Duquemin, that took the eye, but the defence was a vital part of the jigsaw. It featured the safe hands and acrobatics of goalkeeper Ted Ditchburn, the towering presence of centre-half Harry Clarke, the perfect balance of full-back partners Alf Ramsey and Arthur Willis, and two of the finest half-backs in the league in Bill Nicholson and skipper Ronnie Burgess.

Eddie Baily's inch-perfect passing from midfield was a key factor as Spurs took apart the best defences in the land, scoring seven goals against Newcastle, six against Stoke, five against West Bromwich Albion and defending champions Portsmouth and four in three of the first four matches of the season.

Push and Run became more like push and punish. It was wonderful to watch, provided you were not the team on the receiving end.

In my privileged position as chief football reporter with the *Express*, in later years I was able to ask Arthur Rowe, Alf Ramsey and Bill Nicholson who was the most influential player in that Push and Run team. Each answered without hesitation, 'Ron Burgess.'

Bill Nick even went so far as to add, 'Ronnie was the greatest player ever to pull on a Tottenham shirt. Yes, with a gun to my head, I would even have to put him ahead of Dave Mackay.'

That was some admission, and when I asked Ronnie Burgess the same question while he was managing Watford in the 1960s, he told me in his lilting Welsh accent:

> There was no individual more important than the rest. We had that vital all-for-one-and-one-for-all spirit, which I suppose was a spill-over from the war. We'd all been in the forces during the war and knew the importance of teamwork. If you have to single out one man, then it has to be Arthur Rowe. It was his philosophy that we followed. Keep it simple, keep it quick, keep the ball on the ground and pass with accuracy. Yes, boyo, easy.

Legend has it that Burgess, ex-colliery worker and a powerhouse of a player, trod on every blade of grass on every pitch on which he played. He was at left-half, with Bill Nicholson a perfect balance with his more disciplined and careful approach on the right.

Behind Nicholson was the immaculate Alf Ramsey, a model of calm and consistency. Scottish firebrand Tommy Docherty once said spitefully of him that he had seen milk turn faster, but it has to be remembered that Alf was pushing 30 by the time of the Push and Run era and he had learned the art of conserving his energy by clever positioning and intelligent marking.

Arthur Willis, workmanlike at left-back, was an ideal foil for the more artistic Ramsey, with Charlie Withers as a very capable stand-in. Harry Clarke – recruited from Lovells Athletic in the Southern League – stood oak-tree solid in the middle of the defence. He had a great understanding with goalkeeper Ted Ditchburn, who would have won dozens more than his six England caps had it not been for the powerful presence of Frank Swift.

The attack piston on which Spurs fired was provided by effervescent Eddie Baily, the Cockney 'Cheeky Chappie' who proudly patrolled in midfield with a Napoleonic air of authority. His uncanny passing precision made goal-scoring much easier for twin strikers Len Duquemin and the often lethal Les Bennett.

* * *

Duquemin – 'The Duke' – was the Harry Kane of his day, scoring goals galore. But he was not so much a local hero as one imported from the beautiful Channel Island of Guernsey. And what a story he had to tell his grandchildren.

Len had a pugnacious face that mirrored the way he played the game, with a physical presence that brought muscle to the method of Push and Run. In the days that The Duke operated in the number nine Spurs shirt, centre-forwards had to be bold, brave and a little bit barmy as they took on the challenges of hefty defenders who believed in the principle of 'get your retaliation in first'.

Duquemin was a battering ram of a player, with a cannonball shot in either foot and powerful heading ability that also made him a menace in the air. Just like 'Our Harry' Kane, he always gave 100 per cent to the team effort and was adored by the Tottenham fans. As well as being dubbed The Duke, he was also known – particularly by his team-mates – as 'Reliable Len'. They always knew where to find him on the pitch, and there was a consistency to his play that spoke volumes about him as a person.

His life story would make a great television drama or cinema film. He was born in sight of the spectacular, sweeping Cobo Beach on Guernsey, and when the Nazis invaded the Channel Islands, monks hid him in a Catholic monastery to save him being shipped to a slave labour camp in eastern Europe, the fate of many Channel Islanders.

The surprise to meet Len off the pitch is that he was a quiet, gentle, generous soul and nothing like the warrior who battled his heart out for Spurs. He had clearly been influenced in his behaviour by the time he spent with the monks.

They only spoke French, and he became fluent in the language to such an extent that he toyed with the idea of playing his football in France.

The sixth of ten children with a father who worked in one of the many tomato nurseries on Guernsey, he became famous on the island for his schoolboy football feats. He was not the only Duquemin who could play the game. Five of his brothers appeared with him for Vauxbolets Old Boys. But it was Len who stood out and after one try-out game with Colchester United he signed for a Spurs side languishing in the Second Division. Three decades later, four Le Tissier brothers emerged on the playing fields of Guernsey, with Matt making it to the mainland and fame with Southampton and England. But the Duequemins won the numbers game.

Early in his career with Tottenham, Len was rocked by a family tragedy when one of his brothers, Frank Duquemin, was drowned during a freak storm while sailing to England from Guernsey to watch his brother play for Spurs. He considered packing up and going home, but his parents insisted that his brother would want him to continue to try to make the breakthrough as a Tottenham player.

It was the arrival of Arthur Rowe as manager in 1949 that ignited The Duke, who thrived on the responsibility of spearheading an attack fed by the paralysing passes of Eddie Baily, Ron Burgess and Bill Nicholson, and he was the perfect magnet for the crosses of flying wingers Sonny Walters and Les Medley. He often played in tandem with Les Bennett, and in the back-to-back title seasons they were too much of a handful for even the tightest defences.

One of my good social media friends is Colin Bennett, son of Les, who told me:

> My dad was always filling my head with stories of his partnership with The Duke. They were both so proud to be Lilywhites. Dad had a completely different war to The Duke, and collected more medals on the battlefront than on the football pitch. Like so many of his club-mates, he was a hero on and off the pitch. He used to tell me that he and the Duke would have run through brick walls for Arthur Rowe.

* * *

Both Les and The Duke were members of the exclusive Spurs 100 club of players who scored 100 or more league and cup goals in a Tottenham shirt. There are only 18 of them. For the record, this table shows their Spurs career span, their total goals scored, and the order in which they reached the ton:

Billy Minter, 1908–20 (101)
Herbert (Bert) Bliss, 1912–22 (104)
Jimmy Dimmock, 1919–30 (112)

George Hunt, 1930–37 (138)
Johnny Morrison, 1932–39 (101)
Les Bennett, 1939–54 (107)
Len Duquemin, 1946–58 (134)
Bobby Smith, 1955–64 (208)
Cliff Jones, 1958–68 (159)
Jimmy Greaves, 1961–70 (266)
Alan Gilzean, 1964–74 (133)
Martin Chivers, 1968–76 (174)
Glenn Hoddle, 1975–87 (110)
Teddy Sheringham, 1992–97; 2001–03 (124)
Robbie Keane, 2002–08; 2009–11 (122)
Jermain Defoe, 2004–08; 2009–14 (143)
Harry Kane, 2009– (more than 200 and counting)
Son Heung-min, 2015– (more than 100 and counting)

It is interesting to note that Son is the only foreign player to join the ton-up club.

* * *

In my 70 years following Spurs I have never been slow to collect trivia. How about this gem: If you ever get to see the 1947 film *Odd Man Out* starring James Mason, look out for the pedestrian in the street who suddenly reveals football skills. That's our Les Bennett!

He always had to carry the scar of being an Arsenal fan when he was a kid growing up in Wood Green, to the point where he was a Gunners ball boy at the 1932 FA Cup Final where Newcastle beat Arsenal with the infamous 'over the line' goal that would never have got past VAR today.

Proud-as-punch son Colin – a comedian, musician, artist, cab driver and deposit-losing politician – shared this story: 'It was Christmas in the 1951/52 season, and Dad decided he wanted to spend it at home with the family in the days when they played Christmas Day and Boxing Day. He told manager Arthur Rowe, "Sorry, Boss, but I don't feel too good … and will give the Christmas visit to Middlesbrough a miss." Arthur sweet-talked him into playing, Spurs won 5-1 and Dad scored four of the goals. Arthur said to him in the dressing room afterwards, "When you feel better, Les, I'll expect FIVE goals.'"

Les would have been first to admit that he played second fiddle to the great soloist that was Duquemin, who had the full confidence of Rowe from day one. The fabled manager had often talked to him about his football philosophy when in charge of Chelmsford, for whom Len played several games on loan from Spurs.

He rewarded Arthur's faith by plundering 134 goals in 307 games for Tottenham, 16 of them in the Second Division title-winning season of 1949/50, and then 15 in the following campaign when Spurs lifted the cherished Football League championship.

The Duke dropped the curtain on his Tottenham career when Bobby Smith arrived from Chelsea to take over his beloved number nine shirt, and in 1958 he moved into less demanding non-league football with Bedford Town, Hastings United and, finally, Romford.

He ran a newsagent's shop in Tottenham's Northumberland Park before becoming mine host at the Lord Nelson pub in Barnet and then the Haunch of Venison close to the old Spurs training ground in Cheshunt. Len used to hold court in his pub surrounded by Tottenham fans and joke, 'If it wasn't for her [pointing at his wife, June] I'd be living on my treasure island of Guernsey. My fault for going and falling in love with a London girl.'

He talked with warmth to his patrons – many of them Tottenham fans visiting his pub just to meet their hero – about his goal-scoring days at White Hart Lane:

I'd never swap anything about my career. I played with the greatest side of the day. What a team that was. We did not have a single weakness. When the Boss, Arthur Rowe, talked football with the likes of Bill Nicholson, Eddie Baily, Ron Burgess and, of course, "The General" Alf Ramsey, it was like being at a university for footballers. I felt the luckiest man alive to be in that squad. We lived and breathed the game, and during the two seasons when we were beating every team in sight it was like being on top of the world.

There were lots of brains in that team, and Les and I were the brawn. I could have played blindfolded. I knew that if I got in the right position at the right time Eddie would find me with a pass. He could land a ball on a handkerchief from 30 yards, and made the team tick with his passes I had a good understanding with Les Bennett and we each knew where to go to get the best out of each other. There were no Big-Time-Charlie "stars" in the side and we were all dedicated to putting the team first. It was a joy to play with them and for a couple of seasons we were just about untouchable. Arthur Rowe was a manager we all liked and respected and there was a great dressing-room atmosphere.

Arthur's secret was keeping everything simple. He used to have lots of little sayings like "when not in possession get into position" and "it's better to run to the ball than chase after it". People are always asking me if we could have beaten the Double side. I usually tell them you can only be the best of your time, and under Arthur we were easily the best. And to think we got paid to do it. Every day was a joy. I'm proud to have been the first Channel Islander to make an impact on the Football League. There are a load of outstanding youngsters on the islands. Just watch out for them. I think back to when I was living with the monks and wonder what they would make of what I've done with my life. Who knows what would have happened if the Nazis had dragged me off to Poland. I've been a very lucky boy. '

In retirement, Len lived within a ten-minute walk of the White Hart Lane ground where he had so often stoked the roar of the crowd, and his old team-mate Bill Nicholson always used to make sure he had a seat of honour on his regular visits before cancer claimed him at the age of 78.

June, his wife of 50 years, said, 'He was the sweetest man who ever lived.'

And he couldn't half play football. The Duke.

* * *

These were the wonderful days of flying wingers and they did not come much better or more of a handful for full-backs than Sonny Walters and Les Medley. They used to park themselves close to the touchline and both could really motor and were accurate crossers of the ball.

They were encouraged to make their touchline dashes by fans belting out choruses of the following song based on the old Bing Crosby classic 'McNamara's Band' (which had been a Fife and drum band that featured four McNamara brothers; not a lot of people want to know that!):

We are Spurs Supporters and we love to watch them play
We go to all the home games and we go to those away
With us supporters following them we know they will
    do right
We loudly cheer when they appear, the lads in blue and white
We're very proud of our football ground it's known
    throughout the land
And while we wait for the game to start we listen to the band
Then when we see the teams come out you should
    hear the roar
We know it won't be long before the Spurs, they start to score
The ref his whistle proudly blows, the linesmen wave
    their flags
The Duke is ready to kick off as he hitches up his bags
We cheer Sonny Walters as he toddles down the line
And the ball like magic is in the net and makes us all
    feel fine
There's Ronnie Burgess with his skill holding up the line
With Alf, Bill, Harry and Charlie way up there behind
And not forgetting good old Ted whose hands are sure
    and strong
And Eddie and the Leslies who are always up-a-long
And when the game is over, when the game is through
We cheer the winners off the field and the gallant losers too
The Cockerel proudly wags his tail, he gave the Spurs
    their name
In honour of the Lilywhites who always play the game
Now come on all you supporters and join our merry band
No matter what your age is, we'll take you by the hand

We'll pin a cockerel on your chest, it shows the world that we
Are members of that loyal band, the S.S.C.

If you want to sing along with me on this classic old Spurs
theme song, just go to Google and type: Norman Giller
YouTube Spurs theme song (with apologies to music lovers
everywhere). Back to the Push and Run season when
Tottenham were kings of the castle ...

* * *

There was something almost inevitable about Tottenham's
great escape from the Second Division in the early weeks of
the 1949/50 season. It was an attitude about the team that
set them apart from the opposition, almost as if they were
strutting their stuff and saying, 'With this sort of football,
we deserve a place at the top table.'

Yes, there was a touch of arrogance about it, and much
of the cockiness emanated from pass master Eddie Baily. A
fellow East Ender of mine and an old and treasured mate,
Eddie spent a couple of wind-down seasons at Leyton
Orient when I was sports editor of the local paper.

A quick anecdote about the swaggering, larger-than-life
Baily that deserves re-telling. During one of my midweek
visits to the O's ground at Brisbane Road he summoned
me to join him on the pitch. 'What odds on any of today's
prima donna players being able to do this?' he challenged,
then deliberately putting three successive penalty kicks
against the bar. It was an exclusive close-up view of the
skill that put the precision into Push and Run.

He described the 1950/51 championship-winning team
as 'the perfect football machine'. Never one to hold back on
an opinion or three, Eddie told me:

' We were far too good for the Second Division, and played our way to promotion with ease. I remember we were top of the table from September and had a run of 23 matches without defeat. These days I suppose I would be called a playmaker, but then I was just a good old-fashioned, deep-lying inside-forward. My job was to provide the passes for the goalscorers, and I think you'll find I had a foot in the majority of the goals we scored. That's not me being big-headed. That was fact.

An important aspect is that we had a very good dressing-room spirit. There were no stars. We all took equal praise when winning, and shared the blame if things went wrong. Max Miller was the big comedian of the time, and I was given his nickname "Cheeky Chappie" because I was always clowning.

We were the thinking man's team. Players like Alf, Bill Nick, Vic Buckingham and Ronnie Burgess were obsessed with tactics, and of course dear Arthur Rowe was the man who led us with clear and concise instructions. There was no mumbo jumbo. We just got on with playing the game in a simple, direct way that bewildered the opponents. '

A goal that Eddie scored against Huddersfield in the 1951/52 season is still talked about by fans who know their Tottenham history. His corner kick whacked against the back of the referee, knocking him to the floor. He collected the rebound (illegally touching the ball twice) and crossed for Duquemin to head into the net. The ref, still scrambling to his feet, awarded the goal which gave Spurs victory and pushed Huddersfield towards relegation. It would never have got past VAR today.

Eddie was to feature again with Spurs as he started a new life as a coach. More of that later, but back to the team he helped make tick.

By New Year's Eve 1950, they were top of the First Division following a sequence of eight successive victories, and they stayed at the top of the mountain until they clinched the championship on 28 April 1951. Among their devastating performances was a 7-0 destruction of FA Cup giants Newcastle United. They achieved that without skipper Ronnie Burgess, who sat in the stand nursing an injury. 'That was the finest exhibition of football I have ever seen,' he said later. 'It was only by becoming a spectator that I realised just how special this side was. We paralysed Newcastle with our push and run tactics that a lot of so-called experts had said would not work in the First Division.'

In this truly golden season, White Hart Lane attendances averaged 55,486 as Tottenham captured their first league championship. They notched 82 goals and were beaten only seven times. In their post-championship campaign it looked as if they were going to lift the title again as they finished like trains, taking 20 points from the last dozen matches. But Matt Busby's Manchester United hung on to win the crown after finishing runners-up four times in the previous five years.

Tottenham beat Chelsea 2-0 at Stamford Bridge on the final day of the season for the considerable consolation of pipping Arsenal to second place.

It was the FA Cup that brought Tottenham's greatest success the following season, when they finished an unimpressive tenth in the First Division. They battled through to the FA Cup semi-final after surviving four away ties. Waiting for them at Villa Park, as in 1948, were the Matthews- and Mortensen-motivated Blackpool.

Victory was handed to Blackpool on a plate by, of all people, safe-as-houses Alf Ramsey, who in a rare moment of carelessness played a back-pass intended for Ted Ditchburn into the path of Blackpool poacher Jackie Mudie. It became a skeleton in Alf's closet, and I hardly dared mention it in the many hours we spent together during the 1960s. He once confided, after a G and T too many, that the memory of it kept him awake on many nights, playing over and over again what he should have done. But his poker face never conveyed to the Tottenham fans that he was even more devastated than they were. Alf was always harder to read than a closed book.

Remarkably, Spurs managed to produce their flowing football on a White Hart Lane pitch that was little more than a mud-heap during the winter months and was a disgrace when compared with the original billiard-table surface laid by the legendary John Over, who had been trusted with preparing the first-ever Test match pitch at The Oval. The erection of stands right around the Tottenham ground was good news for the spectators but not for the groundsmen, who were dismayed to find their grass refusing to grow properly without full sunlight. The players joined Arthur Rowe in pleading for a surface suited to their on-the-carpet passing style. When the pitch was finally dug up in 1952, workmen were amazed to find the remains of an old nursery so lovingly tended by original ground owner George Beckwith, Victorian-age publican at the White Hart Lane Inn. There was a concrete water container, snaking rows of iron piping and greenhouse foundations.

Floodlights were erected the following year, set high on four corner poles. Racing Club de Paris accepted an invitation to become the first visitors to appear under the lights and were beaten 5-3 in what was something of an exhibition match. Spectators complained about dark patches on some poorly lit parts of the pitch, and the lights were upgraded in 1957. This meant a transfer of the symbolic cockerel from the roof of the West Stand to the East Stand. It had been a quiet, noble witness to all comings and goings at the Lane for many years (surviving Hitler's bombs and, much later, an air rifle attack from 'potty' Paul Gascoigne).

Unfortunately, the stress and strain of managing Spurs took its toll on Arthur Rowe and he reluctantly had to stand down in 1954, with the team he had created, cajoled and championed showing the sign of advancing years. His last signing for the club was a player who was to become a Lane legend – Danny Blanchflower, bought from Aston Villa for £30,000 and in Arthur's expert estimation the perfect player to carry on the Push and Run philosophy.

Push and Run was poetry in motion, and it was Arthur's lasting legacy. They should build a statue to him at the new Lane in memory of the man who pumped the pride and the passion back into Tottenham.

There were problems on the horizon. The new master schemer, Danny Blanchflower, and the new manager, Jimmy Anderson, could not stand each other. They talked different football languages.

3

JIMMY ANDERSON
A Bridge too Far

Born: London 1893
Died: 23 August 1970
Appointed: 18 April 1955
Resigned: 11 October 1958
Games managed: 153
Won: 72
Drawn: 32
Lost: 49
Goals scored: 311
Goals conceded: 245
Win percentage: 46.58

JIMMY ANDERSON had been a member of the Tottenham backroom staff since way back in his teens in 1908, and he found his promotion to manager a burden rather than a blessing.

He filled in as emergency manager when Arthur Rowe became unwell, and was then given the job permanently in July 1955. After years of playing second fiddle he suddenly found himself conducting the orchestra, and he just could not get the rhythm right.

A man of few words, Anderson would not have lasted five minutes in today's world in which Premier League managers are expected to give regular one-on-one interviews and press conferences. They have to know how to please and satisfy not only newspaper reporters but television, radio, internet and social media interrogators. Jimmy was from the Victorian school philosophy: speak only when spoken to and treat the press like you would treat the police. He considered the press a pain in the derrière.

Anderson said following his promotion from the back room to the top job:

> Spurs have been my life virtually since I left school and I will do my best to meet the standards that Arthur Rowe set in his championship-winning season. All I ask from the players and supporters is patience while I settle into the job. I have inherited a talented team that is a little lacking in confidence. We must all pull together to get back into a winning groove. I ask the press to leave me to get on with the job without unnecessary interference. Matters of club business will be dealt with by our secretary. My one priority will be dealing with the players and getting things right on the pitch.

There were encouraging signs that Anderson was starting to get it right when Tottenham reached the FA Cup semi-final in 1956, going down 1-0 to a Don Revie-inspired Manchester City, again at Villa Park. But it was another false dawn, and suddenly all the media attention centred on an earthquaking bust-up between Anderson and his outspoken skipper Danny Blanchflower.

It reached the point where Danny was telling the newspapers how Spurs should be playing the game and how the club should be managed. Anderson blamed Danny for the semi-final defeat, because he made tactical changes during the game without even a glance in the direction of the manager.

It is on record that he said to Danny in the dressing room immediately after the semi-final, 'You have made me look a fool in front of the directors. I'm manager of this club, not you. In future don't make any tactical changes without my say-so.'

Danny, never one to take a verbal volley without retaliating, replied, 'I'm as disappointed as you and the directors. I tried to win the game by taking a gamble. You think I made a mistake. I think it's better to make a mistake trying something than to accept things and do nothing.'

Blanchflower had still not taken his boots off, and was fuming that Anderson had gone for him so soon after the final whistle and the disappointment of defeat. From then on there were at daggers drawn.

Anderson always cut something of a comic figure because he used to wear his trousers with the bottoms tucked into socks, like golfing plus-fours. But there was nothing amusing about his conflict with Blanchflower, and he stripped him of the captaincy after a row during which he accused Danny of trying to knife him in the back.

According to Danny, he was innocent of any wrongdoing. It kicked off when he telephoned the London *Evening News* to discuss an article he was due to write for football editor J.G. (Jack) Orange. He had been left out of the team to play in a crucial relegation match at Cardiff, and Anderson had told Orange earlier in the day that it was because of an injury, which led the early editions.

I was working at the *News* as a sports room assistant and took the call. Danny asked for Jack Orange, and I told him he was out of the office. I passed the telephone to his deputy Vic Railton, who was establishing himself as one of the hungriest news-gatherers in Fleet Street sports history.

Vic asked Danny about his injury, being polite rather than seeking a story. Danny was puzzled and answered truthfully, 'Injury? What injury? I'm in fine shape. I've just been left out.'

The *Evening News* ran a 'Blanchflower dropped' exclusive under Vic's byline in the last edition, and Anderson went ballistic, accusing Danny of trying to undermine him and stir up trouble. Ironically, the next day the veteran, bowler-hatted Orange accused Railton of trying to steal his job by making him look a fool by rewriting his story. It's a funny old world.

It became the talk of football and the Tottenham board of directors had to choose between the manager they had just put in charge or the articulate but prickly Blanchflower, who had arrived from Aston Villa in 1954 in the Arthur Rowe era for a then club record £30,000, with promises of putting himself and Spurs on top of the tree.

The directors told Danny to button his lip, which was like asking a chaffinch not to chirp. The garrulous Irishman had a perfect understanding with Arthur Rowe, but when Anderson took over he just could not get on the same wavelength. This was old school meeting new school, and a collision of ideals, ideas and personalities.

Danny and I later became good pals when we were both writing for Express Newspapers and during our many one-sided conversations (when I listened and Danny talked) he told me:

(My dispute was not so much with Jimmy as with the directors, who were guilty of massive interference. They got it wrong in the first place by promoting a man beyond his capabilities. He was a fine backroom worker, but was just not cut out for managing, and he had never played at the top level.

It made no sense that he was managing a major club. You don't put an able seaman in charge of the ship. That way you will eventually hit the rocks.

The Hungarians and Brazilians had recently shown we were light years behind with our methods, and it was so obvious that Jimmy Anderson was still living in the *Ark*.

He never forgave me for sending Maurice Norman up from defence to lead the attack when we were battling to pull back the Manchester City lead in the FA Cup semi-final. I could not be one of those captains who just spun the coin. I saw it as my duty to make changes in the heat of battle rather than save it for the after-match inquest.

Sadly, my argument with Jimmy dragged our then coach Bill Nicholson in, and for a while I was at loggerheads with a man for whom I had utmost respect. I went on the transfer list and when Bill finally took over from Jimmy he played me in the reserves. That hurt like hell. It all came right in

48

the end, but I was never on Jimmy Anderson's Christmas card list. 〞

In fairness to Anderson, he should not be judged on his managing stint at Spurs. Let's remember that his great service to Spurs included playing a vital part in the foundation building of the Push and Run team while in charge of the Northfleet nursery team from 1934 to the outbreak of war. This meant he was effectively the Tottenham youth team manager and brought along the likes of Ted Ditchburn, Ron Burgess, Bill Nicholson, Les Bennett and Les Medley. Jimmy also set up the deal with Southampton for Alf Ramsey in March 1949.

There were signs of better things to come at Tottenham when big Maurice 'The Ox' Norman signed from Norwich as reinforcement for a creaking defence, and another beefy player – Bobby Smith – arrived from Chelsea to help power Tottenham to a runners-up finish in the 1956/57 title race. By then, super coach Bill Nicholson was virtually running the show, as Anderson – in his mid-60s – battled with what had all the signs of the sort of nervous illness that had ended Arthur Rowe's reign.

Jimmy was finally beaten by his health issues, and his long-anticipated resignation was announced in October 1958. He had just celebrated 50 years with the club, loyalty beyond the call of duty. But – like his old friend Billy Minter from back in the 1930s – he was not cut out to be a manager. And, just like Minter, it all became too much for him and he became the third Spurs manager to have a breakdown because of the enormous pressures and stress of the job.

The man who took his place was to become, without argument, the greatest and most successful manager in

Tottenham's history. For me, it remains the most momentous and significant moment in my 70-year Spurs watch.

Enter 'Sir' Bill Nicholson, and what an entrance!

4

BILL NICHOLSON
The Master of White Hart Lane

Born: Scarborough, Yorkshire, 26 January 1919
Died: Hertfordshire, 23 October 2004
Appointed: 11 October 1958
Resigned: 29 August 1974
Games managed: 832
Won: 408
Drawn: 196
Lost: 228
Goals scored: 1,596
Goals conceded: 1,095
Win percentage: 49.03

BILL NICHOLSON was officially announced as the new Tottenham Hotspur manager at midday on Saturday, 11 October 1958. At 3pm his team greeted him with an astonishing 10-4 victory over Everton. No manager in the history of the game has been given such a remarkable welcome. How on earth could he follow that? Well, how about within three years becoming the first manager of the

20th century to lift in the same season not only the league championship trophy but also the FA Cup: the elusive Double.

Welcome to the legend that is Bill Nicholson: 'Sir Bill', the Master of White Hart Lane.

I had conversations with Bill scattered over four decades, and for the purposes of this 70-year journey through my Tottenham memories I am going to focus on our very last one-on-one meeting. But first I need to share an off-beat story involving Graeme Souness, the Scot who Bill always considered 'the one that got away'.

By accident, I got an astonishing insight into the real Bill Nicholson. This was when he was overwhelmed by a story that made its way on to the front as well as back pages and which gave him more distress than almost any other event in his career.

It was during the 1970/71 season and Bill was losing a battle to hang on to one of the finest young prospects in British football: Graeme Souness. Born in the tough Broomhouse district of Edinburgh on 6 May 1953, Graeme went to the same Carrickvale school that Dave Mackay had attended a generation earlier. They must have been hewn out of the identical lump of granite, because Souness had all the Mackay motivating mannerisms and liked to boss the pitch in the same intimidating way as his schoolboy idol.

His encyclopaedic knowledge of all that Mackay achieved swayed him to join Tottenham at the age of 15 when any of the Scottish clubs would willingly have opened their doors to him.

I learned earlier than most that Souness was not only a star in the making, but also a headstrong boy who knew his own mind. Jim Rodger, the sleuth of a reporter on the *Scottish Daily Express,* was so close to Bill Nicholson that he knew all the Spurs secrets and kept most of them tucked close to his chest, never sharing them with readers or colleagues. He earned a mutual trust with chairmen, managers and players that got him an ear in boardrooms and dressing rooms throughout football.

Jim, almost as wide as he was tall, was a legend in Scotland, on nodding terms with prime ministers and princes as well as most of the people who mattered in football. He telephoned me in the Fleet Street office of the *Express* one day in 1970 and whispered in the conspiratorial tone that he always used, 'Get over to the north London digs of Graeme Souness and talk him out of doing anything silly. Bill Nick thinks he's going to walk out on the club.'

'Graeme who?' I said. 'I wouldn't know what he looks like, let alone where he lives.'

'He's the hottest young prospect in the country,' Jim said in a scolding tone, and proceeded to give me Graeme's address. 'You'll be doing Bill Nick a big favour if you can tell him to just be patient and wait for his chance. He couldna' be with a better club. If you get him, put him on to me. I'll talk some sense into him.'

That was how Rodger the Dodger operated, working almost as a secret agent on behalf of managers across Britain and then being rewarded with some of the hottest exclusive stories in the game.

In those days, I was more concerned with trying to dig out stories on first-team players at all the London clubs, and could not see the point of chasing after a youngster whose career had hardly started.

But I had so much respect for my Glasgow colleague that I drove to Graeme's North London digs, only to be told by his landlady that he had gone home to Scotland an hour earlier.

What a waste of time, I thought. As if anybody apart from Jim Rodger is going to be the slightest bit interested in this story.

Wrong!

It got to the point over the next few days when questions were asked in the House of Commons, as the story crossed from the back to the front pages. Graeme, then 17, had spent two years at Spurs as an apprentice who considered himself more of a sorcerer. He had gone back to Edinburgh because he said he felt homesick.

Spurs reacted by suspending him without pay for two weeks. Graeme's local MP took up the case, and questioned in the House what right a club had to deal with a minor like this when his only crime was to suffer from homesickness. 'Is homesickness something that should be punishable?' demanded the MP, managing to make Souness sound as hard done by as Oliver Twist.

The story became the property of columnists with poison pens, and Bill Nick, a fatherly manager if ever there was one, was unfairly pilloried. Souness, without having kicked a ball in senior football, was suddenly the best-known young player in the land.

The suspicion at Spurs was that their hot young property had been got at and was being tempted away from Tottenham.

I went hunting Bill for quotes and found he had gone home from his Lane office. It was never my style to trouble managers by invading the privacy of their homes, but I was under pressure from my editor to get a Nicholson slant on the story. So I drove down the road to Bill's nearby house.

There was no reply when I knocked on his door and I was just about to return to my car when an elderly lady sweeping the pavement in front of her house next door asked, 'You looking for Mr Nicholson?'

I nodded, and she pointed to a side drive. 'You'll find him around the back,' she said. 'He's in his allotment.'

Allotment? Bill Nicholson, manager of Spurs, in his allotment?

Sure enough, I found Bill dressed in shorts and Tottenham tracksuit top digging with a spade in an allotment around the corner from his home.

'What the bloody hell do you want?' he said, as astonished to see me as I was to find him up to his ankles in shovelled soil.

'You spend a lot of time here?' I asked, my reporter's antenna on red alert.

'I'd like to so that I could escape the likes of you,' he replied, without a hint of humour. 'One day I want to find more time to take it up as a proper hobby and if you say one word about it in your paper I will hang you from the nearest lamppost.'

Goalpost would have been a better simile, but I kept that thought to myself.

I swore to secrecy and have never told this story until now, and I hope Bill Up There forgives me. I just feel it captures his (literally) down-to-earth personality. One of the nicest, kindest and most modest men ever to cross my path, but he could be brutal when necessary.

I pressed him for a response on Souness.

'I have never known such an ambitious and impatient young man,' an exasperated Nicholson told me, putting his spade aside. 'He has a wonderful future in the game, but he wants to run before he can walk. He can't understand why I'm not already considering him for the first team. He wants to jump ahead of established professionals like Alan Mullery and Martin Peters, and the very promising Steve Perryman. His chance will come, but he must show patience. If he's ever picked for Scotland, I wonder if they'll find a cap big enough for his head.'

A suitably repentant Souness returned to the Lane after Bill had travelled to Scotland to have quiet, fatherly words with him, but he wore out the carpet to Bill's office to the point where the Spurs boss decided he had no option but to let him go.

He had made one brief first-team appearance in a UEFA Cup tie (substituting for Martin Peters in a match in Iceland) before being sold to Middlesbrough in December 1972 for £27,000, which was a hefty fee in those days for a virtually unknown and untried player. Graeme went on to become one of the most formidable midfield forces in football, his peak coming when he joined Bob Paisley's Liverpool.

For ever after, Bill 'Digger' Nicholson considered Souness the one that slipped through the net, and I kept quiet about the allotment. Until now.

* * *

When I had first interviewed Bill Nick in 1958, I was a raw young reporter and had travelled to White Hart Lane by bus. Now here I was 43 years later in my Spurs-blue 4.2 Jaguar driving to see The Master for what was to prove the last face-to-face interview. It was the week before the 2001 testimonial Tottenham were belatedly giving him at White Hart Lane and I was sounding him out for a proposed appearance on a television programme I had devised.

This was a series called *Who's the Greatest?*, and we were planning to feature Jimmy Greaves against Kenny Dalglish in a revival of the show that had run on ITV in the 1980s. I wanted to know whether Bill would be prepared to appear as a witness for Greavsie, while also craftily picking his brains for more treasured recollections about all things Spurs.

I prepared to park my flash car outside his modest but welcoming 71 Creighton Road N17 home, a small, unpretentious house once owned by Spurs and rented to him until he became sole owner in the 1960s for a couple of thousand pounds. It was close enough to the Lane that on match days you could hear the roar of the crowd.

Bill opened his front door as I pulled up, leaning heavily on a stick that was his one concession to galloping old age. 'I remember you when you couldn't afford a bike,' was his opening shot, immediately reviving memories of the banter we always used to share when I was doing my bread-and-butter job of football reporting.

'You can't park there,' he said. 'You'll get a ticket. Drive round the back where you'll find our garage in a block. I won't charge you for taking our space. First right and then an immediate left.'

Bill Nick, looking all of his 82 years, was still showing the way, still giving directions. 'Keep it simple. Give it and go. When not in possession get in position.'

His delightful wife Grace – commonly known as Darkie – demanded I have a cup of tea and then disappeared to the local shops, walking I noticed rather than cycling as in the old days, and leaving her beloved Bill and me to our rose-coloured recollections; or perhaps that should be blue and white (matter of record before the diversity merchants dive in: Bill's wife was known as Darkie to differentiate her from her blonde twin sister).

The Nicholsons, approaching their diamond wedding, had one of those end-of-terrace houses that hug you, nothing whatsoever ostentatious about it but warm, welcoming and filled with friendliness. Their snug lounge led into an extension that was decorated with family photographs, mostly of daughters Linda and Jean and much-loved grandchildren. Just a framed photo of Bill proudly showing off his OBE in the Buckingham Palace forecourt gave any hint that this was the home of a hero. This was the comfortable sanctuary to which Bill used to escape after all those triumphs in vast stadiums filled with cheering, chanting fans. What a contrast.

'Still tending your allotment?' I asked from my seat on the sofa, with him relaxed opposite me in his favourite, well-worn armchair, wearing a fawn cardigan and Marks and Spencer slippers. His hair was still military-short, but the once gingery, then steel grey had surrendered to a whiteness that would have matched a Spurs shirt.

'No, the old joints are not up to it now,' he said. 'But the neighbours keep it tidy and under control. The blackberry bush I planted is still there and giving us fruit.'

Just a few months earlier during the welter of litigation that tarnished the club in what were uncertain times there had been a tense exchange in the High Court. Former chairman Sir Alan Sugar, in his libel action against Associated Newspapers, denied vehemently the accusation by the newspaper's QC, 'On one occasion you were introduced to Bill Nicholson and were heard to say, "Who is that old git?"'

When it was reported, I remember all supporters with Spurs in their soul were outraged. This was like not knowing who lived at Buckingham Palace.

'What did you think of that?' I asked Bill, convinced he would give me one of his famous blanks.

'I thought it was hilarious,' he said, unexpectedly. 'I could have said exactly the same thing about Sugar!'

When I tried to press Bill on the subject of boardroom battles and bungs, he waved a finger at me like an admonishing headmaster. 'How long have we known each other?'

'More than 40 years,' I said.

'And when have you ever known me get involved in politics? It is just not my scene. All I was ever interested in was the football. Keith Burkinshaw shared my views on that and it's why he quit the club. He was a first-class manager and I thought it was bonkers when the club let him go. The only time I got into politics was when I tried to get Danny Blanchflower appointed as my successor as manager, and all that got me was the embarrassment of having the board completely ignore my advice.'

I could sense Bill was uncomfortable talking club matters, perhaps conscious that he was still Tottenham's honorary president, so I changed the subject.

'We are reviving a TV series I dreamt up in the 1980s called *Who's the Greatest?*' I explained, 'and one of our first shows will feature celebrities arguing the case for Jimmy Greaves against Kenny Dalglish.'

'Hasn't that already been on?'

'That was Greaves against Ian Rush. We had a jury of 12 people and they voted eight-four in Jimmy's favour.'

It set Bill off on the road down memory lane. 'Should have been 12-nought! Jimmy was the greatest scorer of them all. I've never seen a player touch him for putting the vital finishing touch. While others were still thinking about what to do, whoosh, he would just get on and do it. He would have the ball into the net in the blinking of an eye and then amble back to the centre-circle as casually as if he'd just swatted a fly. A genius.'

Bill's mind was now filled with action replays of golden goals from the boots of our mutually favourite footballer, Greavsie. Not the rotund, funny one on the telly. This, the 10st 8lb lightning-quick, darting, dribbling, twisting, turning and passing the ball into the net Jimmy Greaves, the Artful Dodger of the penalty area, a pickpocket who snaffled more memorable goals than many of us have had hot baths.

'He never gave me a spot of trouble, you know,' Bill continued, now thinking aloud rather than talking direct to me. I need not have been there. He was wandering around a precious past, and did not need any prompting or interruption.

'Even when it came time for us to part company he knew in his heart he'd lost his appetite for the game. People who didn't know what they were talking about sometimes described him as a bit of a faint-heart, but in all the years I watched him I never ever saw him shirk a tackle. And I'll tell you what, there were at least ten goals that should have been added to his career total. Time and again he would be flagged offside simply because his movement was too quick for the eye of the linesman. The hardest of all to take was in the 1962 European Cup semi-final here (Bill waved a gnarled fist at the wall in the direction of nearby White Hart Lane) when he scored a perfectly good goal that was ruled off-side. That broke all our hearts. We might have beaten Jock [Stein] and his great Celtic to become the first British team to win the European Cup.

'Jimmy had two great partnerships for us, first with Bobby Smith who provided lots of muscle in making openings for Jimmy, and then with Alan Gilzean, one of the most elegant forwards I've ever clapped eyes on. Greavsie and Gilly together were like poetry in motion. I was hoping for a third one when I put Jim together with Martin Chivers, but by then he was only giving half his attention to the game. He was quite the businessman off the pitch, and that took the edge off his appetite for football.

'But even with half his concentration he was still twice as good as any other goalscoring forward. It hurt like hell the day I decided to let him go in part exchange for Martin Peters. But as a manager you often had to do things that hurt you inside but were necessary for the team and the club. Martin was another wonderfully gifted footballer, but completely different to Jim. Alf [Ramsey] described him as being ten years ahead of his time, and I knew exactly what he meant. He was an exceptional reader of the game, a bit like Danny and dear John White, and knew where to be before anybody else had spotted the gap.

'Nothing's changed. The ball is still round and the game is still all about positioning. If you're not in the right place, then you're not going to be able to do the right thing. Positioning, positioning, positioning. The three Ps. Now Jimmy always knew where to be to make the most of a goal-scoring opportunity. It came naturally to him. You couldn't teach it. Quite a few of his goals were tap-ins, and people said he was lucky. He made his own luck by being in the right place at the right time.'

* * *

I reluctantly brought Bill out of his golden reminiscing. 'Would you be prepared to come to the studio and say that on camera?' I asked.

Bill looked at me as if I had just awoken him from a wonderful dream.

'You know I hate appearing in front of TV cameras,' he said. 'Hated it when I was a manager, hate it now. I'm a football man, not a song and dance man. Mind you, I got a lot of pleasure watching Jimmy on the *Saint and Greavsie* show. Why did they take that off? I thought it was a good thing to show football could laugh at itself.'

My eyebrows reached for the sky. 'That s rich coming from you, Bill. You were Mr Serious throughout your managerial career.'

'That's true,' he admitted. 'I found it difficult to unwind. I could never understand how the likes of Tommy Docherty, Cloughie and Malcolm Allison could sometimes act like clowns. I never had that sort of release. For me football was, still is, much more than just a game. It was my life.'

Bill then shared a thought with me that he had kept buried for all the years he was in charge at the Lane. 'You know what was the hardest thing about my job?' he asked, then answering himself, 'Being told how to do it by people who couldn't trap a bag of cement. But don't make a thing of it. All part and parcel of being a manager. Everybody thinks they can do the job better than you.'

I could sense he was uncomfortable with the topic, and so brought the conversation around to a happy time for him and Spurs.

'You and Tommy Doc were big rivals in the 1960s. But you got the better of him in the one that really mattered, the 1967 FA Cup Final.'

Suddenly the years fell away from the octogenarian as he dipped back into his peak seasons. 'I was really worried about that one because Chelsea had stuffed us good and proper at the Bridge, 3-0 and it could have been five,' he recalled. 'They were playing a sweeper system, with Marvin Hinton very efficient in the role. Alan Gilzean detested the system and was much less effective against it. I was really concerned. Then, during the week of the final, talkative Tommy gave an interview in which he said he was dropping the sweeper formation and playing orthodox. I was delighted to hear it, and we were able to beat them 2-1.'

Which was the most satisfying of your FA Cup Final victories?

Bill gazed into space, like a man trying to choose between sparkling diamonds sitting in his memory bank, 'Obviously from an achievement point of view it has to be the 1961 final because it completed what people described as the impossible Double, but to be honest I felt flat at the end of it because we didn't play anything like our best against a Leicester team playing above itself. They were down to ten men because of injury, and it somehow made the game lop-sided. There was no rhythm or pattern, while most of that season we'd played some of the finest football I've ever seen from a club side. You could have set it to music, it was so rhythmical. But the final turned out to be a big anti-climax. We got the Double, yes, But I wanted us to do it in real style, as much for our wonderful fans as for me.

'The following year Jimmy gave us a great start with a magnificent goal after just three minutes and we beat a very talented Burnley side 3-1. That was probably the most satisfying, because we played it the Spurs way. Quick, simple, beautiful football. Never complicate what is basically a simple game, and treat the ball with respect, not as if it's your worst enemy and needs a good hard kicking. Caress it, play it with care, make every pass count, and when not in possession get into position.'

I dragged Bill away from the mantra he had been preaching for more than 60 years. 'If you had to pick one match from all those in which you were involved as manager, which gets your vote as the most satisfying?'

Back to the bank vault, and this time he had little hesitation in replying. 'It has to be the 5-1 victory over Atlético Madrid in the 1963 European Cup Winners' Cup Final,' he said firmly. 'This made us the first British team ever to win a major European trophy. That's in the history books forever. A bit special. That was little Terry Dyson's big night. He scored two storming goals. I remember that old rascal Bobby Smith saying to him in the dressing room afterwards that he should retire because he would never top that performance. Terry played on for another six years!'

Bill chuckled to himself over that suddenly uncorked memory, and I stupidly ruined the mood by introducing a sombre topic.

'Eddie Baily told me he was disgusted with the pay-off he got from Spurs, and that you didn't get much more.'

I had dropped winter's discontent into his glorious summer.

Bill was clearly not keen to discuss the subject, particularly with his testimonial match just a few days away. 'Let s just say it was more a paper tissue than golden handshake,' he said. 'Eddie was bitter for a long time, and we fell out over it. We've since patched it up and when we get together we talk about the many good times we enjoyed rather than the unhappy finish.'

Insensitively, I continued with the negativity, 'Martin Chivers gave you a lot of headaches in your last couple of seasons as manager.'

'Yes, he became a real handful,' Bill admitted, shaking his head as if to get rid of bad thoughts. 'He and Eddie really disliked each other, which led to a heavy atmosphere. There were a couple of seasons when Martin was comfortably the outstanding centre-forward in the country, and it seemed to go to his head. He more than anybody put me in the mood to resign with his continual beefing about his wages, that and the terrible hooliganism that started to ruin so many games.

'Since he retired, Martin has gone out of his way to make amends by visiting me a lot, and he has apologised for his behaviour. He has developed into a really nice person, and we get on just fine. When Darkie meets him he makes a fuss of her, and she says, "How on earth did a nice young man like that manage to upset you so much? You were always moaning about him, yet he strikes me as being a real charmer." But Darkie did not have to put up with him constantly complaining about his wages and sulking when things didn't go his way.'

I was kicking myself for bruising our conversation by bringing in bad vibes from the past, and put us back on happier hunting ground.

'Of all the managers of your era, Bill, who did you get on with best of all?'

This was much more acceptable. 'No question, it had to be Bill Shankly,' he replied, his eyes twinkling at the thought of his old friend. 'We used to talk regularly on the phone at least once a week. Bill was a very funny man, but deadly serious about football in something of a fanatical way. Once after Jimmy had scored one of his magical winning goals against Liverpool, he phoned me on the Monday and said, "Bill, there's one thing wrong with that wee Greaves feller of yours. He wears the wrong colour shirt. He deserves to be in Liverpool red, playing for a proper team."

'We would discuss all the football gossip, and put the world to rights. Darkie used to tease that we were like a couple of old women. Both Bill and I agreed that Brian Clough needed reining in. Bill used to say to me, "When I talk to that man on the phone I'm never sure if he's drunk with arrogance or alcohol."'

Bill Nick peered into his tea cup as if searching for a lost memory. 'I don't think Brian ever forgave me for dropping him when I was manager of the England under-23s,' he confided. 'It probably held back his promotion to the senior team, because I told England manager Walter Winterbottom that I considered him a bit of a lazy so-and-so who played more for himself than the team. I had to call it as I saw it.'

And there it was. Bill Nicholson, in a sentence, 'I had to call it as I saw it.'

As honest as the day is long, he was the most refreshingly candid and trustworthy man I ever met in football.

He tossed in one surprise that took my breath away as I was preparing to leave. 'I wonder how different my life would have been,' he said, 'if I had taken the offer to manage Sheffield Wednesday?'

'When was that?' I asked, wondering if he was pulling my leg.

'After the World Cup in 1958, 'he said. 'Wednesday general manager Eric Taylor sounded me out. He said he'd been impressed by my coaching work with England during the World Cup finals in Sweden and wanted to know if I would be interested in taking over as team manager at Hillsborough. "Come home to Yorkshire," he said. But I was happy coaching at Tottenham, and living here with our young family. Within a few weeks of being offered the job, I was promoted to manager at Spurs. Wednesday appointed Harry Catterick, and he turned them into our biggest rivals in that Double season. As your mate Greavsie would say, "It's a funny old game."'

I could not get my head round what Bill had told me. Manager of Sheffield Wednesday rather than Spurs? No, that was too much for my poor old brain to handle.

Incidentally, I never did get him to appear in front of the cameras, but he will always remain on my memory screen.

My last view of Bill that memorable day that I visited him at home was him leaning on his stick, waving me goodbye with a wide smile on a friendly face far removed from the 'dour Yorkshireman' description that accompanied so many of his interviews in his managing days. He was enjoying the last of the summer wine, and it was vintage Tottenham.

Just for the record, my *Who's the Greatest?* idea morphed into *Petrolheads*, a series I devised for BBC2. I could not see Bill appearing in that. The panel, headed by *Top Gear*'s Richard Hammond, would have mocked him unmercifully for driving an unfashionable Vauxhall Cavalier.

Bill would not have cared less. After all, he had driven the best: a Rolls-Royce of a football team called Tottenham Hotspur.

* * *

Bill Nicholson's first match as manager was one of the most extraordinary games ever played at the old and original White Hart Lane. Bill Nick (literally a nickname) had been virtually running the playing side of the club as his predecessor Jimmy Anderson battled with health issues brought on by the pressures of management. A key player at right-half in the Push and Run team, Bill joined the Spurs coaching staff after a knee injury forced his retirement.

The quiet, dignified Yorkshireman supervised the Tottenham team during Anderson's illness, while also holding the job of assistant coach to England manager Walter Winterbottom. It was Bill Nick's clever and suffocating tactics during the summer of 1958 that had earned England a goalless draw against the Pelé-propelled eventual champions Brazil in the World Cup finals in Sweden.

Providing the opposition for his first match officially in charge at the Lane were Everton, struggling three from the bottom of the First Division, a point behind 16th-placed Spurs.

The first decision Nicholson made in his new role was to recall the impish inside-forward Tommy Harmer, known to the White Hart Lane fans as 'Harmer the Charmer'. But that afternoon Everton found him more like 'The Harmer' as he pulled them apart with an astounding individual performance.

He had a hand – or rather a well-directed foot – in nine goals and scored one himself as Everton were sunk without trace under a flood of goals. The final scoreline was 10-4. It might easily have been 15-8.

Harmer was the 'Tom Thumb' character of football. A nerves-jangling chain-smoker throughout his career, he stood just 5ft 5.5in tall and was a bantamweight who looked as if he could be blown away by a strong wind. But he had mesmeric control of the ball and when conditions suited him could dominate a match with his passing and dribbling.

Born in Hackney on 2 February 1928, he joined Tottenham at the age of 14 and was farmed out to amateur club Finchley. He returned to the Lane in 1951 and over the following eight years played 205 league games and scored 47 goals. There will be witnesses from my silver-top generation who will confirm that he was one of the most skilful players ever to pull on a Lilywhite shirt. He would have been deadly on today's billiard-top surfaces, but he often struggled in the cloying mud that handicapped him on the pigsty pitches of his day.

For the record, this was Bill Nicholson's first selection as Spurs manager (in a 3-2-1-4 formation):

Johnny Hollowbread

Peter Baker   John Ryden   Mel Hopkins

Danny Blanchflower   Jim Iley

Tommy Harmer

Terry Medwin   Bobby Smith   Alfie Stokes   George Robb

There was a hint of what was to come in the opening moments when Spurs took the lead through Alfie Stokes after an inch-perfect diagonal pass from Harmer had split the Everton defence. The Merseysiders steadied themselves and equalised eight minutes later when Jimmy Harris side-footed in a Dave Hickson centre.

The unfortunate Albert Dunlop, deputising in goal for injured first-choice Jimmy O'Neill, then suffered a nightmare 30 minutes as Spurs ruthlessly smashed five goals past him through skipper Bobby Smith (two), schoolmaster George Robb, Stokes again and Terry Medwin.

The foundation for all the goals was being laid in midfield where Harmer and Danny Blanchflower, both masters of ball control, were in complete command.

Jimmy Harris gave Everton fleeting hope of a revival with a headed goal to make it 6-2 just after half-time, but bulldozing Bobby Smith took his personal haul to four and the irrepressible Harmer helped himself to a goal that was as spectacular as any scored during this gourmet feast.

Bobby Collins lost possession just outside the penalty area, and the ball bobbled in front of Harmer. He struck it on the half-volley from 20 yards and watched almost in disbelief as the ball rocketed into the roof of the net. It was the first time Tommy had scored a league goal from outside the penalty area.

Everton refused to surrender and the industrious Harris completed his hat-trick from a centre by dashing centre-forward Dave Hickson. Then Bobby Collins, just half an inch taller than Harmer, showed that this was a magical match for the wee people when he hammered in a 25-yard drive as both teams crazily pushed everybody forward.

All the goals were scored by forwards until centre-half John Ryden, limping on the wing in pre-substitute days, scrambled in Tottenham's tenth goal – the 14th of the match – in the closing minutes.

Bill Nicholson, finding it hard to believe what he had witnessed, was close to speechless. It was quite some time later when he told me, 'I have never believed in fairy tales in football, but this came close to making me change my mind. In many ways it was a bad advertisement for football because so many of the goals were the result of slip-shod defensive play. But I have to admit it was magnificent entertainment. Little Tommy Harmer played the game of his life. On his day he was as clever a player as I have ever seen, but he was too often handicapped by his small physique. On this day, he was a giant.'

Everton's Jimmy Harris commented, 'It was a good news, bad news day for me. I was able to tell people that I had scored a hat-trick against Spurs, and would then mumble the bad news that we had lost 10-4. It's no exaggeration to say we could have had at least four more goals. I don't know who were the more bewildered by it all – the players or the spectators, who got tremendous value for their money. Tommy Harmer was the man who won it for Tottenham. It was as if he had the ball on a piece of string.'

Hero Harmer said between cigarette puffs, 'I had been out of the league team for the previous four matches and was half-expecting to be left out again when I reported for the match with Everton. But Bill Nick told me I was in, and it became one of those games when just everything went right for me. I particularly remember my goal because it was about the only time I ever scored from that sort of range.'

As Tommy came off the pitch to a standing ovation, he said to Bill Nicholson, 'I hope you're not going to expect ten goals from us every week, Boss!'

We Spurs watchers were brought down to the White Hart Lane turf with a bump when the team managed to win only two of their next 12 matches as Bill Nick struggled to get all the players to sing from his song sheet. There was a lot of disharmony, with Bill and Danny Blanchflower yet to find a rapport. Can you imagine how today's impatient keyboard warriors would have reacted to the situation? They would have been demanding Nicholson's P45.

It was the peak performance of Harmer's career. He lost his place in the first team when John White arrived from Falkirk in 1959, then moved on to Watford and then Chelsea, where he earned hero status by scoring the goal that earned promotion back to the First Division in 1963. Joker Tommy said, 'The ball went in off my groin. I felt a right knob.'

For Tommy Harmer, that 10-4 was his Everest, and he never scaled the same heights again. Still chain-smoking after his retirement, he became a messenger in the City of London and in later life got lost in the fog of dementia that so many ex-footballers experience. When he passed on at the age of 79 on Christmas Day 2007, Tommy Docherty – his Chelsea manager – said, 'He had the best ball control of any English player I've ever seen, but very little self-belief. If he had been three inches taller and more confident, he would have been one of the world's great schemers.'

Only three players from the Spurs team that scored the knockout ten goals survived as regular members of the Double-winning side of 1960/61– right-back Peter Baker, artistic right-half Danny Blanchflower and biff-banging centre-forward Bobby Smith. The 14 goals equalled the aggregate First Division record set in 1892 when Aston Villa annihilated Accrington Stanley 12-2.

The attendance was 37,794 but if you believe everybody who has since said, 'I was there,' it was more like 250,000!

This was just the start. The Glory-Glory days were around the corner.

Now, with the old Lane demolished, that 10-4 result still sits pleasantly in the memory of Tottenham fans of a certain age, and we quietly smile when we recall the part Harmer the Charmer played in the goals banquet.

Can Harry Kane and Co. ever match it? That would really take us down Memory Lane.

* * *

How best to cover the scintillating Jimmy Greaves reign at White Hart Lane in my 70-year memory march? We have always had a special relationship since his earliest days at Chelsea and from when I was just starting out on my football reporting career. His wonderful wife, Irene, and my late wife, Eileen, were best friends and the Greaves/Giller rapport transcended football.

We have written 20 books together and if it had not been for his paralysing stroke of 2015 he would have been heavily involved in helping to trace my journey. As Jimmy can sadly no longer express himself, I have decided to dip into earlier interviews to cover his golden days as a White Hart Lane idol.

Jimmy was – in my admittedly biased opinion – the greatest British goalscorer ever to illuminate a football pitch. There are plenty of stats and facts to support my view, and I know I could call on an army of Spurs spectators to swear eyewitness evidence that he was simply the best.

To save you from my emotional, over-the-top hyperbole it is best that I just stick to the facts. Let's start at what Spurs supporters would consider the beginning, the day that he joined Tottenham.

Bill Nicholson did not want to burden Jimmy with being the first £100,000 footballer, so he negotiated a £99,999 fee to bring him home from Italy where he had spent a miserable five months after joining them from Chelsea in May 1961. It was the start of a mutual love affair between Greavsie and the Tottenham fans as he set about building a mountain of goals that lifted him into a lasting place in White Hart Lane legend.

Those 1960s were about much more than just England's long-awaited triumph in the World Cup. The decade heralded the first success in Europe of British clubs – led by Tottenham – saw the long overdue introduction of substitutes, ushered in the ee-aye-adio revolution on Merseyside, and witnessed the kicking out of the maximum wage to lead the way to today's professional footballers swimming in money. The 1960s were all about the Beatles, rock 'n' roll, Mini cars, miniskirts, the psychedelic, Ali-psyche and, of course, George Best. In London N17, we had Greavsie.

It was a swinging time for everybody apart from those footballers who found themselves redundant as clubs made swingeing cuts to help pay their suddenly inflated wage bills.

Spurs prudently paid each of their first-team players £65 a week, with built-in bonuses for capturing silverware. These are the terms to which Jimmy agreed, even though Chelsea had been willing to pay him £80 a week to take him back to Stamford Bridge.

Fulham's bearded wonder Jimmy Hill led the PFA's campaign to kick out the £20 maximum wage as the eloquent union chairman, and it was his Craven Cottage team-mate Johnny Haynes who made the quickest profit. Comedian Tommy Trinder, chairman of Fulham, announced to the press in 1961 that he was making England skipper Haynes

British football's first £100-a-week footballer. 'It was,' admitted Johnny, 'the funniest thing Tommy ever said.'

The Football League caved in after the players once again threatened strike action, and this time they really did mean it. In the space of a week in January 1961, the maximum wage was kicked out and the restrictive contracts scrapped. Suddenly the likes of Greavsie, Denis Law, Joe Baker, Gerry Hitchens and the great John Charles found they could earn the same sort of money in England that had tempted them to be lured by the lira to Italy.

Here's Greavsie talking to me long before his disabling stroke about those early days as a Spurs player and his move from Milan to Tottenham in that extraordinary £99,999 deal:

I considered myself the luckiest footballer on earth the day Bill Nick arrived in Milan to sign me for Tottenham. Not only was he rescuing me from what I reckoned was the prison of Italian football, but he was also giving me the chance to join what I believed was the finest club side in Europe. It was in the previous season that Spurs had pulled off that historic Double. I had played against them with Chelsea, and I can vouch for the fact that they were, to use a Cockney understatement, "a bit tasty".

They purred along like a Rolls-Royce, with Danny Blanchflower, John White and Dave Mackay at the wheel. When they wanted to touch the accelerator, there was Cliff Jones to break the speed limit down either wing; and if they needed a full show of horsepower, Bobby Smith was put in the driving seat. These were the nucleus of five world-class players around which Bill Nick had built his team. He had got the perfect blend and I remember thinking when I played against them, "Blimey, there's not a weakness in this team. They can win the lot."

"The lot" in those days meant the league championship and FA Cup, two trophies that were harder to win then because – and of this I am convinced – the game was a lot tougher and more demanding. In comparison, today's football has become a virtual non-contact sport. And remember we were all on a 20 quid a week maximum wage at the time, which is why I nipped off to Italy.

Just to give you an idea of the overall standard of the First Division in 1960/61: I was playing in a Chelsea side that included such international-class players as Peter Bonetti, Frank Blunstone, Peter Brabrook, the Sillett brothers, Bobby Evans, Bobby Tambling and Terry Venables. I managed to bang in 41 goals that season. We finished in 12th place in the table.

Wolves, dripping with international players, scored 103 First Division goals and could do no better than third. Defending champions Burnley, blessed with the talents of Jimmy McIlroy, Jimmy Adamson, Alex Elder, Jimmy Robson, Ray Pointer, John Connelly, Brian Miller and Gordon Harris, netted 102 First Division goals, and were back in fourth place. We were all puffing and panting trying to keep up with Spurs.

Runners-up Sheffield Wednesday had England internationals Tony Kay, Peter Swan, Ron Springett and John Fantham at their peak. Blackpool missed relegation by a point, despite being able to call on such skilled players as Tony Waiters, Jimmy Armfield, Ray Parry, Ray Charnley and the one and only Stanley Matthews.

Each team also had at least two hatchet men, with instructions to stop the clever players playing. The likes of "Bites Yer Legs" Norman Hunter, Tommy Smith and Chopper Harris were coming through the ranks and about to make themselves felt. Just talking about them brings me out in bruises. In today's game, they would have been red-carded every time they stepped on a pitch if they tried to tackle as they did in those 1970s and 1960s when football was not for the faint-hearted.

There was class running right the way through the First Division – and not a foreign player in sight. This was the quality of the opposition that the "Super Spurs" side had to overcome to pull off the league and cup Double that had eluded every great team throughout the 20th century. They did it with a style and flair that made them one of the most attractive teams of all time. There were defensive deficiencies, but you never heard a murmur of complaint from the spectators, who were always given tremendous value for money.

For me to join the team in 1961 was like being given a passport to paradise. I considered it like coming home. I was a Spurs fan when I was a kid, and it was odds-on my joining them from school until a lovely rascal of a Chelsea scout called Jimmy

Thompson sweet-talked my dad into encouraging me to go to Stamford Bridge.

I wondered how the Tottenham fans would react to me moving to their manor at White Hart Lane, and realised they were quite keen on the idea when I played my first game in a Spurs shirt in a reserve match at Plymouth. There was a record crowd for a reserve game of 13,000 and I know many of them were Spurs supporters, because over the years I have met loads that say they were there!

My other concern was how the Spurs players would take to me. They had been reading the day-to-day accounts of my exploits in Italy, where I had been waging a verbal war in a bid to get back into British football. Those who knew me only by reputation must have been thinking I was a real troublemaker, and – having just won the "impossible" Double without me – understandably looked on me as an intruder who could possibly rock their happy and successful boat.

Thank goodness it didn't take me long to kick their doubts into touch. I got lucky and kicked off with a hat-trick against Blackpool in my first-team debut, and I settled into the side – both on and off the pitch – as if I had been at Tottenham all my life.

I am never comfortable talking about goals that I scored, but I have to admit that one of the goals in my first match was a little bit special. Dave Mackay took one of his long throw-ins, Terry Medwin flicked the ball on, and I scored with what the newspapers described as "a spectacular scissors kick". From that moment on I was accepted by the Tottenham fans and players as "one of them".

All these years later I can say that the Tottenham team of that period was the best side I ever played with, and that takes into account England matches. I get goosebumps just thinking about some of the football we used to play: it was out of this world, and I consider myself as fortunate as a lottery winner to have had the chance to be part of the dream machine. **'**

Tottenham made a monumental bid for the major prize – the European Cup – in Jimmy's first season, during which the 'Glory, glory hallelujah' choruses raised the White Hart Lane roof. There are conflicting opinions as to when the 'Battle Hymn of the Republic' was adopted as the club's theme song. Some insist it was being sung by Spurs supporters at Molineux in April 1960 as Tottenham powered to a 3-1 victory that stopped Wolves being first to the league and cup Double.

Older supporters vaguely remember it being sung back in the early 1950s after a cartoon had appeared in the Tottenham match programme showing Arthur Rowe day-dreaming of the Double. The caption read, 'While the Spurs go marching on.'

There was an explosion of noise every time Spurs played European Cup ties at White Hart Lane in 1961/62 as they saw off Gornik, Feyenoord and Dukla Prague. There was also good humour to go with the fanatical support. A small group of Spurs fans always dressed as angels, carrying witty placards and waving them – without malice – at opposition followers. There was never a hint of hooliganism. That scar on the face of soccer was a decade away.

Tottenham were desperately unlucky to lose a two-legged European Cup semi-final against eventual champions Benfica, propelled by the rising master Eusebio. To this day, Greavsie insists that a 'goal' he scored, which would have put Spurs into the final, was wrongly flagged offside by the linesman.

They quickly picked themselves up after their exit from Europe and the following month retained the FA Cup, with Jimmy scoring an exquisite goal in the third minute to put them on the way to a 3-1 victory over Burnley. My Greavsie bias coming out again, but I think it rates with the finest goals scored at old Wembley. He was 15 yards out and passed the ball along the ground into the net through a forest of players' legs and with all the unerring accuracy of a Jack Nicklaus putt. Jimmy, never one to boast in his playing days, said just before the players left the dressing room, 'I'm going to get an early one today, lads.' If it had been a fluke it would have been an outstanding goal, so the fact that Greavsie meant it puts it up into the classic category.

The Tottenham team that day was, Brown; Baker, Henry; Blanchflower, Norman, Mackay; Medwin, White, Smith, Greaves, Jones. Goals from Bobby Smith and skipper Danny Blanchflower clinched Tottenham's win after Jimmy Robson had equalised for Burnley. Danny's goal came from the penalty spot in the 80th minute after Tommy Cummings had handled a Terry Medwin shot on the line.

As Blanchflower was placing the ball on the penalty spot, his Northern Ireland team-mate and good friend Jimmy McIlroy said to him, 'Bet you miss.'

Danny did not say a word. He calmly sent goalkeeper Adam Blacklaw the wrong way as he stroked the penalty home. As he ran past Burnley schemer McIlory, he said, 'Bet I don't!'

The victory earned Tottenham a place in the European Cup Winners' Cup, and the 'Glory-Glory' chanting supporters roared them all the way into the final in May 1963. No British team had won a major trophy in Europe when Spurs travelled to Rotterdam and hopes that they could break the duck were suddenly diminished when their main motivator, Dave Mackay, failed a fitness test on the day of the match. The absence of Mackay was a devastating blow because he had been a major force in Tottenham's magnificent success over the previous two seasons. As it sank in that they would have to perform without his battering ram backing, a blanket of gloom dropped on the Spurs camp.

Atlético were suddenly considered by neutrals to be warm favourites to retain the trophy they had won in impressive style the previous year, when they mastered a high-quality Fiorentina side.

Mackay's absence plunged manager Bill Nicholson into a morose mood, and he added to the air of pessimism when he ran through the strengths of the opposition during a tactical team talk. He made Atlético sound like the greatest team ever to run on to a football pitch, and he bruised rather than boosted the confidence of his players.

Skipper Blanchflower was so concerned about the sudden gloom and doom environment that he summoned all the players to a private meeting and made one of the most inspiring speeches of his career. Using a mixture of fact and blarney, word-master Blanchflower pumped confidence back into his team-mates and made them believe in their ability to win. He countered every point that Nicholson had made about the Madrid players by underlining Tottenham's strengths, and he convinced them that they were superior to the Spaniards in every department. It was a speech of Churchillian class and content and Tottenham went into the final with renewed determination to take the trophy back to White Hart Lane.

This was how Tottenham lined up for the game of their lives, with Tony Marchi stepping into Dave Mackay's place: Brown, Baker, Henry, Blanchflower, Norman, Marchi, Jones, White, Smith, Greaves, Dyson.

Nicholson, one of the finest tacticians in the game, deserved the credit for the fact that Greavsie was in position to give Spurs the lead in the 16th minute. He had spotted, during a spying mission to Madrid, that the Atlético defence was slow to cover down the left side, and he instructed that full use should be made of the blistering speed of Cliff Jones. Moving with pace and penetration, Cliff sprinted to meet a neatly placed pass from Bobby Smith and Greavsie drifted into the middle to steer his accurate centre into the net with his deadly left foot.

The goal was a real pick-pocket job, and Tottenham's fans roared their 'Glory-Glory' anthem as the Spaniards suddenly wilted.

It was on the wings that Tottenham were monopolising the match, with Jones and tiny Terry Dyson running the Spanish full-backs into dizzy disorder. Atlético, strangely enough, also had a winger called Jones, but he was not in the same class as Tottenham's Welsh wizard.

Dyson and Jones combined to set up goal number two in the 32nd minute, exchanging passes before releasing the ball to Smith, who laid it back for John White to rifle a low shot into the net.

It was a rare but crucial goal from White, who had made his reputation as a maker rather than taker of goals. His signature was stamped on most of Tottenham's attacks as he prised open the Atlético defence with beautifully weighted passes.

Blanchflower, White and the tall, stately Marchi were working like Trojans in midfield to make up for the absence of the one and only Mackay.

At most clubs, Marchi would have been an automatic choice for the first team, and he played with such skill and determination that his contribution was in the Mackay class. There can be no higher praise.

Atlético revived their flickering flame of hope in the first minute of the second half when Collar scored from the penalty spot after Ron Henry had fisted the ball off the goal line. Today, Ron would have been red carded.

For 20 minutes, there was a danger that Spurs could lose their way as the holders forced a series of corner kicks, but the defence managed to survive the Spanish storm.

Goalkeeper Bill Brown took his life in his hands as he threw himself courageously at the feet of Mendonca to snatch the ball off the forward's toes. Chuzo broke free and Tottenham's fans sighed with relief as he shot the wrong side of the post, then Ramiro drove the ball just off target. This was when everybody connected with Tottenham began to wonder and worry whether they were going to get by without the great Mackay, who in a situation like this would have been breaking Spanish hearts with his thundering tackles and brandishing a fist in a demand for extra effort from all his team-mates.

It was 'Dynamo' Dyson, having the game of a lifetime, who ended the Atlético comeback when his hanging cross was fumbled into the net by goalkeeper Madinabeytia, who had one eye on the menacing presence of big Bobby Smith.

Dyson became a man inspired and laid on a second goal for Greavsie before putting the seal on a memorable performance with a scorching shot at the end of a weaving 30-yard run. His first goal was something of a fluke, but the second was a masterpiece.

As Tottenham's triumphant players paraded the trophy in front of their ecstatic fans, Bobby Smith shouted at Dyson in his typically blunt way, 'If I were you, mate, I'd hang up my boots. There's no way you can top that. You were out of this world.'

The following season dawned with no hint that it was to see the break-up of the 'Super Spurs'. The heart was ripped out of the Tottenham team in a tragic and painful way, and a black cloud of despondency enveloped the club.

The nightmare was slow and drawn out. It started on the evening of 10 December 1963 at Old Trafford, when Tottenham were playing Manchester United in the second leg of a European Cup Winners' Cup tie. Dave Mackay broke a leg in a collision with Noel Cantwell that surely left the United skipper losing sleep about the validity of his challenge.

Just a few weeks later, Danny Blanchflower was forced to retire because of a recurring knee injury. Tottenham had lost the brains of the team and the heart of the team, and worse was to follow at the end of the season. John White, the eyes of the team, was sitting under a tree sheltering from a storm on a north London golf course when he was tragically killed by lightning. Tottenham had lost the three most vital cogs in their machine.

John's tragic death came only a matter of months after the passing from cancer of his father-in-law and popular Spurs assistant manager Harry Evans. It was Bill Nicholson, along with trainer Cecil Poynton, who had to go to the mortuary to identify John's body. 'The worst moment of my life,' was how Bill described it to me. White was a master footballer and the Nicholson plan was to build his new Tottenham team around the immense talent of the 27-year-old Scot.

There is no way you can measure the grief that engulfed John's 22-year-old widow, Sandra, who had lost her dad and husband in quick succession, and I have often thought that Spurs did not do nearly enough to look after her properly following the double tragedy.

Rob White, John's son and now a respected photographer, captures his mother's misery in a beautifully composed book written with 'Dame' Julie Welch, *The Ghost: In Search of My Father The Football Legend*.

But the game, and life, had to go on.

Bill Nick got busy in the transfer market and bought Alan Mullery from Fulham, Laurie Brown from Arsenal, Cyril Knowles from Middlesbrough, Pat Jennings from Watford, Jimmy Robertson from St Mirren and Alan Gilzean from Dundee.

He took a breather, and then went shopping again, this time buying centre-half Mike England from Blackburn and Terry Venables from Chelsea. He also tried and failed to buy Bobby Moore.

Bill Nick was trying to build another 'Super Spurs'. He never quite made it. The new Tottenham team had some memorable moments together in the mid-60s, but they never touched the peak performances of the Blanchflower-White-Mackay era.

You cannot dwell on the Tottenham Double season without giving special attention to the man whose goals made the feat possible, top marksman Bobby Smith. He was the first Spurs player to hit the two-century mark for the club, and at the Everest peak of his playing career he was as powerful and potent as any player who ever pulled on Spurs' number nine shirt.

Sadly, Bobby never knew prolonged prosperity and he spent most of his life after football in debt and in despair. He and I were due to chronicle his life and times when he passed on in the late summer of 2010, and this is how I recorded his passing in my Spurs Odyssey blog:

'It's the ghosted book that I will never publish – *Bobby Smith: Secrets of a Soccer Slave*. Everything was planned and I had collected and collated much of the material, which would have shocked the life out of today's pampered footballing millionaires. And there is a generation of sports journalists coming through to whom it would have read like fiction.

'But the secrets will go to the grave with Bobby, who lost his fight with cancer at the weekend (18 September 2010). I had put the book on the back burner when, just a few weeks ago, it became obvious that he was struggling.

'The moving minute's applause in his memory before the game against Arsenal at White Hart Lane on Tuesday would have been even warmer if the crowd had been fully aware of the facts of Smithy's footballing life.

'He was 28 before he earned more than £20 a week, and when joining Spurs from Chelsea in 1956 he was taking home just £17 a week.'

In the 1960/61 season that he blasted Tottenham to the First Division championship and FA Cup Double with 33 goals, the maximum wage was lifted. The following season – along with the rest of the Double-winning players and newcomer Jimmy Greaves – he was paid a princely £65 a week. But these relative riches had come too late for Bobby. He was a wreck from recurring injuries, and had to play through a pain barrier every time he went on to the pitch.

He told me how on the morning of the 1961 FA Cup Final he made two secret journeys from the team's Middlesex hotel to see his GP near his home in Palmers Green for painkilling injections on his knee.

'If our manager Bill Nicholson had known the pain I was in, he would have left me out,' said Bobby. 'This was the game of my life and I was determined not to miss it.'

Bobby played through the pain and scored the first and laid on the second of the goals in the 2-0 victory over Leicester City that clinched that historic Double.

There is cruel irony in the first legal betting shops in the UK being opened in May 1961, the very week that Smithy enjoyed his Wembley glory.

What few people knew is that he was hopelessly addicted to gambling, and betting shops became like his second home.

When Tottenham were checking out of their hotel after the away leg of their European Cup first round tie against Feyenoord in 1961/62, Bill Nicholson called a meeting of the players to say in the pre-STD (subscriber trunk dialling) days, 'Our telephone bill is ten times what we expected. Somebody has taken liberties calling home.'

Bobby snapped, 'All right, all right. Keep your hair on. I'll pay it when I get home.'

Nobody except his room-mate Jimmy Greaves had known that Smithy had been on the phone throughout the trip to his bookie in London. 'He just couldn't resist it,' Jimmy told me. 'If two flies were running up a window pane he would want to bet as to which would get to the top first. I know what I'm taking about when I say gambling is a drug worse even than alcoholism.'

After the historic 1960/61 Double, Bobby had two barnstorming seasons alongside Greavsie before his injuries caught up with him. 'He was the perfect partner for me, knocking defenders down while I concentrated on knocking the ball into the net,' Jimmy said. 'We had an instinctive feel as to where to be to get the best out of each other. I had him to thank for many of my goals both for Spurs and England in an era when it was acceptable to hammer into defenders. He would run through brick walls for the team, and I would pick up the pieces.'

With his body protesting and his gambling debts mounting, Smithy moved on to Brighton in May 1964 for a trifling £5,000. 'That money should have gone into my pocket,' he moaned. 'Spurs should have given me a free transfer in return for all those goals I scored for them.' At the time, he was the most prolific goalscorer in the club's history and there were many who thought Spurs were being mercenary for demanding a fee, even though it was peanuts.

I just happened to be interviewing Brighton manager Archie Macaulay when Smithy reported for pre-season training at the Goldstone Ground on the south coast, and I arranged for *Daily Express* sports photographer Norman 'Speedy' Quicke to take a picture of him weighing in on the club scales.

It was going to be just an innocent 'atmosphere' picture. Smithy had weighed 13st 9lb according to the Spurs records. Archie Macaulay hit the roof when the arrow on the scales shot up to 16st 9lb! That was more than a stone heavier than the newly crowned world heavyweight champion Cassius Clay, the difference being that Clay (later Muhammad Ali) stood 6ft 3in, Bobby Smith 5ft 9in.

It went from being a run-of-the-mill photo to supporting a back page lead story under the headline 'Blobby Smith!' He was given extra training and got himself in good enough shape to help shoot Brighton to the Fourth Division title before moving to Hastings for the final shots of his goal-gorged career. As he signed off, he sold his story to the *Sunday People*, which ran the front-page banner headline 'MY LIFE OF BIRDS, BOOZE AND BETTING'.

'I made most of it up,' Bobby told me. 'I was desperate for cash to clear gambling debts. But the bit about birds virtually ended my first marriage.'

He became a painter and decorator and drove a minicab before the crippling injuries he had collected on the football field finally caught up with him, not helped by a fall through a manhole which damaged his already wrecked legs.

Bobby had to take a disability pension after suffering heart problems and having a hip replacement. The Tottenham Tribute Trust quietly did its best to help him through his financial maze.

It would have been handy if he could have sold his championship and FA Cup winners' medals from 1961 and 1962, but they were stolen, and he had the heartache of hearing how the 1961 cup medal had turned up at an auction and sold for £11,200.

Here's something for Spurs fans to chew on. Bobby told me, 'I am always made very welcome when I go to White Hart Lane, but my first club Chelsea go further. Every Christmas they send a cheque for £1,500 to all those who were in the squad for the 1955 league championship win – and I hardly got a kick because manager Ted Drake hated my guts!'

If he had been playing today, Bobby – who mixed cruiserweight strength with subtlety on the ball – would have been revered as a player in the Alan Shearer class, and rewarded with the riches that his ability warranted.

But he played in the soccer slave era. His rewards were pain in the limbs and – much of it self-inflicted – poverty in the pocket.

Bobby's story deserved to be told. But he has taken his secrets with him. Rest easy, old friend.

* * *

Secretly, Nicholson had also tried to bring Edmonton-born England skipper Johnny Haynes to White Hart Lane to team up with his old England sidekick Jimmy Greaves. But the bold attempt fell through, and the Blanchflower-White roles went to Mullery and Venables; good as they were, they struggled to be accepted by the hard-to-please Spurs fans used to the Blanchflower-White chemistry.

Greavsie had become accustomed to the pace set by Danny and John, and he struggled to adapt to their style of delivery.

Both were given a tough time by the Spurs supporters, who had been spoiled over recent years. They unkindly but understandably compared the newcomers with their great idols.

Venables was not always happy playing at White Hart Lane after his success as the midfield boss at Chelsea, and when he eventually moved on to Queens Park Rangers, who would have taken any bets that one day he would return and buy the club. Yes, as Greavsie says, it's a funny old game.

One of the new-look Tottenham squad who did win the hearts of the fans was Alan Gilzean, who formed a wonderful partnership with Greavsie. Jimmy found Gilly a joy to play with, and he felt that Alan was never given sufficient credit for his delicate touch play and finishing finesse in the penalty area. He was a master of the flick header, and could bamboozle defences with deceptive changes of pace and clever ball control.

Missing the command of Blanchflower, and the drive of Mackay, the 1963/64 season was relatively barren for Spurs after three years of non-stop success. But they still managed to finish fourth in the league in a season that would be remembered for the start of Liverpool's 'Red Revolution' under the mesmeric management of Bill Shankly, a close friend yet fierce rival of Bill Nick.

Ownership of Spurs had moved from the Bearmans to the Wales late in 1960, with first Fred Wale and then Sidney as chairman. They considered Tottenham a family club, and allowed Bill Nick to get on with the job of managing without interference. Under the Wale influence, the Tottenham directors ran a tight, well-organised ship, but they were also tight with their wage policy and Bill Nick was never ever paid what he was worth.

The Masters of White Hart Lane's latest team saved their peak performances for the FA Cup in the 1966/67 season, culminating in a well-earned FA Cup Final triumph over London neighbours Chelsea at Wembley. Of the side that won the trophy in 1962, only Dave Mackay and Greavsie had survived, along with Cliff Jones on the substitutes' bench.

Greavsie had recovered from the hepatitis that had robbed him of half a yard of pace during the build-up to the 1966 World Cup finals; nobody ever takes that illness into account when discussing Jimmy's contribution to the World Cup triumph, halted by a shin injury received in a group game against France.

The fact that Mackay was there at the 1967 FA Cup Final to lead out the Tottenham team as skipper was the sort of story that you would expect to come from the pages of *Roy of the Rovers*. 'Miracle Man' Mackay had made an astonishing recovery after breaking his leg a second time following his controversial collision with Noel Cantwell at Old Trafford in 1963.

Mackay motivated a team that had Pat Jennings building himself into a legend as the last line of defence. Baby-faced Irish international Joe Kinnear had come in as right-back in place of the energetic Phil Beal, who was unlucky to break an arm after playing an important part in getting Spurs to the final. Joe, a neat, controlled player, was partnered at full-back by Cyril Knowles, a former Yorkshire miner who took the eye with his sharp tackling and some polished, if at times eccentric skills. He was to become a cult hero, with anything he attempted – good or bad – accompanied by chants of 'nice one, Cyril' from the White Hart Lane faithful.

Standing like a Welsh mountain in the middle of the defence was the majestic Mike England, one of the finest centre-halves ever produced in Britain. He was a class player from head to toe. Just imagine if Bobby Moore had arrived to play alongside him. Bill Nick tried hard to sign him.

Dave Mackay was the immoveable link between defence and attack as he adapted his game from buccaneer to anchorman, helping to stoke the fires of the engine room where Alan Mullery and Terry Venables were forging a productive partnership. They never quite touched the peaks that Spurs fans had seen in the 'Glory-Glory' days of Blanchflower–White–Mackay, but – let's be honest – few midfield combinations have ever reached that sky-scraping standard.

Jimmy Robertson was a flying Scot on the right wing, where his speed was a vital asset for Gilzean and Greaves, who had a radar-like understanding for where to be to get the best out of each other.

For the final, Bill Nick preferred Frank Saul to the veteran Cliff Jones for the number 11 shirt. Frank, who had been a fringe player in the Double-winning squad, was more of a central striker than a winger, but he was a direct player with a good nose for goal. Cliff, and Joe Kirkup for Chelsea, were the first players to wear No 12 shirts in an FA Cup final.

The Tottenham team was: Jennings, Kinnear, Knowles, Mullery, England, Mackay, Robertson, Greaves, Gilzean, Venables, Saul. Sub: Jones.

Facing Tottenham in the first all-London final were Tommy Docherty's elegant but unpredictable Chelsea. They had gone through an even more drastic rebuilding programme than Spurs, and Terry Venables was part of the upheaval when he moved on to Tottenham to make room the previous year for the arrival of Scotland's 'Wizard of Dribble', Charlie Cooke.

Masterminding the Chelsea team was manager Tommy Docherty, one of the game's great personalities. He had a razor-sharp Glaswegian wit and was in complete contrast to the dour and often tight-lipped Bill Nicholson.

On paper, it looked certain to be a cracker of a match. But on the pitch it turned out to be something of a damp squib. The whole day fell a bit flat, mainly due to the fact that both teams were from London. That robbed the match of much of its atmosphere, because the supporters were not in that bubbling 'Oop f'the Coop' day-out mood.

Spurs skipper Mackay had a personal mission to win after having been inactive for so long, and he drove the Tottenham team on like a man possessed. They were always playing the more positive and purposeful football, and deserved their lead just before half-time. Jimmy Robertson crashed a shot wide of Bonetti after Alan Mullery's long-range piledriver had been blocked.

Robertson, proving one of the most effective of all the forwards, set up a second goal in the 68th minute when he steered a typical long throw-in from Mackay into the path of Frank Saul, who pivoted and hooked the ball high into the net.

Bobby Tambling was allowed in for a goal five minutes from the end, but Tottenham tightened up at the back to hold out for victory.

Three months after this triumph, Tottenham drew 3-3 in the Charity Shield against Manchester United at Old Trafford, a match that has gone down in footballing folklore because of a goal scored by Pat Jennings. The Irish international keeper hammered a huge clearance from his penalty area which went first bounce over the head of Alex Stepney and into the back of the United net. The bewildered look on the faces of the players of both teams was hilarious to see.

I was reporting the match for the *Daily Express,* and afterwards Pat told me:

> I decided to clear the ball up to Greavsie and Gilly, and a strong following wind grabbed it and took it all the way to the United net. Jimmy and Alan had their backs to me and could not believe it when they realised it was me who had scored. Greavsie said he told Alan, "D'you realise this makes Pat our top scorer for the season? He'll never let us forget it."

The Greavsie era at Tottenham was drawing to a close, leaving a remarkable legacy of a club record 220 First Division goals (including a record 37 in 1962/63), 32 FA Cup goals and 266 in all competitions. Those bare statistics hide the fact that many of the goals were of the spectacular variety, fashioned like a skilled sculptor with clever feints, dizzying dribbles, astonishing acceleration and then finished with a pass rather than a shot into the net.

Those old enough to have witnessed a Greaves goal will confirm that I am not exaggerating when I say we actually felt privileged to have been there to see it. We were keeping company with a genius, a Goya of goals. How many would a peak-powered Greaves score in today's game, with no Norman Hunter-style bites-yer-legs tackling from behind, billiard-table surfaces and the relaxed, often-confusing offside law? And what would he be worth in the transfer market? Let the bidding begin at £99.999m!

There were calls for Greavsie to be reinstated in the England team when he hit a purple patch with 27 First Division goals in 1968/69, but Jimmy seemed to be almost visibly losing his appetite for the game the following season.

Bill Nick told me privately that he was concerned that the Artful Dodger of the penalty area seemed to be showing more enthusiasm preparing for driving to Mexico in a 1970 World Cup rally than playing football. By this time, Jimmy had built up a flourishing sports shop and travel business with his brother-in-law Tom Barden, and football was no longer the be-all-and-end-all for him. Yet he was still by some distance the most dynamic finisher in the First Division. To try to bring the best out of Greavsie, Nicholson went shopping and bought Martin Chivers as a new play-mate from Southampton.

Sadly, he arrived at Jimmy's side just as the goal master was losing his motivation. The crunch came when Spurs wore their white shirts like flags of surrender against Crystal Palace in an FA Cup fourth round replay at Selhurst Park. Palace striker Gerry Queen dismantled the Spurs defence for the winning goal, and I recall that the headline on my report for the *Daily Express* announced, 'Queen Is King at the Palace'.

Greavsie, trying to settle into his new partnership with Chivers, was dropped for the first time in his nine years at Spurs. It was his final curtain at Tottenham. With many Spurs fans in tears, genius Jimmy was allowed to move on to West Ham for an unhappy last season in league football, while Martin Peters came the other way from Upton Park.

* * *

Without doubt, two of the greatest Tottenham players during my 70-year vigil have been Greavsie and the indomitable Dave Mackay. I have dug out a Q&A feature Jimmy and I produced when we were in harness for *The Sun* back in the 1970s after Dave had followed Brian Clough as Derby manager. Jimmy, a recovering alcoholic, had just started out on his TV and media career and Dave had that season lifted the league championship.

Here's the great Mackay answering questions about his career from Greavsie, with me as the privileged observer and note-taker:

Did you always want to be a footballer?
Not just a footballer, a Hearts footballer. They have always been my favourite club. When I was just a kid I used to walk three miles there and three miles back to get to watch them play at Tynecastle, and I was so small I could nip under the turnstile and get in without paying. My one dream was to play in the maroon and white shirt.

You're the most competitive bloke I've ever known. Were you like that at Hearts?
As you know, whether I'm playing football, golf or tiddlywinks, I HAVE to win. I used to be the smallest player on the pitch and to win the ball I had to tackle twice as hard as anybody else and I never got out of the habit. Even now I'm retired my players fear me in six-a-side kick-abouts, because I only know one way to play and that is to win. My two brothers also played for Hearts, and the three of us had a reputation for being ultra competitive. Fitba's a man's game.

Yes, you used to kick lumps out of us in the Tottenham gym. But you were about much more than power and strength, Dave.
I like to think I could be as accurate with my left foot as the great Danny Blanchflower was with his right. I made a few goals for you, Jim, with my passes. I was lucky to play for a

Hearts team that put the emphasis on skill and then joined a Tottenham side that played pure football, because that was the way manager Bill Nicholson wanted it. Anybody thumping the ball without thought got a right mouthful.

Which was the greatest team you played for?
Well obviously the Tottenham team that won the Double in 1961, but the Hearts side with which we won the Scottish championship ran them close. I skippered the team that banged in a British record 132 league goals that season. Even you, Jim, didn't rattle in that many! You made our Spurs side even better when you signed from Milan, and we deserved to be European champions in your first season but were robbed in the semi-final against Benfica by some diabolical refereeing decisions.

How difficult was it combining National Service in the Army with your football?
I got off lightly. There was no war to worry about and I had a sergeant major in the Royal Engineers who was a football nut. He used to make sure I got home every weekend to play for Hearts, provided I got him a ticket. I also played for my regiment in midweek and was as fit as a fiddle. I did more running about on the pitch than square bashing.

You won only 22 Scotland caps when players with half your ability got picked many more times. Why was that?
I played in the days when the selectors considered you something of a traitor for taking the English pound. A lot of Anglos were often ignored. I was always proud to play for Scotland, and if you mention the 9-3 game, Jim, this interview is over. That still hurts to this day. It was a freak

result and is the only game people seem to remember me playing at Wembley.

The worst thing for all of us in those 1960s was losing dear John White.

Yes, I still well up when I think of it. He had asked Cliffie Jones and me to play golf with him, but we turned him down because there was a lot of rain around. He went out on his own and got hit by lightning. It was a tragedy that affected everybody at the club, particularly his best mate Jonesie and me. I had been responsible for him joining Spurs, because I'd played with him for Scotland and told Bill Nick that he had to sign him. He was a magnificent footballer, a real players' player who always put the team first.

Breaking your leg twice and then coming back to lead Tottenham to the 1967 FA Cup earned you the nickname of the 'Miracle Man'.

Well it was something of a miracle really when you think of the mess my leg was in when Noel Cantwell did me at Old Trafford. I'm not going over old ground, but you saw it, Jim – one of the nastiest tackles ever! Then I got it broken again in a reserve match and for a while it looked as if it was curtains. But I was determined to play again, and that was a marvellous Spurs team I captained at Wembley. You and Gilly [Alan Gilzean] were two of the best striking partners I ever saw. Poetry in motion.

You looked a giant on the pitch, Dave, and people would never believe me when I said I was taller than you.

How many bets did we win in pubs when we'd challenge people to guess which of us was taller. You beat me by half an inch when we stood back to back. Those were the days when any pressman joining us for a drink were told, one, everything you hear is off the record, and, two, make sure you get a round in.

Talking as somebody who is a recovering alcoholic, we certainly used to hit the old hooch back in our playing days. Aye, we were a good drinking club, that's for sure. You and Gilly could really knock it back. I don't encourage my players to booze like we did. For us it was a sort of bonus, but now players are sensible enough to know that they should only drink in moderation. It's a classic case of, 'Don't do as I do, do as I say'. I'd come down on them like a ton of bricks if they drank like we did.

Remember that game when the ref sent you off and you talked him out of it?
For all my reputation for being a tough guy, I was never ever sent off and I was not going to let the referee spoil my record when I knew he was making a mistake. It was in a cup tie against Bristol City and that little so-and-so Johnny Quigley kicked me up in the air. All the ref saw was my retaliation and he said. 'Off, Mackay.' I grabbed hold of Johnny and marched him to the ref and he was honest enough – or scared enough – to tell the ref what had happened, and he let me off.

The fans loved the way you used to always kick the ball miles in the air and trap it as you ran out for the start of a match. It started off as me showing off, but then it became something of a superstition, and I also did it to let the opposition know I had a bit of skill. A lot of people thought

I was all about tackling. But I could play a bit. You will confirm, Jim, that I could beat all of you at keepy-uppy and I can still lob a two bob bit into my top pocket.

There's that famous picture of you grabbing Billy Bremner by the scruff of the neck that proves your competitive nature.
I hate that bloody picture. It shows me in a terrible light. People see that and think what a bully I must have been. But I was just putting young Billy in his place. I had not long come back after breaking my leg a second time and he jumped in with a reckless tackle. He and I have always been big mates and roomed together on Scotland trips. That was just a moment when I felt I needed to give him a bit of fatherly advice about watching his tackles. We often laugh about it.

When you at last won the Footballer of the Year award in 1969 you had to share it with Man City's Tony Book. Did that spoil it for you?
No, I was just proud to have won even if it was a joint award. Tony Book is a smashing bloke and he had an outstanding season. I would have been choked if I had gone through my career without getting the award because I never had false modesty and knew I deserved it. The fact that you never got it, Jim, is a joke.

I was shocked when you signed for Derby, because you told me you were going home to Scotland.
That was the plan. I was all lined up to go back to Hearts as player-manager when I got a call from Brian Clough. He locked me in Bill Nicholson's office and said he was not going to let me out until I'd signed for Derby. He is the

most persuasive guy I've ever met and he convinced me I could still play at the top level.

You changed your style completely when you moved to Derby.
Cloughie knew my legs had gone and told me just to use my positional sense and guide young Roy McFarland at the heart of the defence. Brian wanted me for my leadership qualities and I slotted in comfortably, more as a conductor than the old-style competitor. Others did the running for me and I just kept motivating them with the odd tackle and a flourished fist. I think opponents were frightened of my reputation, not realising that I was nothing like the player I'd been at Tottenham. But it all worked very well and I was nicely paid.

Now, you've taken over from Cloughie as Derby manager and have won the league championship. Do you remain a Cloughie fan?
Of course, he is a master and I've been lucky to play under three of the greatest managers ever in Tommy Walker at Hearts, Bill Nick and then Cloughie. I have learned so much from the three of them. They are completely different personalities but have the same fundamental belief that football is a game of skill. The principles I hold are the same as when I first started out with that wonderful Hearts side.

What was the best advice you got from Cloughie as a manager?
That I should burn his desk! That's what he did to Don Revie's desk when he took over at Leeds, and when he came here to do some transfer business he said I should set fire to his desk because it gets rid of the stench of the old regime.

With a gun to your head, who would you say was the most important influence on your career?

Without question, my wife Isobel. She is the perfect football wife. Knows when to encourage and when to shut up. Without her, I would not have been half the player or half the manager. She is my strength and I'm not saying this only so she'll let me off the shopping tomorrow so I can play golf. I'd have loved to have been a golf professional. Now there's a life, almost as good as being a footballer.

That interview from nearly 40 years ago gives the perfect insight into Dave Mackay the football man. He was a hero for all seasons.

* * *

Now for something completely different (*Monty Python*, circa 1969).

During my 14 years as a member of the *This Is Your Life* scriptwriting team, I was continually trying to get Bill Nicholson booked. One of my roles was to prepare dossiers for the show's producer, Malcolm Morris, who would run them past Eamonn Andrews and, for the later series, Michael Aspel and director Brian Klein.

Sadly, a much deserved tribute never got past the programme planning stage. But at least this 70-year journey gives me the chance to take a microscope to Bill's life and times.

One of the reasons the programme producers were nervous about featuring Bill was that his close confidant, Danny Blanchflower, had famously turned down Eamonn and told him politely where to stick his red book. It cost thousands to scrap the planned show, because relatives, club-mates and friends had been brought from all parts of the globe to join in a tribute to Danny Boy that never took place. The fear was that Bill, a shy, private man, might be tempted to 'do a Danny'.

As I had learned from my first meeting with him in 1958, Bill was very much a tracksuit manager, and only really content when at the Cheshunt training ground working on tactics and theories with his other family, the players.

I have fished out the dossier I compiled for the eyes of Eamonn Andrews in 1981, and here it is in the original note form (the quotes were put in to give Eamonn a taste of what the guests might say). We had to give each proposed subject a codeword, because if ever it leaked out that a *Life* show was being planned it would be instantly shelved. These are my confidential notes, exactly as they dropped on to the desk of that legendary broadcaster:

TIYL BILL NICHOLSON DOSSIER
Suggested codeword: Cockerel
Confidential: From Norman Giller

Subject summary: William Edward Nicholson, ex-footballer and later football manager: born Scarborough, Yorkshire, 26 January 1919; played for Tottenham Hotspur 1936–55, manager 1958–74, managerial consultant West Ham 1975–76; currently chief scout and consultant at White Hart Lane; capped once for England 1951; OBE 1975.

Personal: Married to Grace (known as Darkie, so named as a contrast to her blonde twin sister). They have two daughters (Linda and Jean), and throughout his managerial career with Tottenham he and the family lived in an end of terrace house within walking distance of White Hart Lane. Darkie famously cycled to the local shops on a push bike. He banned her from watching them play because he considered her a Jonah.

Quote (circa 1970) from Darkie, a charming and bubbly lady, 'I accept that Bill has two marriages; one to me, the other to football in general and Tottenham Hotspur in particular. Even when we are on summer holiday in Scarborough his mind is eaten up with ideas for the following season. Sometimes I wonder if he should have a bed put in his office at White Hart Lane!'

EARLY LIFE: Born and raised between the wars in Scarborough, the second youngest of a hansom-cab driver's nine children. Seven are still alive. Grew up during the Depression, and on leaving school at the age of 14, he took a job as a laundry boy and played his football for Scarborough Young Liberals and Scarborough Working Men's Club. In 1936, aged 16, he was spotted by Spurs and moved south to join their nursery club, Gravesend and Northfleet, before turning professional in 1938. Best person to cover this part of his footballing life is Ronnie Burgess, who captained Spurs and Wales in the 1950s and was Bill's close pal.

Quote (circa 1961) from Ron Burgess, 'Bill was the most conscientious footballer I ever played with. He gave 100 per cent in everything that he did, and would always put the team first. In those early days at Gravesend and then in the first team he unselfishly agreed to play at left-back, even though he was essentially right-footed. He lost his best years to the war, otherwise he would have won a load of England caps.'

WAR YEARS: Bill had just started to establish himself
in the first team when war was declared in September
1939. He served in the Durham Light Infantry, stationed
mainly in England first as an infantry instructor, then a
physical training instructor and he found time for Saturday
Wartime League guest appearances with Middlesbrough,
Sunderland, Newcastle United and Darlington.
When he reported back to Spurs in 1945 he first of all
played at centre-half and then switched to right-half, the
position in which he was to establish himself as one of the
most reliable and industrious players in the league. He
became a key man in the Spurs Push and Run team that
in back-to-back seasons of 1949 to 1951 won the Second
Division and First Division titles.

Note to Eamonn: Ideally we should bring in Alf Ramsey
here, but he always refuses to do the show. I think he is in
fear that he will be the subject, and likes to keep his gypsy
background private. Instead, we can go for Push and Run
schemer Eddie Baily.

Quote (circa 1967) from Eddie Baily, England and
Tottenham inside-left and later coach, who was nicknamed
the 'Cheeky Chappie' after comedian Max Miller, 'Bill
was a players' player. He did not hunt personal glory but
gave everything he had to the team. You could count his
bad games on the fingers of One Arm Lou [a notorious
ticket spiv of the time]. The Push and Run side would not
have functioned nearly so well without Billy's energy and
enthusiasm. He covered for Alf behind him and prompted
the forwards with neat rather than spectacular passes. He
left those to me! He learned a lot from our great manager
Arthur Rowe, and when he retired it was obvious he would

make an outstanding coach and manager. He was a born tactician.'

PLAYING CAREER: Bill played 314 league games for Spurs as a defensive midfield player, and scored six goals. He won one England cap for England as stand-in for injured Billy Wright against Portugal at Goodison in May 1951 when he was 32. Remarkably, he scored with his first kick in international football, netting from 20 yards with a drive in the first minute. He never got another call-up because of the consistency of Billy Wright.

Quote (circa 1980) from Billy Wright, England and Wolves captain, former Arsenal manager and now head of sport at ATV, 'Typical of Bill, when I told him he had deserved another chance with England he said, "No, you're the better player and the number four England shirt belongs to you." I have rarely known such a modest man, and he is the perfect role model for young players coming into the game and also young managers. I may have been a better player, but it was no race as to which of us was the better manager! He was one of the top three in the game. His coaching ability was second to none.'

THE COACH: In 1954, Bill was honest enough to admit that his troublesome knee would not allow him to play at full power any more and he voluntarily stood down from the team and after helping the reserves for a while retired to concentrate on his first love of coaching. He gained his FA coaching badge at the first attempt and worked with the Tottenham youth squad and also with the Cambridge University team. In 1957 he became assistant to manager Jimmy Anderson, who had replaced the unwell Arthur

Rowe. In 1958 he was a member of the coaching staff that travelled to Sweden for the World Cup finals.

Quote (circa 1968) from Sir Walter Winterbottom, England manager 1947–1962 and later chairman of the Central Council for Physical Recreation, 'I assigned Bill to watch the Brazilians during the 1958 games in readiness for our match. He came back with his head full of tactical plans, and we sat down and worked out how we could stop a team that was beating everybody in sight. It was largely due to Bill's creative input that we held Brazil to a goalless draw. It was an extraordinary performance against a team that became arguably the greatest world champions ever. Bill has proved beyond question that he is one of the most astute managers and coaches our game has ever produced.'

Bill juggled his Tottenham manager's role with taking charge of the England Under-23 summer tours for many years, and was the choice of a lot of good judges to take over the England job before his old Tottenham team-mate Alf Ramsey was made manager in 1962.

THE CLUB MANAGER: In October 1958, Bill was appointed manager in place of Jimmy Anderson and on the very day that he took charge Spurs beat Everton 10-4! The star of the match was 'Tom Thumb' Tommy Harmer, who scored one goal and helped create seven others.

Quote (circa 1980) from Tommy Harmer, Tottenham's tiny tot midfield schemer, a chain-smoker and now a messenger in the City, 'It was one of those matches when everything we touched turned to goals. It could easily have been 15-8! When we came off at the end I said to Bill, "Don't expect this every week, Boss."'

The greatest feat with which Bill will always be associated was the league and FA Cup Double of 1960/61, the first time it had been achieved in the 20th century and considered the impossible dream. Bill and his captain Danny Blanchflower were the driving force that lifted Tottenham into the land of legend. Many experts rate that Double team the greatest British club side of all time. Note to Eamonn: The perfect person to produce here would be Danny, but after your previous experience I am sure you will not second that opinion! So I suggest Dave Mackay, the heart of the Spurs.

Quote (circa 1980) from Dave Mackay, 'Bill was a master tactician, who could see a game in his mind before it was played. He had a photographic memory when it came to footballers, and could recall instantly the strengths and weaknesses of almost any player he had ever seen. I considered myself fortunate to play under him and tried to take his attitude and application into management.'

The summer after completing the Double, Bill went to Italy and bought Jimmy Greaves from AC Milan for £99,999 (not wanting to give Jimmy the pressure of being the first £100,000 footballer).

That following season Spurs won the FA Cup and reached the semi-finals of the European Cup, going out in controversial circumstances to eventual champions Benfica. This should be when we spring Jimmy Greaves (with whom I am currently writing our sixth book together).

Quote (1981) from Jimmy Greaves, 'Bill would not be my choice as company for a night out on the town, but he would be first on my list of managers. He can be dour and tunnel-visioned where football is concerned, but he does not see his job to be a comedian. His teams always entertain on the pitch, and that's because he gives them free rein. He never tried to put any restrictions on me and I enjoyed the freedom. We won the FA Cup for Bill in 1962, which was consolation for not beating Benfica in the European Cup semi-final. I had a perfectly good goal ruled offside, which would have given us a chance of reaching the final. It's a cruel old game.'

The following season Tottenham created history by becoming the first British team to win a major European trophy, with a 5-1 victory over Atlético Madrid in the European Cup Winners' Cup Final in Rotterdam. We could have fun here by bringing on Bill's big pal Bill Shankly.

Quote (circa 1973) from Bill Shankly, legendary Liverpool manager, 'Bill is the canniest manager in the business, who always comes up with tactical thoughts that make the difference between winning and losing. He showed us all the way to win in Europe, and has set standards that we are all trying to match. I have enormous respect for him as a manager and as a man.'

In less than a year Nicholson lost the engine room of his dream team. Skipper Danny Blanchflower retired with a knee injury, the swashbuckling Dave Mackay suffered a double leg break, and John White was tragically killed when struck by lightning on a golf course. Bill set about rebuilding his side and brought in Pat Jennings from Watford, Cyril Knowles from Middlesbrough, Alan Mullery from Fulham, Mike England from Blackburn, Alan Gilzean from Dundee and Terry Venables from Chelsea. We can have a walk-on of the players, and include Martin Peters, who can join Terry Venables for a joint tribute.

Quote (circa 1980) from Terry Venables, 'It was close to an impossible job to follow in the footsteps of that great Double side. That is the sort of team that comes along only once in a lifetime. But we did our best and managed to win the FA Cup in 1967. Bill set the benchmarks for all future Tottenham managers.' Martin Peters, 'Alf Ramsey said I was ten years ahead of my time as a player. The same can be said of Bill as a manager. His tactics have been copied by modern managers because they were so effective. He and Alf shared the same standards of perfection.'

There were victories in the the League Cup (1971 and 1973) and the UEFA Cup (1972), but Nicholson set his targets high and disillusioned by the pay demands of several of his players, and hooliganism among a section of the supporters he resigned in 1974, but was coaxed back in a consultancy capacity by manager Keith Burkinshaw after a brief interlude at West Ham.

He was rewarded with an OBE for his services to football, while most in the game and certainly the Tottenham supporters feel he should have been given a knighthood.

As a surprise guest at the end of the show I suggest we spring Arthur Rowe, manager of the Push and Run Spurs who was a huge influence on Bill both as a player and as a coach. Bill will be thrilled to see him.

That was my dossier to Eamonn, but the show producers decided that Bill had led too one-dimensional a football-football-football life, and the risk of him saying no was too great.

* * *

Bill's departure from the Lane was delayed by just a few months after Tottenham 'supporters' had rioted during a losing 1974 UEFA Cup Final in Rotterdam. He festered and fretted throughout the summer, waiting for the new season for the first time in his career without enthusiasm. He felt the club had been badly wounded by the incident in Holland, and he was disillusioned by the way widespread hooliganism was scarring the face of the once beautiful game. His lovely wife, Darkie, confided that she had never known him so low. I would put it at the nadir of my 70 years observing all things Spurs.

He had suddenly lost the ability to motivate his players, and he slipped into a deep depression as Spurs got off to the worst start in their history with four successive defeats. On 29 August 1974, 'Mr Tottenham' handed in his resignation, bringing to an end 39 years of service to the club and 16 of them as the most successful manager in Spurs' history.

It was not only hooliganism that had robbed Nicholson of his appetite, but also player power and greed. He revealed, 'Players have become impossible. They talk all the time about security, but they are not prepared to work for it. I am abused by players when they come to see me. There is no longer respect.'

He dropped a bombshell at a press conference by divulging, 'I have recently found it impossible to get the players I want because at Tottenham we pride ourselves in not making under-the-counter payments. It is expected in the London area for players to ask for £7,000 tax-free. That's the minimum asking price by the agents of players. I want no part of that world.'

Skipper Martin Peters and long-serving defender Phil Beal made a private visit to Nicholson on behalf of the players to ask him to change his mind and stay on, but he said there was no going back. The Tottenham directors wrung their hands and allowed the King to leave, when an arm around the shoulders and warm words of encouragement could have made him change his mind.

Eddie Baily, another long-time Spurs servant and a highly regarded and sometimes acid-tongued coach, departed with Nicholson, complaining loudly about what he considered miserly contract-settlement terms. Bill Nick got a 'golden' handshake that he confidentially described to me as 'pathetic'.

I later learned that Bill received £10,000 and Eddie Baily a derogatory £4,000. Without Bill Nick there would not have been a Double. Without the passes of Eddie Baily, there would not have been a Push and Run title triumph. What a way to treat heroes.

* * *

There were strong rumours that Lane icon Danny Blanchflower would take over. Danny and I kept in close touch with each other after I had gone off into the freelancing world, when one of my roles was The Judge of *The Sun*, answering readers' questions and settling pub arguments. One day I received a question that read, 'If the job offer came along, would Danny Blanchflower consider returning to football as manager of Spurs?'

Danny, who could be witty, wise and weird in equal measure and all within one thought process, prided himself on never ducking a question, but on this occasion he was unusually prickly.

'All right, what do you know?' he asked. 'I'm sworn to secrecy.'

Purely by coincidence I had stumbled on a developing story of major proportions.

'This is a genuine question from a reader,' I told him. 'What's going on?'

There was a long silence, which was a rare thing when talking to Danny, because he liked to fill every waking moment with original ideas and unique observations. To wind him up, I used to call him Danny Blarneyflower.

'I don't want to tell you on the telephone,' he said, mysteriously. 'Meet me at the Alex Forbes café in half an hour.'

This was a coffee house near Blackfriars Station, a short walk from Fleet Street. It was years since it had been owned by former Arsenal star Alex Forbes but was still known to football journos by his name. It was the sort of nondescript place where you could melt into the background while meeting contacts.

There was a touch of a John Le Carré spy thriller about Danny's entrance into the coffee house.

He was looking around furtively as if making sure he had not been followed.

'What's with all the cloak and dagger stuff?' I asked.

Danny was agonising. 'I'm going to have to ask you to give me your word that all I am about to tell you is confidential,' he said. 'You're going to be desperate to break the story, but because I cannot tell a lie I'm going to take you into my confidence. If it leaks, it could stop me getting a job I have always dreamed about – manager of Spurs.'

I spluttered into my coffee cup.

'You've known me long enough to realise you can trust me,' I said. 'Thank goodness I'm not a staff reporter any more. My duty then would be to the newspaper.'

'And then I wouldn't be telling you,' said Danny, with his usual strong logic. 'The fact is that Bill Nick is on the point of resigning from Spurs, and he wants to put my name forward as his successor.'

The newspaperman in me was aching to get that sensational story into print, but Danny had tied me into a straitjacket of secrecy.

'When you rang me and asked that question as The Judge, I thought it was your crafty way of saying you were on to the story,' he explained. 'Bill confided in me a week ago, and I have been trying to talk him out of it. I've never known him so low and so lacking in appetite for the game that has been his life. He is completely disillusioned with football, or the politics of it. Bill doesn't like what he sees with the galloping greed of the players, and the violence on the terraces has sickened him. I said that perhaps he was trying to pass me a poisoned chalice.'

It was a month before Nicholson's stunning decision to quit became public, and the veteran manager made no secret of the fact that he wanted Tottenham icon Danny Blanchflower to take over from him. He had even lined up ex-Leeds playmaker Johnny Giles as player-coach.

The board made a complete botch of it, and decided instead to hand the reins to Danny's fellow Irishman Terry Neill, a man with Arsenal-red blood. A desperately disappointed Danny told me:

It can only end in tears. Terry is an intelligent man with lots of bright ideas, but he has as much chance of being accepted at Tottenham as the Archbishop of Canterbury has of being welcomed at the Vatican. He is Arsenal through and through. If I had got the job I would have kept Bill Nicholson on as a backroom consultant. It was madness that the board let him go with all his experience and knowledge. It was the one management job for which I would willingly have returned to the game. I guess the directors have got their own back on me because I always refused to bow the knee to them. "

Bill Nicholson was devastated that the board had ignored his advice. He told me:

" Danny was perfect for the job. He knew the traditions and the ways of Tottenham, and would have slipped into my shoes comfortably and with style. The fans and the players would have welcomed him with open arms. He had Spurs in his soul. I have never been so embarrassed in all my life when the board totally ignored my advice and just refused to consider Danny. I thought that after all my service to the club I was entitled to think I could give guidance as to who would be right to take over. But they appointed Terry Neill without consulting me. I would have been happy to stay on and advise Danny, without interfering. He has always been his own man, but I know he would have been willing to listen to me when there was any situation with which he needed my considerable experience. Everything I did was with the good of Tottenham in mind. I had given everything to the club and now they had turned their back on me. I was angrier than I'd ever been, and I let the chairman and directors know exactly what I thought of them. "

What shoddy behaviour by the Tottenham directors, and in particular chairman Sidney Wale. These were the men who had allowed Bill Nicholson to drive himself into the ground in the service of Spurs without once paying him a decent wage. Now they were slapping him in the face by ignoring his advice as to who should be his successor as Tottenham manager.

These little men were frightened that Blanchflower would dictate to them, as he would have done. Instead they went behind Nicholson's back and chose another Irishman who was totally unsuitable for the job. Terry Neill's heart always belonged to Highbury. They got the wrong Irishman. How Irish is that?

5

TERRY NEILL
Far Too Red-Blooded

Born: Belfast 8 May 1942
Appointed: 13 September 1974
Resigned: 30 June 1976
Games managed: 89
Won: 31
Drawn: 26
Lost: 32
Goals scored: 127
Goals conceded: 126
Win percentage: 34.83

TERRY NEILL had Tottenham fans seeing red when he
was announced as the successor to the legend that was Bill
Nicholson. If they had tried, the directors could not have
appointed a man more closely associated with Highbury and
all the historical (sometimes hysterical) connotations that
has for Lilywhite supporters. Bill Nick was both incredulous
and furious. He had worked hard and secretly behind the
scenes to try to persuade Danny Blanchflower to take over

from him. I was privy to those hush-hush negotiations between Bill and Danny, who told me, 'I would give my right hand to manage Spurs ... correction, left hand. I will need my right hand to write down my team selection, starting with Pat Jennings in goal.'

But the directors stubbornly cocked a deaf 'un to the Nicholson suggestion and went instead for Neill, who had cut his managerial teeth as player-boss at Hull City after spending most of his life at the Arsenal, joining the club from his Belfast school and giving them sterling service as a disciplined defender, captain and total, dyed-in-the-red Gooner.

Bill Nick told me privately (and prophetically), 'I cannot believe that the Tottenham board have preferred Terry Neill to Danny, who is Spurs through and through. I had suggested Johnny Giles as his number two. But the directors interpreted my attempts to help as interference. They wanted to show they were in charge and made what I believed was the wrong choice. No disrespect to Terry, but he is a Highbury man and will find it very difficult to persuade the Tottenham fans to think otherwise.'

Can you imagine if social networks like Facebook and Twitter had been around when the appointment was made? Facebook would have blown a fuse.

The board had turned the clock back to the Joe Hulme days. A Gooner in charge at the Lane. It made no sense.

For those not familiar with the history of the feud between the two north London rivals, let me take time out from my 70-year ramble to give you the background to the antagonism.

The Football League roared back into action nine months after the 11 November 1918 Armistice, boasting of being 'bigger and better' than ever. It expanded from 40 clubs to 44, with the First and Second Divisions now made up of 22 clubs each. The shock, particularly for Spurs, was that the restructured First Division included their new-to-north London neighbours Arsenal – but *not* Tottenham.

It was naturally assumed – with the extra places available – that the teams who finished in the last two places in the 1914/15 season, Chelsea and Tottenham, would automatically retain their First Division status, with Derby and Preston promoted as the top two teams in the Second Division to make up the 22 clubs. But nobody took into account the Machiavellian manoeuvres of Arsenal chairman Sir Henry Norris. He secretly negotiated behind the scenes and behind backs, and had powerful Liverpool chairman and league president John McKenna – nicknamed 'Honest John' – giving him surprisingly strong support.

Despite finishing only fifth in the Second Division in 1914/15, it was Arsenal who were promoted along with Chelsea, Derby and Preston. The team that lost out was Tottenham, and all these years later it still rankles, itching like an angry red sore that will not go away.

Club chairman Charles Roberts, who always played by the book, was speechless. Privately, the Spurs directors and – more vociferously, the supporters – were wondering just how 'honest' John McKenna was.

Tottenham had finished at the bottom of the First Division in 1915 largely because most of their major players, led by skipper Arthur Grimsdell, took up Lord Kitchener's 'Your country needs you' call and volunteered to fight in France.

Roberts and the Tottenham directors described their treatment by the McKenna-dominated Football League

Management Committee as 'disgraceful'. Vice-chairman Wagstaffe Simmons summed it up as, 'The price paid by Tottenham Hotspur for patriotism.'

It was not only Tottenham who felt left out in the cold. The stench carried all the way up through Wolverhampton and to the coalfields of Yorkshire. Wolves and Barnsley had finished third and fourth in the old Second Division, and they could not fathom how Arsenal had managed to leapfrog them without a ball being kicked.

Norris, the man who stubbornly transferred Arsenal to Highbury from Woolwich against the wishes of most people in 1913, got the comeuppance wished on him by Tottenham. In 1927 the Football Association suspended him and a fellow director, and the club was censured for illegally inducing players, including the great Charles Buchan, to join Arsenal.

Sir Henry became embroiled in a huge libel case against the FA and the *Daily Mail,* which alleged he had been using Arsenal funds to pay his personal expenses and the wages of his chauffeur. The newspaper produced evidence that he had pocketed £125 from the sale of the club team bus, endorsing the cheque with Herbert Chapman's forged signature and paying the money into his wife's account.

The cheers in Tottenham when he lost the case could no doubt be heard all the way to the Law Courts.

Norris, whose ancestor had been beheaded for – euphemistically – flirting with Anne Bolyen, fitted the image of a Victorian villain, complete with a huge twirling moustache and a monocle that distorted his features. One of his first managers at Highbury, Leslie Knighton, revealed in his autobiography, 'I have never met his equal for logic, invective and ruthlessness against all who opposed him.

When I disagreed with him at board meetings and had to stand up for what I knew was best for the club, he used to flay me with words until I was reduced to fuming, helpless silence … he made me abandon the Arsenal scouting system, and ordered me never to sign a player under 5ft 8in or weighing less than 11st.'

A former Conservative MP, Mayor of Fulham and chairman at Craven Cottage when he tried to merge the club with Woolwich Arsenal, Norris was drummed out of football for the rest of his life. Arsenal, the club he talked into the First Division, has been at the top table ever since – without ever earning the right to a place on the field of play.

These shenanigans gave Spurs the motivation to win a First Division place through playing rather than politicking. The on-fire Lilywhites ran away with the Second Division title in 1919/20 with an avalanche of 102 goals and a six-point advantage over runners-up Huddersfield (this, of course, in the days of two points for a win). Their collection of 70 points from a possible 84 was a Second Division record and the best in the league for 27 years.

Now we fast-forward 74 years, and Arsenal-through-and-through Terry Neill arrives to take over the Tottenham reins from a disillusioned Bill Nicholson.

Blarney-king Terry and I were close acquaintances going back to his earliest days as an Arsenal player, when dear old Billy Wright was the manager struggling in the shadows of Bill Nicholson's feats down the road at Tottenham. I used to help him promote his propaganda for the PFA, for whom he was a vociferous, highly intelligent supporter and later outspoken chairman.

He could talk for Ireland, and after accepting the Spurs job he told me:

(I am as surprised as you are to find myself at Tottenham, of all clubs. But I come here with the ambition and hopefully the ammunition to restore the glories once bestowed upon them by the wonderful Bill Nicholson. What an act to follow! He has been one of the greatest club managers in the history of the game, and an inspiration to anybody mad enough to take on the challenge of management. I have told the Board not to expect a magic wand overnight transformation. There is a lot of team rebuilding to do, and some confidence building too. There are some excellent players here who have recently lost their way. The Tottenham supporters will inevitably be suspicious of a man whose past is so steeped in Arsenal, but please assure them that from now on I am a Spurs man and as keen as they are to see the club back at the top where it belongs.)

Yes, Terry could always talk a good game. He quickly set about trying to put action to go with his words and put his faith at the feet of Scottish strikers John Duncan and Alfie Conn, but it was an 'old hand' who saved Tottenham from what looked certain relegation in his early days in charge. Big Martin Chivers, as wide as a wardrobe yet with balletic balance, recalled after two months in the wilderness, scored one of the goals as Spurs just beat the drop with a 4-2 victory over Leeds in a nail-nibbling, end-of-season game at White Hart Lane. 'Nailbiting.' How often do you hear that word in the same breath as Tottenham Hotspur?

* * *

Martin Chivers was an enigma wrapped in a riddle. He had many critics during his Tottenham career, whom he continually silenced with the fairly conclusive argument-settling response of scoring goals. Built like a Greek statue, he sometimes seemed just as immobile but would then make you eat your words by thumping the ball into the net with a power that even Harry Kane would envy.

How times change. In my reporting role for the *Daily Express* I met 'Big Chiv' at Waterloo Station on the day he was transferred from Southampton in January 1968 and travelled with him by tube to Liverpool Street and then on to Tottenham as he prepared to start his new life at the Lane.

These days, reporters cannot get near the primadonna players, who invariably arrive at their new clubs in chauffeur-driven limos with dark-tinted windows and an agent handing out second-hand quotes. To be honest, I think this sort of 'royal' treatment would have been more to Martin's taste. He was suited to the big stage.

Martin, a grammar school boy educated at the highly regarded Taunton's School in Hampshire, spent the train journey from Southampton to Waterloo tackling *The Times* crossword. He was different from most footballers I knew, who preferred Page 3 of *The Sun*.

He told me on the way to the Lane, 'This is like a dream for me. I have always been an admirer of the way Spurs play, and it's going to be a thrill as well as a challenge to play alongside Jimmy Greaves.'

His fee (including Frank Saul as a makeweight) was a then British record of £125,000. It was a fortune at the time, and for a long while it sat on Martin's shoulders like a sack of coal.

Sadly, a horrible knee injury early in his Spurs career stopped him showing his best alongside Greavsie. He later flourished with the silken Alan Gilzean as his sidekick, but there were always sniping comments being made about Martin's perceived lack of determination and commitment whenever the going got tough.

In his early days at Southampton, I had watched him alongside the young Mike Channon, and I knew his apparent casual approach was deceptive. He had the physique of a heavyweight boxer, but to many spectators he seemed too often to have punchless penalty area presence.

I recall helping Martin move into a smart new home in Epping with his first wife, and he seemed like a young man with the world at his feet. 'I've made a slow start,' he said, 'but I know I will start to give the fans the goals they want once I have settled into playing with Greavsie, who has a style of his own and it will take me time to get on his wavelength.'

But all his plans and ambitions nosedived in a home match against Nottingham Forest in September 1968 when he felt a shooting pain in his knee and sank to the ground with his leg locked. It was even painful to watch from the press box, and it signalled a nine-month lay-off that made Martin morose and moody.

He was still not firing on all cylinders when he made his comeback in August 1969, and there was obvious tension in the Tottenham camp. Manager Bill Nicholson got so frustrated with him that he once gave him a ticket to go and watch Geoff Hurst play for West Ham. 'I felt quite insulted,' Martin said. 'But I did what I was told and later thanked Bill, because by watching Geoff's positional play I learned a lot.'

He was always having battles with Bill Nick about his game, but even more so with Cockney coach Eddie Baily. They had a continual war of words, and I was witness to two classic cases of Martin making Eddie hold up his hands in surrender.

The first time was in Romania in 1971 when Tottenham were playing Rapid Bucharest in the UEFA Cup for a second leg that has gone down in the Tottenham hall of shame as the Battle of Bucharest. I reported in the *Express* that 'Spurs were hacked and kicked about like rag dolls'. Bill Nick went on record with the view that Rapid were the dirtiest side he had seen in more than 30 years in football.

The dressing room at the end of the match, won 2-0 by Spurs, was like a casualty clearing station, with six visiting players nursing injuries caused by tackles that belonged in the house of horrors rather than on a football pitch.

I noticed that throughout the game assistant manager Baily had been bawling at Martin Chivers from the touchline bench, calling him every name to which he could put his merciless tongue. You could not help but hear the insults being aimed at the Ambling Alp of Spurs because the huge stadium was barely a third full. Big Chiv finally silenced Baily by scoring a superb goal, and you did not have to be a lip reader to know that Martin responded by shouting obscenities back at his nemesis.

We flew straight back to London after the match, and I took careful note that Baily and Chivers completely ignored each other at the airport and on the flight. Later that week I saw Bill Nick privately and told him I was thinking of writing a story about the obvious enmity between his right-hand man Baily and his most productive forward, Chivers.

Bill looked as pained as if I was telling him I was putting down his pet dog. 'I can't tell you what and what not to write,' he said, 'but let me just say that you'll not be doing me any favours. Off the record, we're having problems with Martin. He is a strong-minded young man who thinks he knows it all. His attitude drives Eddie bananas, but you know Eddie – he often shouts things in the heat of a match that he doesn't really mean. I'm trying to make the peace between them, and any story about them will only make matters worse.'

At Bill's request, I refrained from writing about the feud, and it was forgotten as Chivers hit such a rich vein of goalscoring form that I wrote a feature in the *Express* suggesting he had become as powerful an England centre-forward as legends of the game like Tommy Lawton, Ted Drake and Jackie Milburn.

A frothing-at-the-mouth Eddie Baily went out of his way to confront me about the story, and said, 'You have insulted truly great players. Chivers is not fit to carry their jock straps.'

That's how angry Martin used to make Eddie, but he was forced to bow the knee to him again after the first leg of the 1972 UEFA Cup Final against Wolves at Molineux. Before the game both Bill Nick and Eddie had nagged Martin so much about his expected contribution that he snapped and walked out on to the pitch to get away from them.

During the match, with Baily bellowing from the touchline, Chivers conjured two magical goals that virtually clinched victory, with skipper Alan Mullery making sure of the trophy with a crucial goal in the second leg at White Hart Lane.

After Martin's phenomenal first-leg performance, a contrite Eddie Baily came into the dressing room and bowed down in front of the giant centre-forward, miming as if to kiss his feet. 'Here you are, Mart,' he said in his loud Alf Garnett-style voice. 'Walk all over me. You've won me outright.'

In the early 1970s, Chivers was as potent and productive as any centre-forward in the league. Powerfully built and as wide as a door, Chiv had a deceptively lethargic-looking bearing, but if a possible goal beckoned he would suddenly fire on all cylinders and leave surprised defenders in his wake as he accelerated. He preferred the ball on his right foot, and had a rocketing shot that brought him many of his 118 league goals. He also netted 13 times in 24 England games, and might have plundered many more goals but for a recurring knee injury.

The 1970/71 season was the launch of Martin's peak years, for both club and country. He played in all 58 league and cup games and scored 34 times, including both goals in the League Cup Final against Aston Villa, and 21 in the First Division as Spurs finished the season in third place. The bad news was that Arsenal finished top and completed the league and FA Cup Double on the tenth anniversary of Tottenham's historic achievement.

Chivers also notched his first goal for England in a 3-0 win over Greece at Wembley in April 1971 to put the icing on the cake of his resurgence.

It was in the following season that Chivers went into overdrive, netting 44 times in 64 first-team appearances. His seven goals in as many League Cup ties lifted Spurs to the semi-finals where they eventually lost to Chelsea.

Free of worries about his troublesome knee, the rampaging Hampshire giant saved his most impressive form for the UEFA Cup, scoring eight times in 11 matches, including a hat-trick in a 9-0 annihilation of Icelandic side

This 1950/51 team photo was taken by my former Fleet Street team-mate Norman 'Speedy' Quicke, and hung on the wall in the old Tottenham boardroom. Manager Arthur Rowe is on the left of the back line alongside Alf Ramsey. Skipper Ron Burgess and Bill Nicholson flank chairman Fred Bearman immediately behind the treasured League trophy.

It was love at first flight when I saw Ted Ditchburn saving for Spurs in 1950. I rated him Tottenham's all-time greatest goalkeeper ... until big Pat Jennings came along.

Referee Norman Burtenshaw whistles and sun-bronzed Terry Venables witnesses. Dave Mackay's least favourite yet most famous photo. He felt this 1967 picture of him putting fellow-Scot Billy Bremner in his place after a reckless tackle by the Leeds skipper wrongly portrayed him as a bully. 'Iron Man' Dave was never ever sent off.

An off-beat, side-on view of the untouchable 1960/61 Double team, back row left to right: Bill Brown, Peter Baker, Ron Henry, skipper Danny Blanchflower, Maurice Norman, Dave Mackay. Front row: Cliff Jones, John White, Bobby Smith, Les Allen, Terry Dyson.

Scanned from my 1960s cuttings book, the 'Ghost of White Hart Lane' John White before he was tragically killed by lightning.

He could perform magic with **that** ball and on **that** surface!

Side by side, two Tottenham giants, Danny Blanchflower and Jimmy Greaves. They were so close that Blanchflower was godfather to Jimmy's son, Danny.

Happy days as Spurs parade the FA Cup after their 1962 victory over Burnley, left to right: Ron Henry, Cliff Jones, Dave Mackay, Jimmy Greaves, Maurice Norman, Bobby Smith, Bill Brown.

This is probably the most poignant photograph in my 70-year Spurs journey. It was the last time the G-Men were together. I was there with Alan Gilzean to celebrate Jimmy's 75th birthday, a bash organised by his manager Terry Baker. Just a few weeks later Jimmy was struck down by his paralysing stroke, and Gilly passed on soon after following a short illness. It's a cruel old game.

Spurs squad of '67, back row left to right: Pat Jennings, Mike England, Cyril Knowles, Eddie Clayton, Alan Mullery, Joe Kinnear. Front: Jimmy Robertson, Jimmy Greaves, Alan Gilzean, Dave Mackay, Terry Venables, Frank Saul, Cliff Jones.

The enigmatic Martin Chivers, who at his peak was the most powerful centre-forward in Europe. Note the pristine jersey unmarked by commercialism!

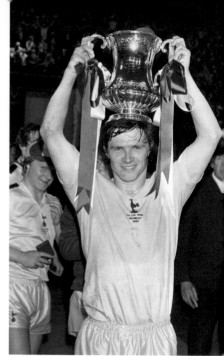

The king wears the crown, Steve Perryman with the FA Cup following collecting the treasured trophy for a second successive year in 1982 after the replay win against QPR.

Pat Jennings does the double at Anfield, saving a penalty against Liverpool's Tommy Smith. He also saved a spot-kick from Kevin Keegan in the same match, prompting Reds manager Bill Shankly to say: 'He should be outlawed because of those shovel-size hands of his.'

I catch up with Big Pat Jennings, who tried and failed to convince me that Hugo Lloris was a better goalkeeper than he had been. Mr Modesty. Pat will always be No 1 in my book.

Time flies, and young managers Alan Mullery (Brighton) and Terry Venables (Crystal Palace) tell me how they plan to beat each other in a 1976 League match. It was only the day before yesterday they were FA Cup winning team-mates at Spurs.

A momentous day for football in general and Spurs in particular when Keith Burkinshaw lands Argentine World Cup aces Osvaldo Ardiles and Ricardo Villa.

Ricky Villa puts the finishing touch to the 'Goal of the Century' in the 1981 FA Cup Final replay against Manchester City. Let the tangoing celebrations begin!

The Pass Master Glenn Hoddle. Has there been a more technically gifted player in a Lilywhite shirt?

Glenn and I were attending the premiere of the classic BTSport documentary, Greavsie. What would you have paid to have seen the jinking genius Jimmy and Hod the God playing together for Spurs?

Together, arguably the two greatest managers in Tottenham history: 'Sir' Bill Nicholson (right) and Keith Burkinshaw. Both proud Yorkshiremen with N17 honorary status.

Keflavik ÍF, and that superb brace against Wolverhampton Wanderers that brought Eddie Baily to his knees. In the First Division, he found the net 25 times in 39 appearances.

Even the bullish Baily had to concede that perhaps my article putting Chivers up at the top of the mountain with greats of his playing days was in no way an exaggeration.

The Tottenham victory over Wolves – 3-2 on aggregate – was a personal triumph for Bill Nicholson. Since taking charge of the club in 1958, he had steered Spurs to three FA Cup finals, one League Cup Final, one European Cup Winners' Cup Final and the UEFA Cup Final. And they had won the lot!

Bill Nick gave his usual level-headed and fair assessment after his latest conquest:

> We won the cup at Molineux with two marvellous goals by Martin Chivers. Give Wolves full credit for the way they came back at us. They were the better team for much of the second leg. The two matches were a fine advertisement for English football, and I wonder what the rest of Europe think of the fact that this is the fifth successive year that the UEFA Cup has been won by an English club [including the final seasons of the old Inter-Cities Fairs Cup].

Martin – with the middle name Harcourt, after his German mother – continued his career in Switzerland with Servette and then had brief appearances with Norwich, Brighton and non-league Dorchester and Barnet, and also tried his luck in Norway and Australia.

He has owned a hotel and restaurant in Hertfordshire, dabbled with club management, is a popular matchday host at Tottenham home games and had a spell as the national development manager to the FA.

Mellowed after all the shooting and shouting was over, he recalled that his career turned round when he started finding the net in 1970/71. 'It was all about confidence,' he said. 'I honestly feared my career was over with that knee injury against Forest. But I began to believe in myself again when I started scoring.'

Remarkably, after he had taken his final shots, he became best of friends with Bill Nicholson, the manager with whom he had a long-running battle over wages, tactics and attitudes. Darkie, Billy's long-suffering wife, used to fume over the sleepless nights he gave her husband, but once she got to know Martin during his many visits to their home she was moved to say, 'How on earth could Bill have got so upset about a proper gentleman like Martin?' Bill looked to the ceiling.

Big Chiv accepts that he had been awkward. He always thought Bill was too miserly with the club's money in an era when players' wages were just beginning to take off. 'Everything Bill did was in the interests of the club,' Martin said. 'He always had my full respect. We got to like each other a lot. And Darkie was a wonderful lady.'

Martin Chivers. Enigmatic, but on his day as explosive as they come. At his absolute peak, as good a centre-forward as was ever bred on the playing fields of England.

* * *

Bill Nicholson and Eddie Baily briefly had the humiliation of signing on the dole before making quiet returns to football in the summer of 1975, both of them joining West Ham in scouting and consultant roles. Bill Nick in claret and blue? I don't think so!

Meantime, Terry Neill was fighting an uphill battle to pump confidence and belief into his Tottenham players. He did not mince words after a goalless draw with Arsenal at White Hart Lane:

> ❛ I apologise to everybody who paid good money to watch this rubbish. It made me feel ashamed. It was the kind of stuff that could kill football. ❜

Don't sit on the fence, Terry. Say what you think.

He was generally a good-humoured man with witty and incisive views on anything and everything, but his happy demeanour was stretched near to breaking point as he struggled to put his big ideas for Tottenham into operation.

The diehard fans struggling to accept him as 'one of us' might have changed their minds if he had managed to pull off an audacious transfer deal in February 1976. He discovered that Johan Cruyff was unsettled at Barcelona, and moved in with a bold bid that was turned down.

Johan Cruyff in a Tottenham shirt. Now that would have been something special.

Three days after he had been rebuffed by the Dutchman, Neill gave a full league debut to a 17-year-old midfield player who would one day become Cruyff class with his passing. Enter Glenn Hoddle, who announced his arrival on the senior stage by firing a spectacular shot past Stoke City and England goalkeeper Peter Shilton.

Terry Neill was not at Spurs to see Hoddle develop into a footballing master. In July 1976, after turning the Tottenham playing staff inside out and upside down, he followed his heart and went home to Highbury as Arsenal manager in succession to Bertie Mee. It is no secret that a lot of Lilywhite supporters said, 'Good riddance.' Terry told me as he settled back home at Highbury:

> Okay, I admit it – I am and always will be an Arsenal man at heart. I gave the Tottenham job my best shot, but there was always a faction – including in the boardroom – who were not going to accept me regardless of what I might have achieved. I could have talked to them until I was blue and white in the face but they would always have seen me in Arsenal colours. I wish my successor luck, and hope the supporters get behind him 100 per cent. I never enjoyed that luxury, and – let's be frank – was never likely to.

He left with a crafty trick up his sleeve: to nick Tottenham's greatest player, the goalkeeper with hands like shovels, the agility of a gymnast and the reflexes of a cat on a hot tin roof. The Tottenham fans were happy to see Neill go to Arsenal. But if they had known he was also planning on taking with him Pat Jennings – a Spurs hero for all seasons – there would have been much weeping and gnashing of teeth. To lose Neill was a topic that caused shrugging. To lose Jennings – and to Arsenal, of all clubs – was a matter of earthquaking concern.

As Neill departed down the road the Spurs directors promoted his 'unknown' coach to the Tottenham hotseat. More by accident than design, they had found a manager fit to follow in the footsteps of Bill Nicholson.

6

KEITH BURKINSHAW
Taking the Tango Route to Success

Born: Higham, Barnsley, 23 June 1935
Appointed: 14 July 1976
Resigned: 31 May 1984
Games managed: 431
Won: 182
Drawn: 118
Lost: 131
Goals scored: 652
Goals conceded: 565
Win percentage: 42.23

KEITH BURKINSHAW is a name that always sits happily on the lips of Tottenham supporters. I even smiled as I typed that sentence. He brought happy, memorable times to White Hart Lane after the sort of nightmare start that could easily have ended his reign before he could show that he was just the manager Spurs needed.

When he was first appointed, many people were asking, 'Keith who?' He had kept a low profile as coach and right-hand man to Terry Neill, and his managerial experience stretched to just a few matches in charge as player-boss at those soccer hotspots of Workington and Scunthorpe.

I was heartened on first meeting him to find him sounding like an echo of Bill Nicholson with his footballing philosophy, and spoken in the same Yorkshire tones as 'Sir Bill'. He said:

> Football is a simple game and should not be made complicated. Pass to a player with the same colour shirt, and then get into position to take the return pass if necessary. If defending, mainly watch the man not the ball and don't commit yourself to unnecessary tackles. Stay upright and get yourself between the opponent with the ball and the goal. I believe in the three Cs – composure, control and concentration. Ordinary players can become extraordinary by doing the simple things well.

It was as if I was back listening spellbound in the 1950s and 1960s to Bill Nick, and my heart soared at Keith's first act after being promoted from coach to boss. He invited Lane legend Nicholson back in an advisory role. I bumped into Bill during one of his last scouting missions for West Ham and he told me in confidence, 'I'm going home.'

How about that to bring tears to your eyes! Bill Nick coming home.

It should be placed on record that the man about to be installed as new chairman – Irving Scholar – played a part in the return 'home' of Nicholson. He was steeped in the history of the club and fully appreciated just what Bill Nick had done for Spurs. And now Burkinshaw was emerging as a manager in the Nicholson mould.

Everybody – fans, players, directors, media circus – liked Keith, an ex-Barnsley miner who came up the hard way and had Nicholson-style principles and work ethic. They gave him a nickname that had once adorned Alf Ramsey: 'The General'.

He had been a peripheral defender at Liverpool before giving long service down the Football League at Workington and Scunthorpe. He learned his coaching trade in Zambia and then with Newcastle, joining Spurs and the Terry Neill backroom team in 1975.

Following the Irishman's decision to return to Highbury, the directors turned to Burkinshaw. Let's be honest, mainly because he was there and available. He was in the right place, but at the right time? His first season in full control climaxed with the ultimate humiliation: relegation in bottom place, ending a 27-year unbroken run for Spurs at the top table.

I felt sure he was for the boot, but amazingly the directors kept faith with him, and he rewarded their confidence by leading Tottenham straight back up again, but not before a transfer in August 1977 that baffled and bewildered just about everybody.

Pat Jennings, arguably the greatest goalkeeper in history, was allowed to join his Northern Ireland buddy Terry Neill – at Highbury of all places. Over the next eight years, Pat went on to give Arsenal nearly as good service as he had given to Spurs. Tottenham had passed Arsenal their safe door. Crazy or what?

Pat told me in that bass-baritone voice of his, 'I asked the board for a loan to help me buy the house we had set our heart on. They ummed and ahhed, and I recall being in the car park when every one of the directors blanked me as they walked past. I decided to teach them a lesson by signing for the Arsenal. It suited us as a family to stay in the same area and I got my house.'

He helped the Gunners reach three successive FA Cup Finals and became a hero at Highbury, burying the hatchet with Tottenham after his retirement and becoming a respected coach at the Lane and then a popular club ambassador. I have not seen a better all-round goalkeeper in my 70 years watching Spurs, or known a more modest superstar. Big pat on the back for Pat.

On their way back up to the First Division – magnificently marshalled on the pitch by giant-hearted Steve Perryman and steered by the gifted Glenn Hoddle – Tottenham found they had still not rid themselves of the curse of hooliganism. There were 85 people hurt when fighting broke out on the pitch between rival fans after Spurs had been beaten 3-1 by promotion rivals Brighton at the Goldstone Ground on 15 April 1978. It was a scar on the face of a great club.

FA supremo Ted Croker told Prime Minister Margaret Thatcher, 'Don't blame football for the hooliganism. Blame your society.' It cost him a knighthood. Forty years later, Ted's grandson would become an idol at Tottenham. Take a bow, Eric Dier.

With the 1977/78 season into its last embers, Tottenham, Bolton and Southampton were neck and neck at the top of the table, with Brighton just two points behind. Spurs, playing it the simple, uncomplicated way preached and practised by Burkinshaw, clinched an instant return to the First Division with a tense goalless draw against

Southampton, pipping Brighton on goal average for third place. This was before the play-offs were introduced, and it was a finale that tested nerves like never before.

Many Spurs fans talked of feeling physically sick during that last game against the Saints. Goodness knows how Keith must have felt. He knew in his heart that the Spurs board would not give him a second chance to get the club back into the top flight where they belonged. In fact he had been brutally told when Spurs were relegated, 'You got us into the Second Division, now you can get us out and back to the First Division.' No pressure then, Keith!

Speaking on a personal level, I was so pleased for skipper Steve Perryman, who ran himself into the ground to help push Spurs to promotion. I had seen him grow up from the baby of the team to taking on the role of leader. I remember Bill Nick introducing me to him when he was about to make his debut at 17. 'He's a diamond of a prospect,' Bill told me, deliberately trying to boost the confidence of the young baby-faced teenager who looked as if he should still be at school. It was the launch of an incredible career, and no player before or since has given more to the Lilywhite cause. Steve could not compete with the likes of Glenn Hoddle for skill – who could? – but his explosive effort and energy lifted and inspired those around him. Well done, Skip, and thanks for the fee-free introduction to this book. You are a one-off, young man!

Steve was devastated when Tottenham were relegated, and secretly vowed that they would bounce back immediately. He kept his target to himself. Like so many of the great players, he was a man of action rather than words.

Few will forget the highlight of that promotion season, a 9-0 thrashing of Bristol Rovers at the Lane on 22 October

1977. Colin Lee, signed from Torquay just 48 hours earlier for £60,000 to partner the bullocking Ian Moores, found the passes from Hoddle and thrusting winger Peter Taylor like a silver-plate service after his days labouring with the league's basement clubs. He scored four goals in the humiliation of Rovers.

Just a week earlier, Spurs had gone down to a 4-1 defeat against Charlton Athletic, a game neutrals admitted Spurs should have won 8-4. What was that Greavsie says about it being 'a funny old game'?

While Colin Lee took all the headlines, a rival to him as the man of the match in the destruction of Rovers was the unsung John Pratt, who continually won the ball in midfield and then fed it to Glenn Hoddle, who finished off the banquet with a stunning strike that put a golden seal on Tottenham's record league victory. It was just a glimpse of the Hoddle magic that was waiting to be unwrapped on the return to the First Division stage. But for all the silken skill of Glenn, he would be the first to concede that he could not have produced it without the sweat of the water-carriers like Pratt and Perryman.

Pratt was one of the most maligned footballers in Tottenham history, and warrants a medal for showing bravery and determination in the face of vicious criticism from a noisy minority of Spurs 'supporters'. Modern 'Aunt Sally' Moussa Sissoko would have won a popularity contest compared with the stick that Pratt had to take from people who could not trap a bag of cement.

He finished his Spurs career one goal short of being in the half-century club. I want to shower him with the praise he deserves for his service to the Lilywhites despite a faction of fans who belittled themselves by their behaviour.

In my previous life as a football reporter, I used to get infuriated when at Tottenham matches hearing a small contingent of Spurs fans baying at and booing John while he was running his socks off for the team. He was not blessed with the natural skills of a Greaves or a Gilzean, but I have rarely seen a player working harder for his team-mates. In 11 seasons in the first-team squad, John played in every position apart from goalkeeper, and I am sure he would have willingly taken on that role if asked. He was a specialist midfield anchorman and water-carrier, getting the ball to those team-mates with the skill to dismantle the opposition.

His 49 goals are proof positive that he was often a potent box-to-box fox. John has always shown good humour over the abuse he used to take:

> Bill Nick expected his players to be men, and said that the crowd paid our wages and were entitled to have their opinions. So one day, before I was due to play my first game at Old Trafford, I asked him what I could expect. He replied that it would just be like playing at Spurs, except that up there 55,000 people would hate me, whereas at Spurs it was only 45,000!

He finished his playing career with Portland Timbers in the USA, then continued to serve Spurs as a youth coach and briefly as assistant manager, while running a successful business with club-mate Mark Falco. He is a popular matchday host, and always has positive things to say about the modern Tottenham team without moaning or groaning about the huge salaries the players take home, while he had to work as a window cleaner in the close-season to supplement his wages. Take a bow, John Pratt. Your service at the old Lane was appreciated by this Spurs watcher.

* * *

While most managers were sunning themselves on beaches in the close season, 'General' Burkinshaw made a top-secret trip to South America and, amazingly, returned with the signatures of two of the heroes of Argentina's 1978 World Cup triumph. It rated as one of the most sensational double transfer coups in football history when Spurs bought Osvaldo Ardiles from Club Atlético Huracán and Ricardo Villa from Racing Club in a £700,000 investment that staggered everybody. It ushered in the era of the 'Foreign Invasion'.

* * *

An interlude here while I do some unashamed name-dropping as I recall how I stumbled on the fact that Tottenham were involved in the most sensational transfer business the game had known in an era when British football was played exclusively by British players.

Master of mirth Eric Morecambe, of all people, knew before most of us that Spurs were about to pull off the most sensational transfer coup in British football history in the summer of 1978, and it was the then doyen of Tottenham, Bill Nicholson, who made it all happen.

Please be patient while I explain, or – as Eric would have said – while I try to get the words down, not necessarily in the right order.

For several years I had the privilege and pleasure of working with Eric on regular newspaper columns for the *Daily Express* and the magazine *Titbits*, which was a weekly, all-topics chat publication. Eric's share of the fees used to be paid to Luton Town Football Club, where he was the jester director who got the Hatters more publicity than they'd had before or since.

The manager at Luton for much of Eric's time on the board was a charismatic character called Harry Haslam, who was rarely seen without a smile on his face as he lived up to his nickname 'Happy Harry'. Whenever I used to be in the company of Eric and Harry at Luton's Kenilworth Road ground, it was a toss-up for who got more laughs. Yes, Harry was that funny.

Now to get to the point. In 1978 Haslam took over at Sheffield United but still kept in close contact with the Harpenden-based comedian. I was discussing our column with Eric when he said, 'Shall we write about the two Argies who are going to play in England? You know, lines like it takes two to tango but it will be more of a knees-up when Bites Yer Legs gets stuck into them.'

Eric often had me speechless with laughter, but this time I was lost for words because of the unusual facts he was offering. 'What two Argentines?' I asked. 'Is this a joke?'

He then explained how Harry Haslam had told him that his Argentine coach Oscar Arce had wanted him to buy two members of the squad who had just won the World Cup in Buenos Aires. Sheffield United could not afford them so Harry had tipped off two of his closest friends in the game, Bill Nicholson at Tottenham and Terry Neill at Arsenal.

The names of the two players who were desperate to play in England were Osvaldo Ardiles and Ricardo Villa.

I immediately telephoned Bill Nick, who had been quite properly reinstalled at Tottenham by manager Keith Burkinshaw after a brief spell as a fish out of water at West

Ham. He was now employed at his beloved Lane as chief scout, and was enjoying the role of helping plot the team's future without the crushing pressure of being the manager. Keith, one of the nicest men you could wish to meet, always kept him in the loop and often quietly asked his advice. There was never a hint of interference from Bill, only sincere interest.

As any reader who has stayed with me to this point will testify, I can waffle for England, but I came straight to the point.

'Bill, what d'you know of Osvaldo Ardiles and Ricardo Villa?'

There was a silence on the phone that could have been measured in fathoms. 'What do YOU know?' he finally asked.

I told him about my conversation with Eric.

'Well, Eric is bang on the ball,' he said. 'Even as I speak, Keith is in Argentina, hopefully wrapping up the deal. I passed on Harry's tip to Keith and the directors, and they are as excited as me about the possibility of signing them. We know Arsenal are interested, but thanks to Harry we've got a head start.'

Driven by the hungry writer inside me, I contacted powerhouse *Sun* sports editor Frank Nicklin with the tip. 'Too late, old son,' he said. 'It's just come over the wires from Buenos Aires. Burkinshaw has signed them both. We're leading the front and back pages on it in the morning. It's the soccer story of the century. Spurs Beat Arsenal In Argie Bargie.' Yes, that was how Nicklin talked, in *Sun* headlines.

Sure enough, Ardiles and Villa arrived at the Lane at the start of what was a revolution in the British game. Both were wonderful ambassadors for football, for Tottenham and for their country, and Villa's magical solo goal in the 1981 FA Cup Final replay against Manchester City has been cemented into Spurs folklore. More of that later.

Spurs were boldly making the most of the Professional Footballers' Association's decision to lift the ban on foreign players, and the newly introduced freedom of contract suddenly made the Football League an attractive proposition for overseas players.

PFA officials Cliff Lloyd and Gordon Taylor expressed their concern over the deal, and were worried about a sudden influx of foreign players. 'If the trickle becomes a flow, we will take a very serious view of it,' said secretary Lloyd, the man who with Jimmy Hill negotiated the lifting of the £20 maximum wage just 17 years earlier. 'We are concerned about our members who will not be able to get first-team football because of these newcomers from overseas.'

By the start of the new millennium in 2000, all of Cliff Lloyd's fears would be justified. It was a revolution started by Tottenham, and it quickly brought rewards. After their 'lost' year in the Second Division, Tottenham took a season to find their feet back at the top table and then came into the 1980s with something of a swagger, a lot of style and a hint of a smile. And, of course – almost as footballing folklore demanded – they marked the first year of the decade, 1981, with a major trophy.

There are many Spurs supporters who will tell you that the Tottenham team of those early 1980s played the best football of any White Hart Lane side. Those of a certain age would continue to champion the Push and Run and/or the Double team as the ideal combination. But there can be no denying that Keith Burkinshaw had inspired his team to touch Everest peaks of perfection in the best traditions of Tottenham.

No dispute as to which player did most to motivate the Spurs revival movement with his skill, perfect balance, passing control and shooting accuracy. A fanfare here for Glenn Hoddle, who in that first season back in the First Division revealed that he had matured into a midfield master of international class.

In that regrouping campaign of 1978/79 – while bedding in Argentine aces Ardiles and Villa – Hoddle really flourished, scoring 19 goals in 41 league appearances and winning recognition as the PFA Young Player of the Year. He also managed to fit in a debut goal for England against Bulgaria in November 1979.

Meantime, Burkinshaw had made another imaginative move into the transfer market and brought in Steve Archibald and Garth Crooks as a £1.5m tandem team to give the attack extra authority and artistry.

Gradually, Hoddle and Ardiles got their double act together, perfecting their footballing tango partnership. This was Strictly Come Passing. Alongside them in a magnificent midfield engine room, the perpetual motion man, Stevie Perryman, was more into the hokey-cokey, keeping one foot in defence and one in attack.

Ossie was becoming a White Hart Lane folk hero. A likeable, intelligent man who had studied for a Law degree, he happily went along with Cockney singing duo Chas and Dave turning him into a short-term hit-parade star in 'Ossie's Dream (Spurs Are On Their Way to Wembley)'. A tribute tear here in fond memory of piano-playing genius Chas Hughes who always had Spurs deep in his soul.

A key player in Argentina's 1978 World Cup-winning team, Ardiles was known in his homeland as Pitón (Python) because of his snake-like, low-gravity weaving and dribbling.

He settled more quickly to the pace and demands of English football than his bearded, often brooding compatriot Ricardo (Ricky) Villa. It took him a long time to win the hearts of the Tottenham fans, but in the 1981 FA Cup Final replay against Manchester City he entered the land of soccer legend.

He conjured one of the goals of the century to give Tottenham a dramatic 3-2 victory, tangoing the City defence into such a tangle with a run past five players that two defenders almost tackled each other. In a nationwide poll, it was voted best-ever FA Cup Final goal. Who's arguing?

Once the ball bulged the back of the City net it became South American carnival time as Villa raced around Wembley on a wild dance of delight, with his diminutive countryman Ardiles trying to catch him. The celebration was as unique as the goal.

A match that had almost died on its feet on the Saturday had been given the kick of life and it guaranteed that the 100th FA Cup Final would be remembered through the following century of matches. Villa, who sulked off the pitch after being substituted in the first match, said:

On Saturday I was so unhappy. Now I am the happiest footballer in the world. When I ran towards the goal the ball seemed to stick to my feet. I did not think of passing because I enjoy running with the ball. My big thanks to the manager Mr Keith Burkinshaw for picking me. I did not think he would ever select me again after the way I left the field when I was substituted. But now I have repaid him with the greatest goal of my life. I am so happy I did this for the Spurs supporters who have always made me feel so at home here in England. **)**

The winning Spurs team was: Aleksic, Hughton, Miller, Roberts, Perryman, Villa, Ardiles (Brooke), Archibald, Galvin, Hoddle, Crooks.

While Spurs were purring to the FA Cup, White Hart Lane was being given a facelift. The old West Stand was demolished to make way for a smart, state-of-the-art new structure that cost £4m to build. It was officially opened on 6 February 1982, with Wolves the visitors in a First Division match. Cup hero Ricky Villa led the celebrations with a hat-trick as Tottenham walloped Wolves 6-1. Tottenham were tasting heady Nicholson-style success under Keith Burkinshaw.

At one stage in the 1981/82 season, 'Burkinshaw's Beauties' had White Hart Lane fans dreaming of not just another Double, more like a a Treble or even a Quadruple. They were in the hunt for the league championship right up until Easter (finally finishing fourth behind winners Liverpool), and went all the way to the European Cup Winners' Cup semi-final – going down 2-1 on aggregate to eventual winners Barcelona. This was not the smooth, stylish Barca of 2011 but an irritating team that angered Spurs with their cynical and clinical win-at-all-costs tactics.

But let's remember that Spurs could also put it about a bit. In centre-back partners Paul 'Maxie' Miller and Graham 'Hard As Nails' Roberts, they had two of the hardest men ever to pull on the Lilywhite shirt. I have come out in bruises just typing about them. Both of them would kick their granny for a win bonus, and then would have their team-mates falling about in helpless laughter with their dressing-room banter and behaviour. Happy days!

Burkinshaw twice led out Tottenham at Wembley in that always exciting, often explosive and never less than eventful season, first of all in the League Cup against Liverpool. It was the first League Cup Final sponsored by the Milk Marketing Board, and it turned sour for Spurs, even with ex-Anfield goalkeeper Ray Clemence bringing Pat Jennings-type quality to the goal line. They grabbed the lead through Archibald, but ran out of steam against a mighty Liverpool team powered by the likes of Kenny Dalglish, Graeme Souness and Ian Rush. Spurs conceded a late equaliser to Ronnie Whelan, and were buried in extra time by a goal from Rush and another from Whelan.

For the first time, Spurs had lost a domestic final and this defeat ended an astonishing run of 25 consecutive unbeaten cup games.

There was laughter to go with the tears. The TV cameras panning the crowd settled on a waving Tottenham banner, but quickly moved on when the message registered, 'Hold on to your knickers, it's the year of the Cock.'

Two months later Burkinshaw's Tottenham were back at Wembley to defend the FA Cup, but without Ardiles or Villa. The misfortunes of war meant they had to temporarily leave the country while Britain and Argentina battled over the Falklands – or, if you listened to Ossie and Ricky, the Malvinas Islands. In Wearsider Micky Hazard, Spurs had signed a midfield player almost in the Hoddle class; there can be no higher praise. He really knew his way around a football pitch, just as after his career he knew his way around London as a black-cab driver. Micky went off for five years to Chelsea, but came back to what he described as 'my first love, Spurs'. It was witty Micky who once said, 'The Spurs motto of "To Dare is to Do" has been my motto for life. You dare me, I'll do it!'

Waiting for Tottenham in the 1982 FA Cup Final were London neighbours Queens Park Rangers, under the management of former White Hart Lane schemer Terry Venables. Two largely unforgettable games were finally settled in the replay by a Glenn Hoddle strike from the penalty spot.

The FA Cup winning team in 1982 was: Clemence, Hughton, Miller, Price, Hazard (Brooke), Perryman, Roberts, Archibald, Galvin, Hoddle, Crooks.

While on the pitch everything looked smooth and well organised, there were the beginnings of upheaval in the boardroom that was to become commonplace. The Wale family took over from the Bearmans and had a stranglehold on the club for many years, until they made way for the Richardsons – Arthur and Geoffrey – but the cosy family image that had been so jealously guarded became a thing of the past as money began to poison football.

Douglas Alexiou took over as the first of a procession of high-powered businessmen filling the chairman's seat. Pulling the strings were future chairman Irving Scholar and his business partner Paul Broboff, who had taken effective control when trend-setters Tottenham became the first football club to float shares on the London Stock Exchange. From now on, profits were as important as points for Tottenham Hotspur PLC. I was into my fourth decade as a Spurs watcher and suddenly felt as if I should be writing my reports for the *Financial Times*.

What would those pioneering boys who gathered under the gas-lit lamppost in Tottenham High Road back in 1882 with an idea to form a club have made of it all?

Burkinshaw was making no secret of the fact that he was unhappy with the high-pressure business approach to the game and was having regular battles in the boardroom.

He was further unsettled by a running dispute with 'magnificent but moody' Steve Archibald that spilled over into the newspapers. This was Jimmy Anderson-Danny Blanchflower revisited, with the disagreement reaching the ridiculous point of player and manager refusing to speak to each other.

Burkinshaw's disillusionment reached new depths as he steered his stylish side to the 1983/84 UEFA Cup, with a dramatic penalty shoot-out victory over Anderlecht. Even before one of the biggest matches of his career, he indicated he would be quitting the club.

The teams were deadlocked at 2-2 at the end of extra time in the second leg at White Hart Lane, and – with agile young goalkeeper Tony Parks the hugely celebrated hero – Spurs won 4-3 on the Russian roulette penalties system. There was general agreement that Tottenham would have lost the final if skipper Graham Roberts had not produced a barnstorming display over the two legs that knocked the breath out of a polished Belgian side. Heart-of-a-lion Graham lost three teeth in a collision during one of the matches and played on as if nothing had happened. 'It was the most handsome he's ever been, toothless and ruthless,' said 'Maxie' Miller, who like the old music hall comedian he was named after could never miss the chance of cracking a joke.

Tottenham captured their latest trophy without key man Hoddle, who was being continually troubled by niggling injuries. The highlight of the run to the UEFA Cup was a 6-2 aggregate second round victory over Feyenoord, who had the veteran Johan Cruyff controlling their midfield. Hoddle out-mastered the master to confirm that he had now established himself as a player of world class. I described it as like having Van Gogh and Turner painting against each other, and it was the Englishman's brushes that provided the winning strokes. Yes, I have always over-decorated my sentences.

The winning team in 1984 was: Parks, Hughton, Miller (Ardiles 77), Mabbutt (Dick 73), Thomas, Roberts, Galvin, Hazard, Stevens, Falco, Archibald.

The UEFA Cup triumph marked the end of Burkinshaw's reign, which had brought promotion and three trophies, along with stylish football that was easy on the eye in the best traditions of Tottenham. Totally disenchanted with the boardroom situation, he kept to his pledge issued earlier in the season to quit. As he made his sad exit, he tossed a verbal hand-grenade, 'There used to be a football club here.'

Now, more than three decades later, we can put the Burkinshaw reign into perspective, and the quiet Yorkshireman can be hailed as the second most successful manager in Tottenham's history behind the man on whom he modelled himself, Bill Nicholson. Will we see their like again?

Returning to the club to be inducted into the Spurs Hall of Fame, Keith got a welcome that had enough warmth to melt an eskimo. He was clearly delighted to receive the honour and told master of ceremonies John Motson:

> Most of my time here was the happiest I have ever been in football. How can I ever forget that FA Cup win in 1981, and the magical goal by Ricky. I am so pleased to see him here being part of this special

event in my life. It was always my intention to run the club as one big happy family, and I think I achieved that until the game suddenly became more about making profit. Once the club became a limited company the heart went out of it, in my opinion. The directors, driven by having to satisfy their shareholders, made it clear to me that in future they would be making all the crucial decisions on footballing matters. Sorry, but that was not the way I wanted to do things. You don't hire a dog and then bark yourself. I was suddenly the manager only in name. I would like to see Tottenham getting rid of the City finance mentality and going back to being a football club. I am honoured to be following my hero Bill Nicholson as a member of the Hall of Fame. He set the standards we have all tried, and mostly failed, to meet. He was The Master.

Keith virtually disappeared off the radar after leaving Spurs on his strong point of principle, and hardly made ripples on the game in Bahrain, Portugal (with Sporting Club), briefly back home with Gillingham, West Brom and Aberdeen before winding down his career as assistant manager to Graham Taylor at Watford. He will always be affectionately remembered at White Hart Lane as a manager supreme, until the money men took away his pride. The General won many more battles than he lost. This was his finest hour.

With Irving Scholar now in the chair, Tottenham first of all looked north of the border for a successor but then again turned to their own doorstep for the new manager.

7

PETER SHREEVE
A Welsh Hand on the Tiller

Born: Neath, Wales, 30 November 1940
Appointed: 25 June 1984
Sacked: 13 May 1986
Appointed: 23 July 1991
Sacked: 15 May 1992
Games managed: 177
Won: 79
Drawn: 37
Lost: 61
Goals scored: 283
Goals conceded: 294
Win percentage: 44.63

PETER SHREEVE – for that is the correct spelling – had
two shots at managing Spurs, first as successor to Keith
Burkinshaw and later as surrogate for Terry Venables. But
he never got the breaks he deserved and finished his two
stints without silverware and the humiliation of twice
getting the sack.

Perhaps it might have helped if the newspapers and the club directors had got his name right. They were less than polite to Peter in that they got his name wrong when announcing his appointment, and he went down in the newspaper reports and the record books as Shreeves.

I stumbled on the fact that he was Shreeve and not Shreeves when he brought the Tottenham squad down to Dorset to train, staying in the old Dormy Hotel next to the Ferndown Golf Course and a short chip shot from my home.

I was standing in the reception waiting to be reunited with my old pal Steve Perryman when I could not help noticing that Peter was signing the hotel register as Shreeve. When – inquisitive git that I am – I queried it he told me:

> I've had it all my life. My proper name is Shreeve. That's what it says on my birth certificate. But everybody, including the Tottenham directors, calls me Shreeves, so I just shrug it off and go along with it. I don't mind what people call me as long as it's in time for breakfast.

Well, Peter was being called only good things in his opening months as manager. By Christmas 1984, he had steered Tottenham to the top of the table. But they stuttered in too many home games, losing seven and Merseyside rivals Liverpool and Everton eventually overtook them. The consolation of a place in the UEFA Cup was snatched from Shreeve by the blanket ban on English clubs following the Heysel Stadium tragedy (when 39, mainly Juventus, supporters were killed during a crowd stampede just before the 1985 European Cup Final against Liverpool, whose fans were held responsible for the riot).

Tottenham disciples wondered if they were dreaming in May 1986 when world master Diego Maradona appeared in a Spurs shirt. But it was only a one-off appearance for the Ossie Ardiles testimonial match. The supporters were only half-joking as they chanted every time Maradona settled on the ball, 'Sign him, sign him.' I wonder what they were chanting eight weeks later when he used the 'Hand of God' to help put England out of the World Cup.

Here's a trivia question with which to test and tease your Spurs mates. Who is the only Welshman to have managed Tottenham?

The answer is Peter Shreeve, an accidental Welshman. His mother was evacuated to Wales from north London in the Blitz year of 1940 just in time for her son to be born in Neath. But if you ever talked to Peter, you heard pure Cockney. He was brought up in the Gooner territories of Islington and Finchley, where he started playing as an amateur inside-forward in the Athenian League.

Shreeve was signed by Reading but had his career wrecked by a badly broken leg after 113 league appearances and 17 goals. He switched to playing non-league football with Wimbledon and Chelmsford before landing a coaching job with Charlton Athletic.

Peter and Keith Burkinshaw met on numerous coaching courses and became close friends, sharing a passion for football tactics and training methods. When Keith became Spurs manager he put Peter in charge of the youth team, then the reserves, and later promoted him to assistant manager. 'I started out as Uncle Peter to the kids,' he joked, 'and then became "that son-of-a-bitch Shreevsie" to the older players.'

Plans to bring in a Scotsman from Aberdeen called Alex Ferguson fell through, so Shreeve was the easy choice for the directors to make as the new manager when Burkinshaw announced that he was off to Bahrain to coach.

When I think of Peter Shreeve, I think of what Napoleon said when selecting generals for his army, 'I don't just want courageous and brilliant generals, most of all I want *lucky* generals.'

A likeable man, Peter, sadly, was not a lucky manager. In his second season in charge, the directors ran out of faith with the team stuck in mid-table and he was unceremoniously sacked in May 1986 to make way for the arrival of David Pleat.

He took his exceptional coaching skills to QPR and Watford and became assistant manager of the Welsh international team before again accepting the challenge of managing Tottenham after Terry Venables had moved 'upstairs' in 1991. But again there was no luck on his side and he was booted out after just one season back in the box seat, with the team stranded in 15th place in the table.

Shreeve, warm, engaging and with a quick, cutting wit, did not deserve such a swift exit, and he gets full marks as a manager from the old pros he coached. Ossie Ardiles described him as 'a top-class coach, a conscientious manager and a bloody nice bloke'. To hear the intellectual Ossie using a phrase like 'a bloody nice bloke' shows that being among Tottenham folk for so long rubbed off on him.

Shreeve was just as warm about Ossie and his team-mates:

It was an honour for me to manage Tottenham. I just wish I'd been given longer to make things happen, My happiest days with the players were when I was coaching them. We had a great rapport and it was a joy to work with them at the training ground. Ossie was my personal favourite. He never gave a moment's hassle and showed the enthusiasm of a schoolboy just coming into the game. His ball skills were astonishing. I have rarely known anybody as laid back as him in the dressing room before a match. He used to do the *Times* crossword and would be reading out clues to try to get help right up until just before the kick-off. All right, we didn't win things but anybody who was around at that time will agree we had a great bunch of lads. It was a privilege to work with them.

Peter later managed, briefly, at Sheffield Wednesday, Barnet and Grays Athletic without ever proving he had found that lucky touch. The assessment has to be: An outstanding coach, an unlucky manager. Oh yes, and 'a bloody nice bloke'. But Napoleon wouldn't have liked him.

8

DAVID PLEAT
Sadly, Sent to Coventry

Born: Nottingham, 15 January 1945
Appointed: 16 May 1986
Sacked: 23 October 1987
Appointed: 21 September 2003
Resigned: 3 June 2004
Games managed: 116
Won: 54
Drawn: 21
Lost: 41
Goals scored: 184
Goals conceded: 134
Win percentage: 46.55

DAVID PLEAT is a pleasant, pleasing man who found happiness and heartbreak at Tottenham in equal measure. I came into his life at the lowest point, just five months after he had enjoyed the highs of steering Tottenham to a third appearance in an FA Cup Final in six years. His position at White Hart Lane suddenly became untenable when he got caught up in a kerb-crawling sex scandal that should have remained a private matter. The tabloids treated him appallingly, making him out to appear to be the criminal of the century. Then the Tottenham directors – with Terry Venables in their sights – were quick to accept his resignation, allegedly with 'heavy hearts' but leaving the suspicion that El Tel had been in their sights all the time. It was a murky episode that made me ashamed to be a Fleet Street journalist, but I continued to take my weekly bunce for writing The Judge column in *The Sun*. A hypocrite, moi?

David and I were brought together by our mutual mate, the commentator Brian Moore, to discuss an offer from a publisher who wanted to cash in on the scandal by tempting him to produce a quick book. It was just a week after he had been virtually shown the door and he was still shell-shocked by the humiliating experience. I managed to talk him out of writing a book that would have been seen by his critics as him making capital out of a mainly self-inflicted predicament. Excuse me while I adjust my halo. Seriously, it would have been poor-taste timing for a book and I was not going to be a party to kicking him while he was down.

As I knew he would, David showed enormous character by climbing above his degradation, and over the following years winning respect as one of the most intelligent and incisive match summarisers on television and radio. Revealing what a big man he is, he ignored old wounds and later returned to the Lane to bring stability to Tottenham in critical times.

He first stamped his image into the public consciousness when, as manager of Luton Town, he was captured on TV skipping maniacally across the Maine Road pitch in celebration of his team escaping relegation at Manchester City's expense. It has stuck in the memory that he was wearing a beige suit and grey shoes that were iconic in those early 1980s and the dreadful fashion sense of the time.

Taking over from Peter Shreeve in 1986, Pleat enjoyed a spectacularly successful first season in charge. He steered Tottenham to third place in the First Division and to a best-forgotten FA Cup Final at Wembley.

He was a man with a plan, and made the football world sit up and take notice of his five-fold midfield force (Glenn Hoddle, Ossie Ardiles, Steve Hodge, Paul Allen and the wandering winger Chris Waddle) supporting the dynamic lone striker Clive Allen. It was a tactical formation that worked almost to perfection.

The disappointment of defeat in a three-match League Cup semi-final serial with deadly rivals Arsenal was offset by a thumping 4-1 FA Cup semi-final victory over Watford. Tottenham's opponents in the 1987 FA Cup Final were Coventry City, a club with a history mainly of taking part rather than winning things. The Sky Blues were at Wembley for the first time in their 104 years, while Spurs were bidding for their eighth victory in eight FA Cup Finals.

It would have taken a brave or foolish man to bet against Tottenham continuing their winning streak when, in less than two minutes, Clive Allen scored his 49th goal of the season. There had not been finishing finesse and consistency like this since the days of Jimmy Greaves, who had pushed Clive's dad, Les, out of, first, the Chelsea and then the Tottenham team.

In the end, it all came down to glory and grief for Tottenham's marvellous defender (and marvellous man) Gary Mabbutt, who played at the top level throughout his career despite being a chronic diabetic. He scored Tottenham's second goal to put them 2-1 in the lead, which was cancelled out on the hour by a diving header from Coventry marksman Keith Houchen.

For the fifth time in seven years the FA Cup Final drifted into extra time, and in what was the 97th minute the unfortunate Mabbutt turned a cross into his own net – famously, off his knee – to give Coventry a victory they thoroughly deserved. Football is a cruel old game.

The Tottenham team was: Clemence, Hughton (Claesen, 97), Thomas, Hodge, Gough, Mabbutt, Paul Allen, Waddle, Clive Allen, Hoddle, Ardiles (Stevens, 91).

If anybody deserved a winners' medal in that final it was Clive Allen, who became a supercharged goal machine for Tottenham in the eventful 1986/87 season when he collected a club record 49 goals. He thrived on manager David Pleat's bold plan of making him a lone front man supported by the brilliant midfield 'Famous Five': Glenn Hoddle, Ossie Ardiles, Steve Hodge, Chris Waddle and Clive's cousin, Paul Allen.

Oldest son of Les in the Allen clan, Clive was born in my home borough of Stepney in the May 1961 month that his dad helped Spurs complete the Double. On his way to Spurs he was a prolific goalscorer for Queens Park Rangers before a bizarre non-playing stop-off at Arsenal, then on to Crystal Palace and following manager Terry Venables back to QPR.

He signed for Spurs for £700,000 in 1984 and scored twice on his debut in a 4-1 victory at Everton. His sensational 49-goal season ended with the massive disappointment of defeat by Coventry in the FA Cup Final at Wembley, despite him adding to his goals collection. Consolation came with the winning of both the Football Writers' Footballer of the Year award, and the PFA Player of the Year trophy.

Capped five times by England, Clive moved to Bordeaux in March 1988 and went on to play for Manchester City, Chelsea, West Ham, Millwall and Carlisle and he later coached at Tottenham as part of Harry Redknapp's backroom staff.

In 105 league games he notched up 60 goals, and found the net 24 times in 30 cup matches. There had not been finishing finesse and consistency like Clive's purple patch since the days of Jimmy Greaves, who had pushed Clive's dad out of the Tottenham (and, earlier, the Chelsea) team.

Before finally hanging up his boots, Clive played as a specialist place-kicker for London Monarchs in the European division of the NFL. He then joined the Tottenham coaching staff and had two brief interludes as caretaker manager. Following the departure of Harry Redknapp, he concentrated on work as a television and radio football pundit, and became one of the Tottenham Legends hospitality team. Like his dad, he was a modest, dignified gentleman who has always been a credit to the game.

Allen's importance to the attack was matched by the towering performances in defence by skipper Richard Gough, who Tottenham fans were broken-hearted to lose to Rangers in the first £1m transfer of a player moving from England to Scotland. The Sweden-born Scot was one of the finest central defenders ever to pull on the Lilywhite shirt and it was a pity his stay lasted barely a year. In retirement and living in the United States, Richard recalled:

I played for many good teams during my career, but none better than that Tottenham side of 1986/87.

They were extra special and I look back fondly on playing for Spurs. In fact I don't think I ever played better than in that season we got to Wembley. I have still not got over the disappointment of losing to Coventry in the final. It really hurt. '

* * *

There was an off-beat story that went unreported and which gave unmatchable commentator Brian Moore and I reason to laugh for many years afterwards. At half-time during the 1987 FA Cup Final, five of the Tottenham players switched to short-sleeved shirts because of the sweltering heat at Wembley. Nothing odd about that, of course, but what Brian did not notice from his ITV commentary box is that the shirts were blank and missing the distinctive Holsten logo of their sponsor.

Brian was driving home his neighbour and close friend Lord Ted Willis – the distinguished playwright – when Ted's ten-year-old grandson piped up, 'Mr Moore, why did some Tottenham players have advertisements on their shirts while others didn't?'

'We were going round Trafalgar Square when he made the observation,' Brian told me later, 'and I nearly drove the car into one of the fountains.'

Perfectionist Moore, a master of the microphone and in my admittedly biased view one of the finest-ever football commentators, rang me at home late that evening. 'Notice anything odd about today's game, apart from the result?' he asked in a mysterious manner.

'Uh, you'll have to give me a better clue,' I replied, as if we were discussing a crossword puzzle.

'Just trying to find out if you saw anything odd about the Tottenham shirts.'

I admitted I had seen nothing. 'That's exactly it,' said Mooro. 'Nothing. That's what half the Tottenham players had on their shirts.'

Worried that he had missed a huge story, Brian then telephoned BBC rival and good friend John Motson to ask if he had mentioned it in commentary. Much to his relief, Motty did not know what he was talking about.

Only a sharp-eyed ten-year-old, Tom Willis, had spotted it, and Brian – one of the most conscientious men ever to cross my path – was able to sleep properly. Look up the match on YouTube, if you can bear seeing Tottenham beaten in one of the biggest of all Wembley upsets. It screams out that half the Spurs players are not running advertisements for Holsten.

Brian and I were close pals for many years, and worked together on several television assignments, most memorable of which was when I scripted and co-produced a 1990s documentary for ITV called *Over the Moon, Brian*, which featured Mooro looking back over his commentating career.

We took the cameras to Brian Clough's Derbyshire home for the final interview. Unbeknownst to Mooro, I had organised a framed cartoon drawing of him surrounded by the autographs of every major living British footballer, including legends such as Matthews, Finney, Bobby Moore, Best, Law and Charlton, and Greavsie and Dave Mackay.

The idea was for Cloughie to come in unannounced to make the presentation as Brian was wrapping the programme. The night before the shoot we spent a pleasant – if a little confusing – evening at the Clough home with his wife, Barbara, and Brian. I was accompanied by director and co-producer (and later *Top Gear* director) Brian Klein, which meant there were three Brians in their lounge.

Cloughie insisted on playing his latest Sinatra album and singing along with it in a passable imitation of his idol Old Blue Eyes.

It was in these days that Brian was hitting the sauce. He was as good as gold when we shot the main interview in his garden the next day. Then, while Mooro prepared to do his sign-off to camera, Cloughie went off secretly to collect the framed cartoon. He also had a good secret swig of sherry.

As Brian delivered his closing words in his usual professional style, Cloughie suddenly appeared from behind a hedge carrying the presentation frame. To the surprise of everybody, he made his entrance singing – Sinatra-style – Cole Porter's 'You're the Top'.

He sang the whole song, sitting on the knee of a bewildered Brian Moore, and finishing by saying, 'Mr Sinatra and Mr Porter say it much better than I ever can, Brian. You're the top.'

Cue closing titles.

The last time I saw Cloughie was in September 2001, at the funeral and combined celebration of life for Brian Moore. I had been sitting at home just over a week earlier watching England destroying Germany 5-1 in Munich when I got a telephone call during the match from Simon Moore, telling me his dad had died following a heart problem. As England's fifth goal went in, I was bawling my eyes out.

I was privileged to be trusted with the eulogy to my good friend, paying respects to Moore the man, while Bob Wilson beautifully and emotionally talked about Moore the broadcaster.

As I looked down on the congregation (400 shoe-horned into the Kent country church with hundreds listening outside), my gaze fell on those trademark George

Robey eyebrows of the one and only Cloughie, and I managed to ad-lib how pleased Mooro would have been to see him there.

Cloughie was seriously ill and he had made a monumental effort to get to the service, with Barbara, as ever, at his side.

Brian and I briefly hugged outside the church. 'Well done, young man,' he said. 'You did our Brian proud. But if I'd been in that pulpit, I would have sung "You're the Top".'

You can't top that.

I appreciate this anecdote has nothing to do with my 70 years of Spurs, but I drop it in as a mark of respect for not only a great football commentator but also one of the kindest people ever to light up my life, Brian Moore. It is specially for the attention of his oldest son, Christopher, who has done his dad proud as a vicar-turned-chaplain at a hospice caring and praying for others, a real chip off the old Mooro block. One other thing, Chris is a lifelong Spurs supporter, which is beyond the call of duty.

David Pleat, a family friend of the Moores, will I know be delighted to read that.

Back to my Spurs story.

* * *

The defeat by Coventry signalled the end of an era, with Glenn Hoddle closing his sparkling Spurs playing career after contributing 110 goals and a million spot-on passes in 490 first-team matches. He was signed for £750,000 by AS Monaco, and joined forces with their new manager, a scholarly chap called Arsène Wenger. The move broke up the thankfully short-lived double act of Hoddle and Waddle, who had managed to sing their way into the pop charts with the single 'Diamond Lights'.

Let me go on record by saying that Glenn Hoddle and Chris Waddle will be much better remembered in White Hart Lane folklore for their footballing rather than singing talent. Both can be mentioned in the same breath as any of the all-time Tottenham football idols. For singing, they were up there with Pinky and Perky.

What a pity that a growing cash crisis at Spurs meant they could not be kept together to please Tottenham fans and tease opposition defences with their glorious skills.

But Hoddle would be back, and his standing at Spurs would become dented.

David Pleat was adjusting to the new financial squeeze when his world fell apart in the autumn of 1987. He went from the back pages to the front pages of the newspapers and was ignominiously dispatched. It's to his everlasting credit that he had the character to climb out of his pit of despair and get back to the top of the mountain. We have remained good buddies, and as I was chasing my deadline on this book, David was writing his memoirs, which will be well worth reading for anybody who likes their Spurs history and told by a man who gave great service to the club.

He produced adventurous sides that played the Tottenham way, a style he preached from his young days watching the Spurs Double team:

They truly were Super Spurs. I feel as if Tottenham is my spiritual home because they always try to play the game in the right spirit. I was inspired to want to coach and manage from watching Bill Nicholson at work. He was one of the most honest and conscientious men I have ever had the privilege of knowing. Bill always put the club before himself, and he demanded the highest standards both of football skill and behaviour. What a role model for any aspiring coach or manager. '

As David exited the first time, a Tottenham old boy made his entrance as manager. The fun, the games – and the fury – of the Terry Venables era were about to kick off.

9

TERRY VENABLES
It Became Hell for El Tel

Born: Dagenham, Essex, 6 January 1943
Appointed: 23 November 1987
Moved to chief executive role: 22 July 1991
Games managed: 165
Won: 67
Drawn: 46
Lost: 52
Goals scored: 244
Goals conceded: 206
Win percentage: 40.60

TERRY VENABLES and I have known, and largely avoided each other for 60 years, from when he was first starting out as a 17-year-old boy wonder with Chelsea. I have followed his mercurial career closely every step of the way, and the Tottenham adventure took his ability to surprise to new horizons.

Last time I saw Terry was in the sumptuous surroundings of the House of Lords, of all places, where Lord Seb Coe was hosting a reception to mark 50 years of *Telegraph* writing by the doyen of sports scribes, David Miller. Venners gave me that cheeky grin that I had first seen on his teenage face back in the 1950s, as he said in a deliberately exaggerated Cockney accent, 'Long way from Bonham Road, ain't it?'

Bonham Road in Dagenham was where I first met Terry. His dad, Fred – a larger-than-life character – ran a café in the area. It was where Terry had grown up in the same football-daft road as the Allen brothers Les and Clive, West Ham and England centre-half Ken Brown, Tottenham chief scout Dickie Walker and – around the corner – Jimmy Greaves, just down the road from where Alf Ramsey had grown up and a long goal kick from Bobby Moore's Barking territory.

It was a hotbed of football fanaticism, and Terry followed in Greavsie's footsteps to Chelsea and then Tottenham, where he had a lukewarm rapport with the Spurs fans before moving on to put the midfield oil into one of QPR's finest football machines.

He was poorly rewarded for his exquisite passing skill with just two full England caps, but had the satisfaction of becoming the only player ever to get the full house of England schoolboy, youth, amateur, Under-23 and senior international honours.

In his early playing days he lived a couple of roads away from me in a semi-detached house in Ilford, where east London drifts into Essex. His first wife, Christine, and my wife were on school gate friendly terms while dropping and picking up the kids in an era when professional footballers were not much better off than the rest of us and still living in the real world. I only tell this story to underline how the game has changed.

These days journalists rarely get past agents and minders to befriend the pampered, over-paid Premier League players, most of whom do not have English as their first language. Terry and I have always been able to communicate in fluent Cockney.

He served his coaching and managerial apprenticeship with Crystal Palace and QPR, while – with his left hand – organising and operating businesses on the side, writing books and learning all he could about the media and television world and singing in nightclubs with the Joe Loss Orchestra. He was always an entrepreneur of huge energy and enterprise, and would have made the perfect candidate on Alan Sugar's show, *The Apprentice*.

The occasionally swaggering, often amusing and always-innovative cheeky chappie of football left QPR in 1984 for a spell in Spain where – after winning La Liga – he became affectionately known as El Tel. While in charge at Loftus Road he supervised and encouraged the laying of the first synthetic pitch – and with Gordon Williams wrote a novel about it called *They Used to Play on Grass*. But his vision of the future proved blurred. Luton, Oldham and Preston were the only other clubs who followed Rangers into the plastic revolution, and by 1993 they were all back on grass. Football was not in need of plastic surgery – yet.

Tottenham, however, was a club urgently requiring financial surgery when Venables was tempted back to White Hart Lane in November 1987. His arrival was a prelude to the best of times and the worst of times, with the club making as many headlines on the news and business pages as on the sports pages.

Terry kept the supporters happy by bringing in Geordie entertainer Paul Gascoigne from Newcastle for a then club record £2m, and he then went back to his old club Barcelona to coax that crisp finisher Gary Lineker home to the British game in the summer of 1989 for a fee of £1.2m. Celebrations over this coup were short-lived when – to try to balance the books – Tottenham had to sell the enormously popular Chris Waddle to Marseille for 'an offer they could not refuse' of £4.25m.

Third place in the First Division in 1989/90 was proof that Venables was starting to get things right on the pitch, but there was blood on the walls of the boardroom. The 1990 property slump hit chairman Irving Scholar like a wrecking ball to the wallet, and suddenly Tottenham was a club wide open for a takeover, being bled dry by interest rates on a loan to build a new East Stand.

On the field of play they were touching wonderful peaks of power and poetry, but off the pitch Scholar's Spurs were coming apart at the seams.

The *Financial Times* made much more worrying reading than *Shoot!*:

> Tottenham's losses for the year are £2.6m. Trading profits of £1.3m were erased by interest charges. Delays and rising labour and material costs in the rebuilding of the East Stand have sent the debt to Midland Bank spiralling to £12m.

Cries for a saviour just about stopped short of supporters writing 'HELP' in huge letters on the famous White Hart Lane pitch. It was widely reported that sailing to the rescue was 'Captain' Robert Maxwell, nobody – least of all his staff – realising that he was using Mirror Newspapers pension funds to muscle in on all sorts of business deals.

In the autumn of 1990 Tottenham's shares were suspended at 91p by the City watchdogs, and newspaper maggot (sorry, magnate) Maxwell seemingly abandoned takeover plans that always appeared confused and never set in concrete. If you think I am going over the top with my description of 'Robber' Maxwell, translate it as a few lightweight blows on behalf of my friends at the *Mirror*, who were criminally cheated out of their pensions.

Leading the charge for control of Spurs was a consortium headed by none other than my old friend El Tel. Meantime, 'El Loco' Paul Gascoigne had turned himself into one of the world's hottest properties with his talent (and his tears) on the 1990 World Cup stage in Italy. There was talk of him being worth a world record £15m in the transfer market, which gave a sudden boost to the share price.

Gazza! What an interlude. It was as if Spurs had signed a ball-juggling Marx brother. He not only brought his box of tricks on to the pitch but to every corner of the club. Nobody's belongings were safe from his pranks and any press man who tried to interview him had to vet his answers to make sure he was not telling them a pack of porkies. He once went to a local zoo, 'borrowed' an ostrich and brought it into training. It was Gazza who peppered the club's giant cockerel emblem with airgun pellets, and Gazza who let down the tyres on the cars of team-mates and once tied all the laces of their boots together. He was a laugh a minute, but often went over the top with his madcap humour.

Exciting and excitable, he captured the hearts of the nation with his tears in the 1990 World Cup semi-final and was crying again at Wembley in 1991, this time in pain. Playing for Tottenham in the FA Cup Final against Brian Clough's Nottingham Forest, he made a crazy, scything tackle on Gary Charles in the 15th minute. Gazza injured his knee so badly in the challenge that he was carried off and taken to hospital for an operation that delayed his £8m transfer to Lazio, money needed desperately by near-bankrupt Spurs (eventually, he made the move for a cut-price £5.5m). I remember with a huge lump in my throat skipper Gary Mabbutt taking the FA Cup to Gazza in hospital on the evening of the FA Cup triumph. More tears. Paul had almost single-handedly powered Spurs to Wembley and got himself so fired up that he was like an out of control fire truck when the game kicked off.

If he had not been stretchered off in the final, the likelihood is that he would have been sent off for his recklessly dangerous play, which – in fairness – was completely out of character. He was daft but never dirty. Without a shadow of doubt, he is one of the most gifted footballers ever born in the British Isles, but as nutty as a fruitcake (if any lawyers try to sue me over the description, I could call scores of witnesses to support my claim, including Paul, who admits that Bobby Robson's 'daft as a brush' characterisation early in his career was spot on). But boy, could he play football!

A month earlier, in the first semi-final ever played at Wembley, Gazza had helped beat the old enemy Arsenal with a rifled 35-yard free kick that beat England goalkeeper David Seaman all ends up. 'One of the best free kicks I've never seen,' the affable Seaman told me later when we worked together on a series of football video productions. 'Only Gazza could have come up with that one. It was a beauty.'

Gazza, the most naturally gifted footballer of his generation, was a player and a person of many different faces and moods, and to a lot of us looking on seemed like somebody almost certainly on a collision course with calamity. Gary Lineker plundered the other two goals in Tottenham's so satisfying 3-1 victory over Arsenal, who were being masterminded through a glorious run of success by George Graham.

Terry Venables had been George's best man when they were close chums back in the mid-60s. Here he was, more than 20 years later, best man again.

The Tottenham v Forest final went into extra time. Bizarrely, while El Tel was out on the pitch coaxing and encouraging his players in the short break, Cloughie stood passing the time of day with a policeman. Spurs went on to win 2-1 when Forest's dependable defender Des Walker (one of the few you could mention in the same breath as Bobby Moore) deflected the ball into his own net. It was FA Cup win number eight for Tottenham, and – naturally – in a year ending with the number one.

The FA Cup was the one trophy that always eluded Cloughie, who said of the policeman incident, 'He was a very nice young chap and I was interested in what sort of day he was having. Trying to crowd thoughts into players' minds at that stage is pretty pointless. If they don't know what to do by then they should not be professional footballers.'

There will never be another quite like Brian Clough. Or Gazza.

* * *

The 1991 FA Cup Final triumph was the pinnacle of Gary Lineker's brief but brilliant sojourn with Spurs. He was at the peak of his power at Leicester, Everton and Barcelona, but still had enough gas in the tank to make an impressive impact at Tottenham in the autumn of his exceptional goal-plundering career. In just 138 matches, he managed to bang in 80 goals for Spurs.

Sandwiching World Cup duty in Italia 90, Lineker linked up beautifully with the Geordie wizard Paul Gascoigne to provide Spurs with an exciting cutting edge in the 'El Tel' Venables era.

Gary was a born striker, and surprisingly his only domestic medal came in that 1991 FA Cup Final, which he will look back on with mixed feelings having had a 'goal' controversially ruled offside and his penalty saved.

It was in the semi-final against Arsenal that we witnessed a Lineker masterclass in finishing. His first a typical close-range poacher's goal and his second a 25-yard shot past Seaman.

Gary was a fierce but fair competitor and managed to go through his 17 years of hunting goals without once having his name taken, a display of sportsmanship that earned him the FIFA Fair Play Award in 1990. He did not have the twinkle toes of a Jimmy Greaves but was more direct and always showed positivity in the penalty area, never more evident than with his Golden Boot-winning six goals in the 1986 World Cup finals.

A proud Englishman with the second name of Winston, he scored 48 goals in 80 international matches. His final move to Nagoya Grampus Eight in the Japanese league ended painfully in 1994 with a recurring toe injury that forced his retirement.

Gary then had the drive and intelligence to open a new career for himself as a television presenter, serving his apprenticeship under the guidance of the master Des Lynam at the BBC before emerging as both the voice and face of BBC and BT football coverage. We'll always remember him as a crisp finisher.

Tottenham's team that beat Forest at Wembley was: Thorstvedt, Edinburgh, Van Den Hauwe, Sedgley, Howells, Mabbutt (c), Stewart, Gascoigne (17 Nayim), Samways (82 Walsh), Lineker, Paul Allen. Subs: Nayim, Walsh.

Victorious Venables got his mind back on business rather than football matters, and in June 1991 he joined forces with East End tycoon Alan Sugar in a combined bid for the club as Robert Maxwell came back into the frame.

Scholar, with the Midland Bank breathing down his neck, handed control of Tottenham over to the Venables/ Sugar team. I believe that Scholar genuinely always wanted what was right for Spurs, and was one of the few chairmen who could quote chapter and verse on the history of his club. I'm not sure that Alan Sugar knew a Waddle from a Hoddle.

Venables teaming up with Sugar seemed a marriage made in heaven, but the path was to lead to hell.

Peter Shreeve was briefly brought back as manager, while chief executive Venables concentrated on running the club in harness with major shareholder Sugar. Very quickly, their honeymoon turned into a headline-hitting divorce.

Bill Nicholson, honoured with the club presidency, looked on with increasing disillusionment. He hated it when the activities of the boardroom overshadowed what was happening on the pitch.

Shreeve was dismissed again in 1992 after an indifferent season, with Venables taking on many of the managerial responsibilities, supervising the work of joint coaches Ray Clemence and Doug Livermore.

Sugar was outraged by some of the business transactions that were taken as the norm in football. In 1993 – at the dawn of the age of the Premier League – he sensationally sacked Venables (I wonder if he actually said, 'You're fired!').

During a vicious bout of legal fisticuffs in the High Court, they did not just wash Tottenham's dirty linen in public; they tumble-dried it, and spun it inside out.

Sugar brought a new word into the sporting vocabulary when he talked in court of the 'bung' mentality of football. There were astonishing revelations in the courtroom. The graphic picture painted by the legal eagles was of a football world populated by men on the make, meeting in shadowy secret in motorway cafés to swap bags of money.

In his sworn statement, Sugar alleged that Venables had told him that Brian Clough, the Forest manager at the time of Teddy Sheringham's move to the Lane, 'likes a bung'.

It was claimed by Sugar, 'Mr Venables told me that what actually happened was that people would meet Mr Clough in a motorway café and hand him a bag of money. I told Mr Venables it was out of the question. It was not the way I like to conduct business.'

Clough and Venables both strongly denied the allegation. 'Not a penny was passed between Terry Venables and me,' Clough told me when I contacted him at his Derbyshire home. 'The last time I was in a motorway service station, I went for a wee.'

In his affidavit, Venables said, 'The allegation that I told Mr Sugar that Brian Clough "liked a bung" is untrue. I have never used that expression and I have never used those words or words to that effect to Mr Sugar. As to what I am alleged to have said to Mr Sugar about Mr Clough meeting people in motorway cafés to collect bags of money, it really is a lot of nonsense. Mr Sugar is either making it up or is repeating something he heard from another source.'

It all eventually led to an FA probe and Tottenham being found guilty of making illegal payments to players. They were given one of the severest punishments in English football history: a crippling 12-point deduction, a one-year FA Cup ban, and a £600,000 fine. A police probe of Brian Clough receiving a near-£60,000 'bung' was dropped.

The Spurs owner protested against the FA verdicts and the cup ban was quashed, the fine increased to £1.5m and the all-important points deduction reduced to six (and later kicked out altogether). Sugar won the court case, after Venables departed to start astonishing new chapters in his career, including becoming one of the finest of all England team managers, a leading media pundit, a wining and dining club owner with his second wife Toots, a Spanish hotelier and a man always with a song to sing.

In January 1996, Venables announced he would be standing down as England coach after Euro 96 because of time-consuming court cases due to be heard later in the year. He then became director of football at Portsmouth, but he could not escape his past and one of the most disarming people I have ever known was subsequently disqualified as a company director for seven years.

His squabbles at Spurs with Sugar left a sour taste. No apprenticeship could have prepared him for the experience, but he came through it all with his humour and swagger intact.

Nice one, Tel.

10

OSVALDO ARDILES
Cry for Me, Argentina

Born: Córdoba, Argentina, 3 August 1952
Appointed: 19 June 1993
Sacked: 1 November 1994
Games managed: 65
Won: 20
Drawn: 17
Lost: 28
Goals scored: 91
Goals conceded: 100
Win percentage: 30.76

OSVALDO ARDILES, known and loved by everybody at the Lane as Ossie, was next to take the manager's baton. Despite all the goodwill that came showering down on him, he found it as difficult a challenge as climbing the Andes with a monkey on his back.

He arrived back at Tottenham in the summer of 1993 with another Lane legend in tow as his assistant manager, the one and only Steve Perryman. They were Spurs through and through, but despite boldness in the transfer market and a positive approach on the pitch they just could not produce the results to satisfy the demands of Sugar and the shareholders. They lost more games than they won and scored fewer goals than they conceded. A recipe for a crisis. Even big Pat Jennings as goalkeeping coach could not save then.

The intellectual Ardiles could have been a lawyer, but decided instead to put his superior brain to work in the game of football. If you didn't see him play, you missed a treat. He was all smoothness and skill, slippery as an eel and so accurate with his passes that you felt he could have placed the ball through the eye of a needle. Back in Argentina he was known as 'Python' because of his snake-like dribbling, and he won 52 caps for his country, including playing a major role in the national team's 1978 World Cup triumph.

But for all his intelligence and deep understanding of football theory, he has never been able to make an impressive impact as a manager. It has not been for the want of trying. Before taking on the Spurs challenge, he was in charge at Swindon, Newcastle and West Brom, and after being unmercifully booted out at the Lane he tried his luck in Mexico, Japan, Croatia, Syria, Jerusalem, back home in his native Argentina and in Paraguay. He is Airmiles Ardiles.

Ossie is interesting to listen to on his football philosophy; that could have come out of the Arthur Rowe/ Bill Nicholson manuals:

My principles as a manager are the same as I had as a player when I was fortunate to be a member of the 1978 World Cup-winning team under that fine coach César Luis Menotti. I shared his belief in possession football. You must have the ball to win a match. If you do not let the opposition have it they cannot hurt you.

The team I admired most when I was a young boy falling in love with the game and also the team I most feared when playing was Brazil. They played the way I always tried to play and tried to get my teams to play as manager; controlling the ball and keeping it. Be positive. That is my motto. ❯

Ossie and Steve 'Skip' Perryman took that positive attitude with them into their bid to steer Tottenham into a position of power. They boldly flourished the 'Famous Five': Teddy Sheringham and dynamic German import Jürgen Klinsmann up front, Nick Barmby in a support striker role just behind them, with Darren Anderton and Ilie Dumitrescu attacking from the right and left flanks. It was pleasing on the eye, particularly with Klinsmann bombing in for spectacular goals that made him a huge hero at the Lane.

But in many ways it was suicidal, because there was nobody to shut up shop in midfield when necessary and the defence leaked goals like a sabotaged sieve. As fast as they scored at one end, they surrendered goals at the back. Oh, how they could have done with a young Steve Perryman to shore things up.

An appalling eye socket injury sidelined skipper and chief motivator Gary Mabbutt, and without his on-field leadership the thrilling-to-watch but reckless Ossie-built machine started to lose its way.

Come November 1994, dear old Ossie was 'Tangoed' and told to vamoose. What a way to treat a hero.

Steve had one game in charge as caretaker manager before he, too, was shown the door. 'I was bitterly disappointed,' he told me. 'Ossie and I were not given a proper chance to get things right because there was so much turmoil affecting the club off the pitch. We were there for football, not politics. I felt very sour about the whole thing. It was not the club I had known and loved as a young player.'

By then, Alan Sugar was hands-on and taking no prisoners. He and Klinsmann, who had two spells at the Lane, had an acrimonious spat that led to the Spurs owner saying on television, 'I would not wash my car with Klinsmann's shirt.' Hands up all those who truly believe that Sir Alan – now Lord Sugar – gives himself the task of washing his own car.

Ossie, despite the haste of his dismissal, has never lost his love of Spurs. Whenever he talks about the club he still uses the royal 'we' and he even has 'Ossie's Dream' as the ringtone on his mobile phone. Now a granddad, he still looks on Hertfordshire as his second home, immensely proud of his British-raised grandchildren and regularly dropping in at White Hart Lane, where he is idolised. He has run a successful soccer school where the emphasis was always on playing pure football, as you would expect from a man who was all about performing with passion and panache.

Ossie describes his playing days at Tottenham as the happiest of his life.

Now, from a former Argentine field marshal, Spurs turned to a man who used to captain England.

11

GERRY FRANCIS
The Impossible Job

Born: Chiswick, London, 6 December 1951
Appointed: 15 November 1994
Resigned: 16 November 1997
Games managed: 146
Won: 56
Drawn: 42
Lost: 48
Goals scored: 204
Goals conceded: 188
Win percentage: 38.35

GERRY FRANCIS declared publicly what many have whispered privately, 'Managing Tottenham is an impossible job.' He made his startling statement a decade after quitting the club because he failed to meet the standards he had set for himself.

The ex-England captain, who had made his name as a buccaneering midfield player with Queens Park Rangers, did not wait to be sacked. A proud man, he walked away in

November 1977 at the end of his three-year contract, with Spurs battling against the threat of relegation.

Much later, when back on the football roundabout as coach at Stoke City, he said:

> The thing with Tottenham is it's not just about winning – I didn't have too many problems with that. My record was the best for over a decade until Martin Jol went there and finished fifth twice, and you know what happened to Martin as well. In most clubs winning is what it's all about, and people are happy with that, but at Tottenham you have to win with style as well, which puts even more pressure on. It's a great club, with terrific support and I enjoyed my time there, but it's not easy – in fact there are aspects about the club which makes managing it a lot tougher than others.
>
> When I was there they hadn't done much for four years – but people still thought we would go to Manchester United and win. Then when we got to be top London club, reached an FA Cup semi-final and went into Europe, the expectations just got bigger. It is an impossible job, harder I would say even than managing England.

Francis had been considering taking a complete break from football when Alan Sugar called him following the brutal ending of the Ardiles/Perryman reign. The man who had captained England and Queens Park Rangers and managed Exeter, Bristol Rovers and QPR was ready to turn his back on football to enjoy a quiet family life and concentrate on his hobby of racing pigeons.

But the chance to manage a major club like Tottenham was a challenge he could not resist. He was not doing it for the money, because he was a wealthy young man who had always invested wisely while captaining England and QPR. He owned an antique shop and read the stocks and shares as avidly as Alan Sugar. This was the age of the mullet and he had one that was as good/bad as Chris Waddle's. Hair-raising days.

In his first season in charge, he lifted Spurs from fourth from bottom to seventh in the Premier League, and reached the semi-finals of the FA Cup, despite the distraction of twice being interviewed for the England manager's job.

The following season, Spurs ended up eighth, with a higher points tally than any other manager had achieved at the Lane in the 1990s. Francis genuinely believed he had laid the foundations for a title challenge, but then got hit by a succession of injuries unprecedented in the club's history. After three games of his third season he had lost Chris Armstrong, Gary Mabbutt and – surprise, surprise – Darren 'Sicknote' Anderton, plus Teddy Sheringham.

The season went from bad to worse until, at one point, he had 15 first-team squad players queueing in the treatment room.

'It got to the stage where I was handing out Jelly Babies at half-time to the kids I had to play in the team,' Francis recalled with the ironic sense of humour that kept him sane when the stresses and strains were at their peak. 'If we hadn't have had such a big squad, we would undoubtedly have been relegated.'

The injury crisis got so bad that when Steffen Iversen and Les Ferdinand were injured on international duty, he had to call in his sixth-choice striker from the youth squad.

Then, of course, Spurs also lost Sheringham, who left for Manchester United in the summer of 1997, controversially stating he needed to play for a club that could win trophies. That cut into Francis like a knife stab. He said:

> In reality Teddy wanted to stay. He wanted a five-year deal that would see him through to his testimonial. He came to me personally and said that he didn't want to move. The best the club could offer was a four-year contract, which, under its terms, was a tremendous offer. He left because he didn't get what he wanted, but when you analyse what he later said about his reasons for leaving Spurs, it just doesn't add up. If he wanted to leave us because we weren't going to win anything, how come he asked for a five-year contract?

There was such an upheaval of the playing staff – Klinsmann, Chris Armstrong, Nick Barmby and Popescu all moving on – that Francis could not get any rhythm and consistency in the team, and after two reasonable seasons he found himself struggling to keep the club out of the relegation rat race. In a terrible moment of misjudgement, he turned down the chance to sign Spurs fan Dennis Bergkamp and left the door open for Arsenal to snap up the man who was to be arguably the greatest overseas player to decorate the Premier League. Ouch.

Adding to the pressure on Francis was that down the road at Highbury, George Graham had been hoovering up trophies with Arsenal. In the end it was too big a challenge for Gerry, a sincere and dedicated football man, and he walked before he was pushed.

Gerry kept a diary of his highs and lows at Tottenham and an enterprising publishing company (Pitch Publishing, still available as a Kindle edition) launched it under the title, *The Team that Dared to Do*. The main focus is on the eventful 1994-95 season, with memories galore of the passion and the pain of near-glory, familiar to all Spurs supporters. Jurgen Klinsmann writes the foreword and recalls his goal blitz that became the talk of football. Gerry gives a revealing insight into the pressures of managing at White Hart Lane at a time when there was little money in the kitty.

In the end, Francis proved a more successful diarist than manager as he became the latest to find the Spurs job Mission Impossible. I wonder how this chapter would have ended if he had signed Bergkamp, who twisted the knife by telling the press, 'I modelled my game on that of my hero, Glenn Hoddle.'

Next up, a Swiss grasshopper!

12

CHRISTIAN GROSS
Not Quite the Ticket

Born: Zurich, Switzerland, 14 August 1954
Appointed: 25 November 1997
Resigned: 5 September 1998
Games managed: 29
Won: 10
Drawn: 8
Lost: 11
Goals scored: 40
Goals against: 45
Win percentage: 34.48

CHRISTIAN GROSS spent nine months at White Hart Lane. Somebody (it might have been me) unkindly described it as a pregnancy without a birth. It was an appointment that made little sense, and while he had coaching rather than managerial responsibilities he still gathered all the frustration and the flak that goes with being manager.

Gross had been coaching Swiss champions Grasshoppers when he got the call from Alan Sugar to come and dig Spurs out of their relegation hole. The standard of the Swiss league was the equivalent of about the English Second Division, and it was difficult to see what credentials he had to guide Tottenham back to the glory-glory days.

It became even more illogical when it was later alleged that Sugar was at one time pointed in the direction of Bobby Robson, who was restless in Spain.

Trying to show that he was a people's manager, Gross arrived at the ground at the start of his reign by tube train. He waved his underground ticket at the cameras at his welcoming press conference, saying, 'I want this to become my ticket to dreams.'

A journalist cynically asked if he had bought a return ticket. Welcome to the Premier League, Herr Gross.

Alan Sugar watched the pantomime of the tube ticket with open mouth. 'From that moment on,' he later confessed, 'our new manager was dead meat. The media slaughtered him.'

Gross got off to a promising start with a win at Everton, but a 6-1 defeat at home to Chelsea and a 4-0 setback at Coventry set alarm bells ringing. Just as everybody was writing Gross off as being out of his depth, he managed to tighten the defence and away wins at Palace and 6-2 against Wimbledon – coming from behind twice – lifted Spurs out of the relegation zone.

The incredible match against Wimbledon included a four-goal haul from Jürgen Klinsmann, who made up with Alan Sugar and had come back to Tottenham for a final blitz.

It quickly got around on the gossip vine that all was not well behind the scenes under the whip of Gross. Few of the players could get on with him, and one senior first teamer whispered to me, 'The only player he talks to is his fellow Swiss, Ramon Vega.'

Gross was unfortunate in having a heavy Swiss-German accent that made him sound like a send-up of the Gestapo officer in *'Allo 'Allo!*, and he had the Mickey (or the Manfred) taken out of him unmercifully behind his back.

He fell out with Klinsmann just when he most needed the German's forceful finishing power, and there were rumblings of discontent as the new season started. In all my years observing Spurs I had never known the dressing room so divided, and it was obvious that Gross had lost the confidence and support of the players who could make or break him. When a manager loses a dressing room, he is in trouble. He introduced a training routine that the players quietly reported was torture. 'We just don't look forward to coming in each day,' I was told off the record. 'It's like a hard labour camp.'

Gross was unlucky that Gary Mabbutt, a player of principle who could have pulled the team together, was near exhaustion after his incredible 16 years of service to the club. Every day throughout his career this Miracle Man of football endured without a moment of complaint four injections and eight blood tests. During those 16 years, he had undergone 16 operations. There was not a dry eye in the house when he played the final game of his career against Southampton in May 1998. 'I've had a fantastic innings,' he said. 'I could consider a future in management, but I always remember Bill Nicholson telling me because of the pressure of the job he never saw his daughters growing up. I want to enjoy my family.'

At the start of the new season, Tottenham beat Everton but then in their third game went down to a shocking

3-0 home defeat against Sheffield Wednesday. It was an appalling performance and there was little sign of unity and desire among the players. The directors swiftly dropped the guillotine.

Gross said, with some justification:

> After only three games, I think it is too short a time to judge me and decide my fate. It is not a failure for me to be judged after three games, especially after a big win at Everton. I am more disappointed than angry. There were so many ideas that I had for the weeks and months ahead. I might have understood if I had been asked to go after three months. But after three matches? That cannot be right.
>
> Perhaps things would have been different if I had been able to bring my fitness coach Fritz Schmid as was originally planned, but he could not get a work permit. That was a big blow, because he could have given me the balancing support that I needed. But despite everything and the less than satisfactory manner of my dismissal I will always have good memories of my stay at Spurs.

In classic style, Alan Sugar shot the messengers. 'I think one has to say we were faced with an untenable situation created, with all due respect, by the media,' he said. 'We the board felt that Christian – no matter how professional or how good he is – had been destroyed by the media. It is as simple as that.'

The board then astonished everybody by bringing in a King Gooner. When would they ever learn?

13

GEORGE GRAHAM
The Man in the Raincoat

Born: Bargeddie, Scotland, 30 November 1944
Appointed: 5 October 1998
Sacked: 16 March 2001
Games managed: 125
Won: 49
Drawn: 35
Lost: 41
Goals scored: 177
Goals conceded: 152
Win percentage: 39.2

GEORGE GRAHAM was the third Gooner put in charge at the Lane, and like Joe Hulme and Terry Neill before him he was always made to feel a passing stranger. He had put Tottenham in the shadows during his six-trophies-in-eight-years reign at Arsenal, and his name was poison on the lips of intransigent Spurs supporters. George and I have always had a leg-pulling relationship through the 50-plus years that we've known each other. He telephoned me from Leeds in the summer of 1998 to tell me, 'I'm on the move again. Guess where to?'

I said the daftest answer I could think of, 'Tottenham Hotspur.'

'Bloody hell,' said George, or words to that effect. 'How did you know? I've only just agreed to take the job.'

Now I thought he was countering my joking response with a joking response. It was several minutes before he convinced me he really *was* taking over as manager at Spurs. This was like the Archbishop of Canterbury becoming the Chief Rabbi.

Only three years earlier I had ghosted George's confessional autobiography, *The Glory and the Grief*, in which he told the inside story of taking a £425,000 bung (we were legally bound to call it 'an unsolicited gift') that brought him a year's ban and cost him his Arsenal job. George remains the only manager ever to be caught, a scapegoat if ever there was one.

He had the character to overcome the earthquaking event in his life, and came back into the game as manager of Leeds United. Now here he was accepting the poisoned chalice, manager of Tottenham Hotspur. I told him I thought he was mad.

As I guessed, there was a large faction of Spurs fans who just would not accept him. And even after Graham had steered Spurs to the 1999 League Cup with a last-minute defeat of Leicester City, there were many Lane regulars who would not give him credit.

A section of supporters at Wembley would not even chant his name, instead singing, 'Man in a raincoat's blue-and-white army'.

George told me:

I quickly discovered at Tottenham that there were quite a few fans who would never accept me even if I won them the league. I just had to shrug off their constant criticism and concentrate on doing the job to the best of my ability. It was not worth wasting energy worrying about them. My only concern was getting it right on the pitch, and we were well on the way to getting a settled and successful side when I was kicked out in a totally bizarre way. It was not only some of the supporters who wanted me out.

George had the satisfaction in his first season of giving Tottenham their best spell on the pitch for several years. They secured a mid-table finish, captured the League Cup and were robbed in an FA Cup semi-final against Newcastle, when a definite penalty was turned down with the score deadlocked at 0-0. The Geordies won with two extra-time goals, and went down 2-0 in the final against Manchester United.

The League Cup victory was carved out with courage after Tottenham had been reduced to ten men on the hour, when Justin Edinburgh was sent off after a clash with that annoying wasp of a player, Robbie Savage. The game was into its 90th minute when Allan Nielsen scored the winner with a dramatic diving header.

Tottenham's winning team at Wembley was: Walker, Carr, Edinburgh, Freund, Vega, Campbell, Anderton, Nielsen, Iversen, Ferdinand, Ginola (Sinton).

The icing on the cake of an agreeable season came with idolised French flier David Ginola collecting both the PFA and Football Writers' Association Footballer of the

Year awards. Cross-Channel charmer David was a huge favourite with the White Hart Lane faithful, and Graham's popularity hit freezing point when he sold the entertaining but enigmatic Frenchman to Aston Villa following a disagreement over David's nonexistent defensive qualities that his adoring fans were happy to overlook.

George explained, 'I wanted players who decided matches, not decorated them. David was great on the ball and could do some wonderful, eye-catching things. But when the chips were down and we needed a sleeves-rolled-up team performance he too often went missing.'

It has to be said that there was huge surprise but no mass mourning when George was dismissed in March 2001 for allegedly being too open with the media about his budget restrictions at Tottenham. But the timing of his dismissal was strange, to say the least. He had steered the club to the FA Cup semi-final (against Arsenal, of all teams), and he described his sacking as 'bizarre and inexplicable'.

He kept to himself that while giving 100 per cent to the job he was fighting a private and painful battle against crippling arthritis, which continues to handicap him today.

I know for a fact that George had big, ambitious plans for Tottenham that he was going to put into operation in the following close season, but they were ideas that never got beyond his imagination.

Alan Sugar had meantime sold out to ENIC (an acronym for English National Investment Company), with Daniel Levy installed as chairman and responsible not only for the day-to-day running of the club but also for its future direction.

Sugar – not yet knighted or Lorded – made an astonishing attack on footballers after making his exit, although remaining a major shareholder at Tottenham. He said while promoting a television documentary:

> Footballers are total scum. They don't know what honesty or loyalty is. They are the biggest scum that walk on this planet and, if they weren't football players, most of them would be in prison, it's as simple as that.
>
> Do not believe a word that comes out of their mouths. All they are interested in is themselves. Totally themselves. And if something doesn't go right, they'll go behind you and stab you in the back.

Gary 'Gentleman' Mabbutt, club captain during Sugar's ownership of Spurs, shook his head in disbelief when he heard of the tirade. 'It would be laughable if it were not so serious,' he said. 'It is so unnecessary and derogatory.'

Gordon Taylor, chief executive of the Professional Footballers' Association, commented, 'These pathetic comments say more about Alan Sugar than the people he's talking about. No doubt in the business world people might say similar things about Alan Sugar. It's as offensive as any racist remark. Footballers' organisations have probably done more in this country to try to create respect for other people and anti-racism than anybody and it's not the sort of language we would use.'

I saw it as a dreadful generalisation that was a slur on the countless dignified and honest footballers I have mixed with over the last 60-plus years.

To those of us close to the politics of football it was clear ENIC wanted their own man in charge at Tottenham after they had brutally removed George Graham, who was a completely wrong choice by Sugar. George was too much his own man. He did not fit their mould. His dismissal was handled by vice-chairman David Buchler, who commented, 'We cannot conduct the affairs of Tottenham in the press, and I have summarily dismissed George Graham for breach of contract.'

As somebody who knows George better than most, let me tell you that he is a man of great charisma, style and dignity. Yes, dignity despite that hiccup of accepting 'an unsolicited gift' for giving advice on transfer dealings while manager of Arsenal. He gave into temptations that would have tested most of us. He was later contrite, apologetic and handed the money over to Arsenal. In what I saw as a scapegoat case, he was banned from football for a year. He served his time and was then welcomed back into the game he played with grace and in which he managed with dedication, determination and distinction. But never in a million years was he cut out to be a Tottenham manager. Spurs once again had red blood on their carpet.

The White Hart Lane musical chairs – now more a funeral march – continued. Time to welcome back one of the club's greatest-ever players. But could he manage?

14

GLENN HODDLE
Success Passes Hod By

Born: Hayes, Middlesex, 27 October 1957
Appointed: 30 March 2001
Sacked: 21 September 2003
Games managed: 61
Won: 29
Drawn: 10
Lost: 22
Goals scored: 102
Goals conceded: 73
Win percentage: 39.68

GLENN HODDLE was arguably the most gifted player ever to pull on a Spurs shirt, but what is not in dispute is that he was one of the club's most ineffective and hapless managers. While there were those who almost willed red-blooded George Graham to fail, Hoddle had nothing but goodwill on his side when he arrived – as he put it – 'back home'.

But it all turned sour, and the man who had been hero-worshipped as a player found himself taunted and derided by the same fans who had sung his praises when he was hitting the sort of passes that made spectators purr with pleasure.

Was it only the day before yesterday that walls were daubed with graffiti claiming 'Hod is God'? It would need Sigmund Freud rather than this ancient writer to fathom why Hoddle could not transfer his mastery as a player to management.

Glenn had lit up the Spurs firmament with some of the most spectacular goals ever scored by a player wearing the Lilywhite shirt. For an essentially midfield player, his scoring output was just phenomenal, and Tottenham supporters to this day warm themselves on memories of his classic contributions.

Come with me to Tottenham's old training ground at Cheshunt. It's the summer of 1973 and I am standing alongside veteran manager Bill Nicholson as he watches his youth squad being put through their paces. I am there in my role as chief football reporter for the *Daily Express*.

A gangling young lad effortlessly traps the ball on his right thigh, lets it run down his leg and then sends a glorious chipped pass direct to the feet of a team-mate 30 yards away.

'Very nice,' shouts notoriously hard-to-please Bill, 'but remember you're a footballer not a circus performer.'

Bill keeps his all-knowing eye on the 15-year-old youngster as he tells me, 'That's Glenn Hoddle, from your neck of the woods in Essex. He's been with us since he was ten and we've high hopes for him. We've just got to get some tactical nous into him to go with his natural skill.'

From that day on, I was a Hoddle disciple and this first view of Glenn came sharply into focus on Saturday, 27 October 2018, his 61st birthday, when I got a call from an old television colleague to tell me the Spurs and England legend had collapsed with a heart attack in the BT Sport studio.

I was one of the first to share the news on social media, because I knew how much love and respect there is out there for one of the greatest footballers of his generation. He needed all our thoughts and prayers, and as I write this book I am relieved to report that Glenn is recovering from his life-saving bypass operation and has resumed his TV pundit duties.

'It was shocking to witness it,' my old mate Harry Redknapp reported, still reeling from being just feet away from Glenn when he suddenly collapsed. 'If it hadn't been for BT sound man Simon Daniels who knew first aid and how to use a defibrillator we could have lost him. A few moments earlier he'd been showing all his old skill playing keepy-uppy. He's a smashing bloke and everybody in the game will be rooting for him.'

This is not the time or place to bring out old skeletons, but I have never forgiven some of my former Fleet Street colleagues for the way they mangled him after he had allowed strictly private thoughts to become public when England manager. Each to his own. Let's judge him purely as a football man and he goes right to the top of the tree.

It would need a book rather than this chapter to catalogue Glenn's life and times. Nut-shelled, Glenn won the FA Cup (twice) and UEFA Cup with Tottenham and also had spells with Monaco (under Arsène Wenger), Swindon and Chelsea.

He began his managerial career as player-manager at Swindon before taking over at Chelsea, for whom he signed Dutch icon Ruud Gullit.

From there he managed England for two and a half years, taking them to the 1998 World Cup finals, but his reign ended in controversy when he admitted a 'serious error of judgement' after suggesting disabled people were being made to pay for the sins of past lives.

He went on to manage with limited success at Southampton, Tottenham and Wolves, before embarking on a career as a TV pundit and regular co-commentator, when his grasp of tactics was always on the ball and instructional to viewers.

It was at Tottenham that he had his peak years as a player, and we Spurs disciples bask in the recollections of perfectly placed passes made with a touch of arrogance, and chipped shots delivered with a delicious accuracy that baffled a procession of goalkeepers.

I always remember skipper Steve Perryman once telling me, 'If Glenn was on song, then the team was on song. He was that influential. A sheer genius.'

Glenn was 'on song' from the moment of his first full league game at Stoke on 21 February 1976 when he struck the sweetest of shots past England goalkeeper Peter Shilton to register his first goal for Tottenham, which lifted them to a 2-1 victory. The Hoddle road show was up and running.

Glenn revealed that he could not sleep that night for the excitement that he knew he had found his personal paradise. 'The style of football Tottenham played was made for me and I was made for Tottenham,' he said, not boasting but just brimming with anticipation. 'The club wanted players coming through who were Spurs lads. I had blue and white blood.' The Harry Kane way.

Away from White Hart Lane, the polished and at times peerless performances from Hoddle were mocked by envious rivals as being a luxury. Those of us watching through Tottenham eyes were excited to be witnessing the best thoroughbred football since the glory-glory 1960s. Hoddle, never frightened to speak his mind, countered his critics with the comment, 'A luxury player is the one who keeps giving the ball away and doesn't use it.'

He bristled when people called him lazy. His imaginative passes and innovative positioning shouted in reply that his contribution should be measured not by sweat but by skill.

Each season club-mates queued up to praise Hoddle's elegance. Ossie Ardiles described his midfield partner as 'Maradona without pace', adding, 'He was the most gifted English footballer I played with, the greatest passer of a ball, a magnificent talent who could win a game with just one flash of brilliance.'

Steve 'Skip' Perryman said, 'Glenn is the greatest natural footballer I ever played with. I can never understand people who criticise him. He is class from top to toe. Some of the things he does with the ball are just unbelievable.'

Keith Burkinshaw, manager of the Hoddle-inspired team that won back-to-back FA Cups, said, 'I'd pay to watch Glenn play. England would have been much more successful had they built their team around him. He should have won twice as many as his 53 caps. I've never known a better technical player.'

Who will ever forget the 1983 UEFA Cup tie against Johan Cruyff's Feyenoord, when he steered Spurs to a 6-2 win on aggregate? He managed to outshine the legendary Cruyff over both legs, and the Dutchman came into the Tottenham dressing room to present Glenn with his autographed shirt, a sign of respect from one master to another.

Hoddle stepped out of character to sing his way into the Top 20 in harmony with Tottenham team-mate Chris Waddle, but it was the music he made on the pitch that grabbed the attention and it was like losing a best friend when he ended his Spurs career.

There was the same kind of mourning when Hoddle moved to Monaco that followed the exit of Jimmy Greaves for West Ham, but there was not the consolation of getting Martin Peters in part-exchange. Glenn's silken skill had the Monaco fans purring, and his manager Arsène Wenger persuaded him to think about a switch to management.

As player-manager at Swindon, he was like a mother hen with chicks that he coached and cajoled to a place in the Premier League. He was poached by Chelsea and then – when fellow ex-Spur Terry Venables surrendered the England job ahead of Euro 96 – Hoddle was the popular replacement as national manager.

He was a hero when he plotted the goalless draw in Rome which earned England a place in the France 98 finals, but Glenn was scorched under the microscopic scrutiny of the media. His controversial religious views were brought into focus, and he perished on the altar of belief when he went public with his view that disabled people were suffering for sins committed in a previous life.

Hoddle was a football genius, but he too often seemed frustrated and intimidated by man-management decisions. He fell out with Tottenham favourites Paul Gascoigne and Teddy Sheringham, and many considered he got it wrong when he dropped 'Golden Balls' David Beckham. It seemed the great individualist could not handle great individualists.

After his self-harming cost him the England job, he reinvented himself as Southampton manager before he found the call of Spurs too strong. Saints were disgusted with the way he walked out on them but the lure of managing his beloved Tottenham was too much. Right man, wrong time.

He arrived with the club lost in a maze of its own making and he was unable to give it the direction he had on the pitch as one of the finest players ever to pull on the Spurs shirt.

It was the defeat by Blackburn at Cardiff in the 2002 League Cup Final that marked a turning point in Hoddle's fortunes. Up to that point all had seemed to be going well with player purchases and team performance, and indeed Spurs soared to second place in the Premier League just before Christmas 2001. But after the Blackburn game and the 2-1 loss, Hoddle lost his grip as Spurs went into a slide. Behind-the-scenes rows made their way into the newspapers, and one bust-up with the headstrong England international midfielder Tim Sherwood rumbled on long after they had gone their separate ways.

Hoddle later reflected on accepting the Tottenham challenge:

It was an offer I couldn't refuse because Spurs will always be in my blood. But I let my heart rule my head and lost out to the sort of club politics that are just not part of my make-up. I so badly wanted to succeed but it wasn't to be. I should never have gone back at that time, but 20/20 hindsight is easy.

I have spoken to many footballers who played under him as a club and country manager and, to be honest, few have positive things to say. And you should hear what they think of him at Southampton, the club he walked out on to take the Tottenham job – the one he called 'my destiny'.

The way he was sacked by England for his chillingly tasteless comment about disabled people paying for sins in a previous life and his unfathomable leaning on the word of faith healer Eileen Drewery all added up to Hoddle being considered, well, a sort of oddball.

He made a promising start to the challenge of managing Spurs, with the highlight of his first season being that League Cup Final appearance against Blackburn Rovers at Cardiff's Millennium Stadium. Christian Ziege cancelled out a Matt Jansen goal to make it 1-1 at half-time, and goal machine Andy Cole snatched the winner for Rovers.

In the 69th minute Les Ferdinand missed a sitter, and Teddy Sheringham fumed when referee Graham Poll turned down a last-minute penalty appeal. Spurs finished feeling frustrated, furious and potless.

Hoddle was named Premier League Manager of the Month the following August as Tottenham sprinted to the top of the table. But it was a false start, and there were mutterings of discontent when the team dropped away to a disappointing tenth place.

It was not a happy camp, and stories leaked out from senior players complaining about Hoddle's alleged lack of man-management and communication skills. On the surface an affable character, it was remarkable how many enemies he had made for himself in the media, and there was a constant drip-drip-drip of stories dropping on to the back pages about discontent in the dressing room and disagreements at the training ground.

Just four points from the opening six games of the 2003/04 season confirmed Hoddle's fate, and in September he was politely invited to pack his bags. Perhaps he was being punished for sins perpetrated in a previous life.

In the last ten games that Tottenham played under one of the great attacking architects, they scored just six goals and conceded 25 – this, despite having brought in £7m goal gourmet Robbie Keane from Leeds. In fairness to Hoddle, maybe the defensive record would have made better reading had he not lost the rock-solid Sol Campbell to, of all clubs, Arsenal under the Bosman free transfer ruling.

To many Tottenham fans, that was a deal of the devil that they would never ever forgive. The way I saw it, Campbell – a magnificent footballer – was entitled to ply his trade wherever he chose, just like anybody else in this free country of ours. But there is a faction of myopic supporters who are completely unable to see his side of things. They forgave Pat Jennings for taking the Arsenal shilling. But Campbell? No chance, and to this day he is referred to as Judas. I'll tell you this, there have been only a handful of more talented defenders to pull on the Lilywhite shirt. Many Spurs fans only see red when they hear his name.

Tottenham became a rumour sieve during the Hoddle reign, and there were stories of unhappy training sessions and a divided dressing room. When he offloaded George Graham signing Tim Sherwood, the former Blackburn skipper was overheard saying, 'Nobody would shed a tear if Hoddle was sacked tomorrow.'

The enormously popular Steffen Freund fell out with Hoddle over tactics and reluctantly left a club he described as 'the place where I want to spend the rest of my career'. Instead he went home to Germany and Kaiserslautern.

It all started to fall apart for Spurs and Hoddle and the job of removing him from the Tottenham hotseat fell to fairly new club chairman and former season ticket holder Daniel Levy, who had grown up watching Glenn at the peak of his glorious playing career. Conscious that he was dealing with the dismissal of a Tottenham legend, he interrupted his honeymoon to release a full statement on the decision to sack Hoddle:

> Following two seasons of disappointing results, there was a significant investment in the team during the summer, in order to give us the best possible chance of success this season. Unfortunately, the start to this season has been our worst since the Premiership was formed. Coupled with the extremely poor second half to last season, the current lack of progress and any visible sign of improvement are unacceptable.
>
> It is critical that I, and the board, have absolute confidence in the manager to deliver success to the club. Regrettably we do not. It is not a decision we have taken lightly. However, we are determined to see this club succeed and we must now move forward. Glenn occupies a special place at this club. Today's decision in no way detracts from the fact that he was one of our greatest players. He will always be welcome at White Hart Lane. I should like to personally thank him for his determination and commitment and wish him well.

The honeymoon was over for Hoddle.

The one-time idol of the Lane, Hoddle was the first Premier League manager of the new season to lose his job, just a matter of months after splashing £11m on the summer signings of strikers Hélder Postiga, Freddie Kanouté and Bobby Zamora. All were proven and highly rated goal scorers, but they could not find the net on a regular basis to save Glenn from the ignominy of the sack.

* * *

We Spurs followers were excited when Hoddle signed former Spurs favourite Teddy Sheringham on a free transfer from Manchester United. Two of the finest players of modern times joining forces. But they had a huge personality clash.

Teddy graced Spurs with his goals in two spells at White Hart Lane when he cemented himself into club legend with his cultured performances and cheerful personality. He was very much a modern footballer, and was like Martin Peters – ahead of his time in his reading and execution of the game.

Using his tactical brain like a soccer scientist, Teddy would lie deep as if a hidden assassin and then come through as an unseen support striker to collar goals before defences were even aware of his presence.

He was the thinking footballer's footballer, subtle and cunning and able to almost tiptoe into dangerous areas like an uninvited guest at a party, and invariably the one who took the cake.

His extraordinary career stretched 24 years from when he was first spotted by Millwall while playing youth football for amateur club Leytonstone & Ilford. He was hugely influenced at The Den by manager George Graham, and amassed 111 goals between 1983 and 1991 for the Lions before Brian Clough came calling to whisk him off to Nottingham Forest.

His move to Forest and then to Tottenham was to become the fodder for football folklore. It emerged during the bitter court case between Alan Sugar and Terry Venables that Teddy was the innocent player in cloak and dagger transfer dealings that allegedly involved Cloughie pocketing a famous 'bung'. It was never proved to be true, but the story accompanies every relating of Teddy's colourful life and times.

Cloughie, of course, had an answer. 'A bung?' he said, with his distinctive eyebrows raised. 'The only bung I've ever heard of is the one you plonk in the bath.'

An unashamed playboy who liked a pretty girl on his arm and the challenge of a late-night game of poker, Teddy was a frequent visitor to the celebrity gossip columns. But it was on the football pitch where he always gave us soccer scribes something to write about.

His 11 goals in 51 appearances for England – when he formed the explosive 'SAS' partnership with Alan Shearer – was just part of his success story. Amazingly, he had to wait until he was 27 and an established favourite at White Hart Lane before he got his first cap in a 1993 World Cup qualifier in Poland.

After collecting 75 Premier League goals in his first five-season spell at Tottenham, he moved to Alex Ferguson's all-conquering Manchester United and started to gather the medals his beautifully honed skills deserved.

He was an enthusiastic and productive member of the United team that won three Premier League titles, one FA Cup, one Champions League, an Intercontinental Cup and a Charity Shield, during his dazzling days at Old Trafford, where he was as idolised as he had been at White Hart Lane.

The crowning moment of his career came when he scored the equaliser and then conjured the assist for Manchester

United's dramatic last-minute winning goal in the 1999 UEFA Champions League Final against Bayern Munich at the Nou Camp stadium.

His peak performance in an England shirt was his two-goal man-of-the-match display in the 4-1 hammering of Holland at Euro 96, and being part of Terry Venables' England setup is something he recalls with pride:

> Everybody was tipping the Dutch to tear us apart. We outplayed them and the nation went potty. It doesn't get better than that. Terry could really communicate with his players, Sadly, in my experience, this was not something Glenn Hoddle could do. He had a way of belittling his players. I cannot say I enjoyed playing for him.

Teddy was one of the few players I've seen in a Tottenham shirt who could match Hoddle for technique and ball control. His performances continued to enchant and excite spectators regardless of their club persuasion, and in 2001 while still at Old Trafford he got the distinguished double recognition of both the PFA Players' Player of the Year and FWA Footballer of the Year awards.

From Tottenham, we looked on at his success with a mixture of envy and pride in his exploits. The roars of delight when we heard that he was coming back to the Lane could be measured on the Richter Scale. Glenn Hoddle manager, Teddy Sheringham scorer. It was the dream team.

But the two giants of the game – opposites in life style and tastes – just could not get along with each other, and when Teddy moved on to join Harry Redknapp's Portsmouth on a free transfer in 2003 he made a barbed attack on Hoddle when he said, 'I'm looking forward to playing for a manager who can communicate with his players.' Ouch.

In his second spell at Spurs, Teddy added 26 goals in 80 appearances to join the exclusive 100 club, just as he had at Millwall at the start of his career. To this day he insists he should have had a last-minute penalty against Blackburn in the 2002 League Cup Final, which might just have made a major difference to Hoddle's managerial reign.

From Portsmouth, he moved to West Ham and helped them gain promotion, then reach the 2006 FA Cup Final. At 40 years and 268 days he was the oldest player to score a Premier League goal. He then signed for Colchester United, where he had his final shots at the age of 42. His service to football was marked in 2007 with the award of an MBE.

He later had a crack at management with League Two club Stevenage and ATK of the Indian Super League. But managing did not come as easily to him as playing.

Teddy, happier at the poker table, was quite a card.

* * *

There was a sickening irony for Hoddle in that the team that plunged the final knife into him was Southampton, who he had abandoned to take the Tottenham job. After their 3-1 victory had clinched Hoddle's dismissal, his successor at Saints, Gordon Strachan, said, 'Coaching is an absolute doddle. Man-management is far harder and there's a massive difference between a coach and a manager.'

Nobody knows the truth of that statement better than Glenn Hoddle.

He did not expect the axe although there had been constant rumblings of dressing-room unrest. Glenn said after his dismissal:

I am shocked and disappointed. We are only six matches into the new season. I have been a dedicated professional and also a lifelong Spurs fan, and no one could have tried harder to turn things round for the club. I have built a great squad that when fully fit can go on to do very well this season.

I feel sure this turning point will happen very soon but I won't be around to see the fruit of my labours. It's so frustrating because I know I can do the job.

After an unimpressive spell in charge at Wolves, Hoddle opened a successful soccer academy in Spain, and right up until that frightening heart attack has been one of the most sought-after of all football pundits. Glenn talks a game nearly as well as he played it, which means he is like a football professor.

Of all Tottenham's 18 goal centurions, few were in the Hoddle class for finishing finesse.

Steve Perryman recalls: 'I saw Glenn do things with the ball that were out of this world. He was a true footballing artist and I considered it an honour to be on the same pitch as him. If he'd been French or Brazilian, they'd have awarded him a hundred caps and built a statue to him. He scored goals that no other English player would have even attempted, shots that left goalkeepers beaten and bewildered by his accuracy. The man was a genius. Don't judge him as a manager. Judge him as a player. I've not seen anybody better in a Tottenham shirt.'

He was simply *the* legend of Lane legends. A player from the heavens, but too often finding hell as a manager.

In 2021 he took part in a television series, *The Masked Singer*, disguised as a grandfather clock. His time was definitely up as a football manager who could be taken seriously.

Let's be generous, and remember Glenn in the summertime of his service to Spurs, hitting glorious passes and scoring goals that lifted Spurs supporters to paradise. Sadly, his management exploits plunged them to the dungeons of despair.

As Hod the God became history, director of football David Pleat took over as caretaker, with Chris Hughton as first-team coach.

The next manager brought French farce to White Hart Lane.

15

JACQUES SANTINI
The One Who Got Away

Born: Delle, France, 25 April 1952
Appointed: 1 July 2004
Resigned: 5 November 2004
Games managed: 13
Won: 5
Drawn: 4
Lost: 4
Goals scored: 16
Goals conceded: 11
Win percentage: 38.46

JACQUES SANTINI was the one who got away. He arrived amid much hype and hope with the reputation of being one of Europe's top coaches, and left after just 13 matches. It was the briefest reign of any Tottenham manager. Talk about Jacques be nimble, Jacques be quick. He had been and gone before many supporters even caught a glimpse of him. David Pleat took temporary charge until the Frenchman's appointment at the start of the 2004/05 season, while Jacques was putting the finishing touches to leading France to the Euro 2004 finals. At the same time, the Dane Frank Arnesen was brought in to take Pleat's old job of director of football. This was musical chairs at White Hart Lane played to an international tune.

The lines of duty, so it was claimed, were clearly drawn: Santini to handle the daily training and tactical sessions and to select the team; Arnesen to scout for new talent and to be in charge of transfer dealings. This was football management the modern continental way.

The football world was stunned when Santini announced after five wins, four defeats and four draws that he was quitting, citing personal reasons. In a hastily produced statement, now-you-see-me-now-you-don't Jacques said:

> My time at Tottenham has been memorable and it is with deep regret that I take my leave. I wish the club and the supporters all the best. Private issues in my personal life have arisen which caused my decision. I very much hope that the wonderful fans will respect my decision. I should like to thank football director Frank Arnesen and Daniel Levy for their understanding.

Much later, the apparent true story emerged that Santini and Arnesen were incompatible and continually arguing over responsibilities. So much for Santini thanking Arnesen for his understanding. He had lost a power struggle to the Belgian.

Meantime, Arnesen got caught up in an episode that could have come from a John Le Carré thriller. He was photographed onboard one of the luxury yachts belonging to Chelsea's Russian owner Roman Abramovich, and Chelsea and Spurs got involved in a verbal and legal punch-up. It finished with Chelsea – who had gone a Bridge too far – having to cough up £5m compensation when the Dane, metaphorically, jumped ship and joined the King's Road crew.

To add to the gloom, Bill Nicholson – Mr Tottenham – passed on in the autumn of 2004 at the age of 85. Goodness knows what Bill would have made of the comings and goings at his glorious old hunting ground.

Next on the captain's bridge, so to speak, was a very jolly man, and for a while a good time was had by all.

16

MARTIN JOL
The Jolly Dutch Giant

Born: The Hague, Netherlands, 16 January 1956
Appointed: 8 November 2004
Dismissed: 25 October 2007
Games managed: 149
Won: 67
Drawn: 38
Lost: 44
Goals scored: 242
Goals conceded: 184
Win percentage: 44.96

MARTIN JOL was surprised to find himself Tottenham's manager so soon after being appointed assistant coach to the fast-disappearing Jacques Santini, but the Dutchman quickly brought stability to the team and smiles back to the faces of the long-suffering Spurs supporters.

Working in harness with the ever-popular Chris Hughton, Jol pleased everybody with his warm personality and open-hearted approach to management. Here at last was somebody proving that it was possible to do the 'impossible job'.

His three years in charge were among the happiest Tottenham had known in a long run of broken promises. Martin – full name Marteen Cornelis Jol – guided the club to two successive fifth-place finishes in the Premier League, and encouraged an old-style attacking attitude that cheered up fans fed for too long on a diet of dull defensive football that went against all Tottenham traditions.

Jolly Jol's Spurs looked booked for a Champions League place, but in the final game of the 2005/06 season they were forced to field a team at West Ham that was savagely weakened by the outbreak of a stomach virus. They tried to get the game postponed, but were ordered to go through with it. A defeat by the Hammers meant they lost their Champions League spot to, of all clubs (look away if you are squeamish), Arsenal. It went down in the Tottenham history books as 'Lasagnegate'.

Spurs touched their Everest peak under Jol when on the verge of qualifying for the Champions League for the first time in their history. All they had to do was match 'the other' north London club's result on the final day of the season and they would finish above Arsène Wenger's side and in the top four.

The Gunners, playing their final game at Highbury, were facing Wigan, while Spurs had to go to Upton Park for a showdown with West Ham.

Spirits were high in Jol's camp until the night before the match. Their squad started going down like ninepins with a bout of suspected food poisoning at the team hotel, the Marriott at West India Quay. The football cliché 'sick as a parrot' took on new meaning, with many of the players spending most of the night suffering sickness and diarrhoea.

Chairman Daniel Levy tried to get the game postponed for 24 hours, but the Premier League chiefs insisted they play as scheduled. Midfielder Jermaine Jenas later revealed that several of his team-mates were still throwing up in the dressing room toilets minutes ahead of kick-off.

It was hardly surprising that the drained and groggy Spurs players struggled and went behind to an early goal by Carl Fletcher. Jermain Defoe levelled before half-time, but he and his team-mates were on the edge of exhaustion when Yossi Benayoun scored the winner for West Ham in the 80th minute.

Across London at Highbury, Arsenal walloped Wigan and leapfrogged over Spurs for the coveted Champions League place. Spurs had to make do with the consolation of the UEFA Cup.

The final whistle had hardly blown before there were conspiracy theories floating around, with allegations that a kitchen hand at the hotel where Spurs were staying was an Arsenal fan who had doctored their lasagne.

Spurs demanded that the Premier League order a replay of the game, but the request was denied, with the governing body ruling there were 'no grounds for acceding to your request'.

An official investigation by the Health Protection Agency revealed that norovirus, a form of viral gastroenteritis, had been the cause of the illness.

* * *

Everybody liked the always cheerful Jol, but having recruited the likes of Darren Bent – at a club record

£16.5m – plus Gareth Bale from Southampton and French defender Younes Kaboul during the summer, Spurs suffered a stuttering start to the 2006/07 season, recording just one victory in ten league games.

Suddenly those of us who had got to like the Dutchman and his attitude feared for his managerial life, and you could almost hear the boardroom knives being sharpened. The inevitable end came just hours before Jol suffered through a home UEFA Cup defeat by Getafe.

After the promise of two fifth-placed finishes, Spurs had made their worst start to a domestic campaign for 19 years and were languishing in the Premier League relegation zone. 'For me, the departure of Martin Jol and Chris Hughton is very regrettable,' said Daniel Levy. 'Our greatest wish was to see results turn in our favour and for there to be no need for change. We feel honoured that Martin has been manager at our club, having seen us qualify twice for Europe.'

Jol took the disappointment of his dismissal on his big chin. Pocketing around £4m in settlement of his contract helped soften the blow considerably. He said with his usual candour:

I can understand the position of the club in light of the results. I have thoroughly enjoyed my time here. Tottenham Hotspur is a special club and I want to thank the terrific staff and players. For me, the fans were always amazing with their support, so I would also like to say thank you. I shall never forget them. It has been a wonderful experience, and I am just very sad that we have not been able to get a better start to this season when it seems that everything that could go wrong did go wrong. The

man taking over from me inherits a very talented
squad of players, and I just hope they get the breaks
they deserve. 🙶

Confirmation of Jol's departure drifted through to the
Tottenham supporters during the second half of the UEFA
Cup tie, and the fans stood and chanted their praise in
a clear demonstration of affection. It was surreal to hear
Jol being cheered as the team he was being forced to leave
behind slumped to a 2-1 home defeat against mediocre
Spanish club Getafe. The players had clearly heard that Jol
and Hughton were on their way out and showed little heart
for the game.

An outgoing manager has rarely been given such a warm
send-off. He disappeared to the Bundesliga with Hamburg,
and then in 2009 returned home to Holland to manage
Ajax. He guided them to the Dutch Cup, but then suddenly
resigned in December 2010 with Ajax in 'an unacceptable'
fourth place.

Not-so-jolly Jol made it clear he was going to take a
break from the pressures of football management. but his
self-exile days in the wilderness did not last long. He was
soon back in the mix as boss of Fulham and his itchy feet
later took him to Egypt in the search for his football kicks.

Meantime, at White Hart Lane a Spaniard was about
to be thrown into the works.

17

JUANDE RAMOS
A Spaniard in the Works

Born: Pedro Muñoz, Spain, 25 September 1954
Appointed: 29 October 2007
Sacked: 25 October 2008
Games managed: 54
Won: 21
Drawn: 16
Lost: 17
Goals scored: 84
Goals conceded: 69
Win percentage: 38.88

JUANDE RAMOS was one of the most in-demand managers in Europe after winning back-to-back UEFA Cups with Sevilla, and Tottenham got him at the second time of asking. But his reign would last just one year, and when the axe fell Spurs were bang at the bottom of the Premier League.

It had all looked so promising when Ramos and Gus Poyet first took over, steadying the ship and even capturing the first silverware since 1999. Supporters could hardly believe it when Spurs hammered Arsenal 5-1 in the second leg of the League Cup semi-final at the Lane. It was their first victory over their greatest antagonists for eight years, and it clinched a place in the final against Chelsea at the new Wembley.

Spurs went behind to a Didier Drogba free kick, but a Dimitar Berbatov penalty took the game into extra time. Jonathan Woodgate snatched the winning goal to earn qualification for the 2008/09 UEFA Cup.

Tottenham's team that day was: Robinson, Hutton, Woodgate, King, Chimbonda (Huddlestone), Lennon, Jenas, Zokora, Malbranque (Tainio), Berbatov, Keane (Kaboul).

Spurs had become the only club apart from Manchester United to win a trophy in each of the last six decades. At last, so the fans thought, a settled side and an inspired and rewarding period to look forward to.

Wrong! Following the final, Spurs won only two of their next 21 matches.

Hopes and dreams came tumbling down again as Spurs made their worst start to a Premier League season in 2008/09. It added to the depression caused by the failure to hold on to their star strikers Berbatov and Robbie Keane. The fans saw red as born predator Keane went to Anfield and the gifted yet maverick Berbatov to Old Trafford. Then England striker Jermain Defoe was sold to Harry Redknapp's Portsmouth.

With only two points collected from their first eight matches, Tottenham were in freefall by October 2008. The final straw came as Udinese completely outplayed Spurs throughout their UEFA Cup tie. Spurs looked bereft of ideas and industry, while on the touchline Ramos appeared shell-shocked and at a loss as to what to do.

In fairness to Daniel Levy, when he signed Ramos all good judges thought he had captured one of the finest managers in the game. He had tried to hook him a year earlier, and when he eventually arrived at White Hart Lane it was hailed as a coup.

But Ramos ran into the same problems as his immediate predecessors in that he had power over the team but no responsibility for transfers. The transfers in and out turned the spotlight on director of football Damien Comolli, who had allowed the three main strikers to leave and only signed Roman Pavlyuchenko as replacement.

On what became known as the night of the long knives, Levy acted with the ruthlessness that was required. Operating with an executioner's alacrity, he dismissed Ramos, first team coach Marcos Alvarez, assistant manager Gus Poyet and the under-fire Comolli.

In a brief statement on his personal website, Ramos said:

> The results are what count in football and we all know how this world works. Now we just have to see if this decision is the best one for the team to recover and have a good season.

But in private he spat angrily about not being able to bring in the players he wanted because his hands were tied by the Tottenham transfer system.

Within eight weeks, Ramos – who could barely speak understandable English – was happily counting his compensation money while accepting one of the top jobs in Europe: manager of Real Madrid. Yes, it's a funny old game.

Levy, giving all his energy to pinning down a successor to Ramos, issued one of his now familiar 'sorry, but' statements:

> I have made an important judgement call and in doing so I have taken some very difficult decisions. Relieving Juande Ramos, his assistants, Gus Poyet and Marcos Alvarez, of their posts is not something I have undertaken lightly. Unfortunately, our record of just three Premier League wins since our memorable Carling Cup victory against Chelsea last February, combined with our extremely poor start to the season, led the board and I to determine that significant change was necessary as a matter of urgency.

Levy made it clear that the departure of sporting director Comolli signalled a return to a 'more traditional style of football management'. They don't come any more traditional than the next man on to the Tottenham roundabout. Enter Harry Hotspur.

18

HARRY REDKNAPP
Taxing Time for the Crafty Cockney

Born: Poplar, London, 2 March 1947
Appointed: 26 October 2008
Departed: 13 June 2012
Games managed: 198
Won: 98
Drawn: 50
Lost: 50
Goals scored: 335
Goals conceded: 225
Win percentage: 49.49

HARRY REDKNAPP came swaggering into White Hart Lane in the autumn of 2008, bringing with him a style, a smile and a guile that he transferred to the Tottenham team. Everybody loved 'Aitch', until he rather naively let it be known that he would consider it a privilege to manage England.

Myopic Spurs supporters turned on him viciously and Harry became the victim of his own honesty.

And it was his honesty that was challenged in court during a headline-hitting battle with the Inland Revenue that he won, but not without serious damage to his personal integrity. Only Harry could have bounced back to become a national treasure after winning the immensely popular *I'm A Celebrity Get Me Out of Here* TV show. You couldn't make it up, Aitch.

For the 60-plus years that we've known each other, he has never failed – as with Terry Venables – to surprise me. He first came on my radar as a young flying winger; yes, he is old enough to have played in the days of orthodox wingers.

From day one Aitch amazed me with his encyclopaedic knowledge of the game. He is a walking record book on football and in particular Tottenham history, and he was a schoolboy player with the club when Spurs won the Double in 1960/61. From then on, those were the standards that he set for himself.

Harry eventually started his professional playing career at West Ham, where he came under the influence of a professor of football in Upton Park manager Ron Greenwood, who also believed in the Spurs creed of putting skill and method before might and muscle. Back then, I was a confidant of Greenwood in my Fleet Street reporting days, so I knew before most people that Harry was an obvious manager in the making.

Wherever he has gone on the managerial roundabout, he has been a purist. Yes, perfect for Tottenham. And he speaks understandable English, provided you don't mind a sprinkling of dropped aitches, some strangled English grammar and an occasional reacquaintance with the Anglo Saxon tongue. T'rific!

Let's quickly get rid of the skeleton in his cupboard. His first allegiance as a boy (born down the road to me in Poplar, in the heart of London's East End) was – brace yourself – to Arsenal. But this was before he could think for himself. Harry's dad was a Gooner, and used to take his young son to Highbury.

But as soon as he could appreciate the finer points of the game, Harry realised that Spurs were playing the best football in town. The manager he rated above all others was 'Mr Tottenham', Bill Nicholson.

'I would not be fit to lace Bill Nicholson's boots,' is Harry's as-ever totally frank assessment of Bill Nick's stature in the game. But of all the managers Tottenham had since Nicholson let go of the reins – 16 of them before the Redknapp arrival – he seemed best suited to carry on the Nicholson and Tottenham tradition of winning with a mix of precision, pace and flamboyance.

If chairman Daniel Levy had got his way, the Redknapp reign would have started 18 months earlier, but he finally got his man in return for a whopping £5m compensation fee to Portsmouth, the club Harry had, against all odds, steered to the FA Cup six months earlier.

Harry and I are fellow East Enders who chose dozy, delightful Dorset as our adopted county. We often bumped into each other and discussed the old days when he and I were members of Bobby Moore's Black Lion drinking school back when Mooro was the undisputed king of the Hammers. Redknapp was a skilful, high-stepping and very quick right-winger who was unlucky to establish himself as a touchline-hugging express just about the time Alf Ramsey was making wingers redundant. He was as fast as Lennon, but crossed the ball more like McCartney (excuse the pun, Aitch).

I reported on his debut for the Hammers in the *Daily Express*, and nicknamed him the 'Boleyn Greyhound'.

He was a slimline, thoroughbred of a player, all nervous energy and wanting to be involved in everything; just like he was as a manager. Harry taught his son Jamie and nephew Frank Lampard how to make the ball do the work with passes of Hoddle class, but as a player he liked to run with the ball as if it was tied to his flying boots.

Always inquisitive about tactics, he used to pick the brains of everybody who knew the difference between an overlap and an underpass. It came as no surprise when he switched to coaching and managing at the end of his playing career.

He cut his teeth with Seattle Sounders, Oxford City and then Bournemouth, and it was while putting the Cherries on the map that he nearly lost his life in a car smash when following the 1990 World Cup finals in Italy. He was written off as dead, but came back larger than life and scattered the chirpy Redknapp personality across West Ham, Southampton and Portsmouth.

I knew that he would not be able to resist the Spurs stage when it was offered to him. Tottenham is the big club he deserved. It was something of a sleeping giant, and if anybody could give it the kick of life it was 'Harry Hotspur'.

He was a wheeler-dealer like none other in the transfer market, and was such a good judge of players that he rarely made a mistake. The few times he did get it wrong he was man enough to admit it and rectified it with another lightning buy-and-sell market raid.

When Harry was brought in as successor to Juande Ramos, Tottenham were bang at the bottom of the Premier League, and there was a smell of relegation fear permeating deep into the nostrils of Tottenham players and supporters. Within a few weeks of taking charge, there were smiles where there had been scowls and hope where there had been despair. Harry was not waving a magic wand. He was simply doing what he did throughout his managerial career – quietly motivating players with common sense advice, rollocking when necessary and always spreading an air of self-belief that was contagious.

Unforgiving when any player gave less than his best, Harry set high standards of skill, dedication and sportsmanship. He did not want his players cheating, but he did want them competing at all times. Harry did it the Spurs way. The Bill Nicholson way. Is there a better way?

He pulled no punches when talking about life in general and football in particular, as the directors and shareholders discovered when he addressed the Tottenham annual meeting two months after taking over, making it crystal clear that he meant business.

There was a sharp intake of breath as he said about the club's playing ambitions:

It depends where you want to finish. If you are talking about getting into the top five or the top four, the squad is well, well short of that. There is a lot of work to be done to become a top team. I cannot tell lies. The squad is still well short of challenging for a place in the top four. We are not as good as Aston Villa or one or two other teams, so there is a lot of work to be done to get where we should be.

I have probably upset the chairman now! I have got a good group of lads and they are a very good squad. They come and work hard on the training ground. This is a proper football club, and we need proper players and a proper team that this club deserves. I want to bail out in a few years' time and leave this club in the top four. '

Harry got his first taste of how Tottenham fans can turn when he gave a frank answer at a press conference to the question, 'Would you like to manage the England football team?' A less honest man would have side-stepped and given a non-committal answer. Not Harry. He replied, 'Of course I would. It must the biggest honour you can have in the game to manage your country. I would be very proud to have the job.'

This was interpreted by many fans as Harry fishing for the England job, which was proving a tough challenge for the incumbent (some would say incompetent) Fabio Capello. He had given a straight answer to a question and had the burning oil of criticism poured on him. Those Spurs supporters giving him a good kicking appeared to have short memories. They seemed to have forgotten that when he arrived at the Lane, Tottenham were a club in intensive care.

Harry had arrived at Spurs just as a new phenomenon was taking off: social media. Fans who had only been able to voice their views from the terraces suddenly had a platform. Facebook, Twitter and a billion blogs shook with their rage. Everybody was suddenly a pundit and an armchair expert, many of them keyboard warriors out to injure and intimidate with words aimed mostly from anonymous launching pads. They called themselves supporters, but continually turned their guns on their own players in general and Redknapp in particular. He and Levy became the most pilloried men in football by couch coaches who had never kicked a ball professionally in their lives and could not organise a loft conversion. Suddenly renowned football historians like me (I'm joking, folks) were having to compete with knee-jerk opinions fired without need for accuracy or judgement. And Harry got it from both barrels for saying that he would consider it a privilege to manage his country, Oh dear. Wash your mouth out, Aitch. Who would be a manager!

Spurs were four points adrift at the bottom of the Premier League after taking just two points from eight matches when he took over at the Lane. Harry Hotspur quickly proved himself Harry Houdini, motivating the players into producing a run of five wins and one draw in six games. It was one of the greatest starts to the reign of any Tottenham manager in history.

There was a new bounce and buoyancy on and off the pitch, and he inspired the likes of Roman Pavlyuchenko and Darren Bent to recover their confidence in the penalty area. He showed his typical boldness in the transfer market by bringing back master marksmen Jermain Defoe and Robbie Keane, stiffened the backbone of the team with the purchase of Wilson Palacios from Wigan, motivated jet-paced Aaron Lennon (a winger in the young Redknapp style) and nursed Ledley 'The Legend' King, so that he could continue playing despite recurring knee injuries.

He gave Tom Huddlestone the encouragement to show his wares, and supporters started to rub their eyes. Were they really seeing a player who could strike a ball as well as Glenn Hoddle?

Even Harry had to admit he was astounded by the performance of the reborn Spurs side when they clawed their way back to an amazing 4-4 draw against Arsenal when two goals down with just minutes left to the final whistle. Suddenly the description 'Miracle Man' was tumbling from the lips of Tottenham supporters aching for the return of the Glory-Glory years.

The players revealed there was a new spirit blowing through the club from the moment of Harry's arrival, the fans (their nails chewed to the bone) were for the first time in months becoming relaxed, and the media were reporting events at the Lane without having to resort to words like 'crisis' and 'shambles'.

Harry surrounded himself with a backroom team of people he knew he could trust: the likes of Clive Allen, Tim Sherwood, Kevin Bond and his former Portsmouth right-hand man Joe Jordan. For Harry, familiarity bred content.

Spurs very nearly retained the League Cup just weeks after his arrival, eventually going down on penalties to Manchester United at the new Wembley. Tottenham might have won in normal time but for United's second-string goalkeeper Ben Foster making a stunning save from Aaron Lennon when a goal looked inevitable.

Ryan Giggs, Carlos Tevez, Ronaldo and Anderson found the net for United from the spot in the shoot-out, but only Vedran Corluka scored for Spurs.

The Tottenham team for that final was: Gomes, Corluka, Dawson, King, Assou-Ekotto, Lennon (Bentley 102), Jenas (Bale 98), Zokora, Modric, Bent, Pavlyuchenko (O'Hara 65).

Late in the nerve-jangling, rollercoaster season, Spurs looked on course to end a 20-year drought at Old Trafford when leading 2-0 at half-time. But they came apart at the seams after a disputed penalty decision pumped new life into United. But the only thing that mattered to Harry as the curtain came down on his first season was Premier League survival. He virtually gave up on the UEFA Cup challenge as he concentrated on his one priority of beating the threat of a relegation that would have been disastrous so soon after the unveiling of plans for the new multi-million pound Northumberland Park development project.

With the encouragement and support of chairman Levy, Harry made significant surgery to the squad in the summer of 2009. Bent and Didier Zokora were shipped out, and in came England's Leaning Tower striker Peter Crouch and creative Croatian midfielder Niki Kranjcar from Harry's old hunting ground at Portsmouth, along with defender Sebastien Bassong from Newcastle United.

In an exceptional first full season, Harry guided Spurs to their most successful Premier League season to date. They got off to a flier with four consecutive wins and went on to finish in fourth place with 70 points, getting a passport to the promised land of the Champions League.

The highlight was an astonishing 9-1 victory over Wigan on 22 November 2009, eight of the Tottenham goals coming in the second half and five of them from the boot of Jermain Defoe.

* * *

Born in the same London E6 postal code as one Jimmy Greaves, Jermain Defoe won the admiration of Tottenham supporters with his goals, and the hearts of the nation with the compassion he showed terminally ill Bradley Lowery in a sad episode that transcended the village world of football. He is a great advertisement for his profession and thoroughly deserved the award of the OBE for his charity foundation's work for under-privileged children.

Wherever he has taken his boots, Defoe has always been a prolific goalscorer, no more so than in two periods at White Hart Lane during which he became a highly regarded member of Tottenham's 100 club.

He started his collection with his local West Ham club in 1999, and has also scored for Portsmouth, Toronto FC, Sunderland, Bournemouth and Glasgow Rangers. He has plundered 20 goals for England in 57 appearances.

How best to represent him in this book of a 70-year march through Tottenham time? One match he played for Spurs has gone down as among the most memorable of modern times. It was the day the Lilywhites went one over the eight with a 9-1 whacking of Wigan at the Lane on 22 November 2009. Astonishingly, eight of the Tottenham goals came in the second half.

Defoe scored five goals, including – in just seven minutes – the second-fastest hat-trick in Premier League history. He became only the third player to score five times in one Premier League match, after Alan Shearer and Andy Cole (Dimitar Berbatov and Sergio Aguero have subsequently equalled the feat).

This is how I reported the devastating Defoe display:

> There is something about 22 November. People always say they remember exactly what they were doing on that day in November 1963 when John F. Kennedy was assassinated. On a much happier note, Spurs fans will always recall what they were doing on that day in 2009 when Tottenham walloped Wigan 9-1.
>
> Call it hindsight, but there was something in the air at the Lane on this Sunday afternoon of 22

November 2009. Perhaps it was the fact that Aaron Lennon was back on the right wing after a three-match lay-off with an ankle injury; whatever it was, there was a definite upbeat mood and a buzz of extreme optimism around the ground packed with what was then a near-capacity 35,650 spectators.

For Spurs fans it was great to have high expectations rather than high anxiety.

Manager Harry Redknapp felt relaxed enough to start with Croatian midfielder Niko Kranjcar on the left, ditching his recent diamond formation and resting Robbie Keane on the bench following his midweek World Cup efforts with the Republic of Ireland in France that ended in Thierry Henry's 'L'Hand de God' breaking Irish hearts.

In the pre-match warm-up it was easy to spot that Jermain Defoe had the two recently dislocated fingers on his left hand cushioned in bandaged tubes. Metaphorically, he would be giving more than two fingers to the Wigan defenders before the afternoon was over.

There was just a hint of what was to come in the very first minute when the jet-paced Lennon left his marker for dead before crossing to Peter Crouch, who flicked the ball just wide. Moments later, Wilson Palacios, playing against his old Wigan club, delivered another cross to Crouch for a chance that was squandered.

It could only be a matter of time before a goal came and, sure enough, in the ninth minute Lennon's cross reached the leaning tower that is Crouch, who stooped to conquer, heading the ball from close range beyond the despairing dive of goalkeeper Chris Kirkland.

Soon afterwards, Kirkland smothered a shot from Lennon, and then he stretched to push the ball to safety under the head of Crouch from Niko Kranjcar's deadly accurate left-wing delivery. The overworked goalkeeper also denied Palacios and the silky-smooth Tom Huddlestone thumped an instant shot inches wide. It seemed all too easy for Spurs, and they suddenly took their foot off the accelerator.

There were warnings that Wigan could get back into the game when a Charles N'Zogbia chip scraped the Spurs crossbar, and the underworked Heurelho Gomes made a fine save to compensate for a poor throw-out.

Defoe had been taking up promising positions without getting the ball played to him. He took matters into his own hands with a speculative dipping shot that bounced off the crossbar, and then just before half-time he tested Kirkland with a rasping shot that the keeper tipped off target.

The half-time scoreline greatly flattered Wigan. But for Kirkland's saves it could have been 4-0.

Redknapp looked mightily unhappy on his way to the dressing room.

As we know the final scoreline, it seems crazy that Redknapp gave his players a rollocking that scorched the walls of the Tottenham dressing room at half-time. He felt that Wigan had been let off the hook, and were still in there with a fighting chance when they should have been dead and buried.

Missing the injured Ledley King and Luka Modric, there was satisfaction in the way big-hearted Michael Dawson had slotted in alongside Jonathan Woodgate and Kranjcar was proving a playmaker of the highest quality. But still Spurs led only 1-0. Jermain Defoe revealed, "Harry and the coaching staff had a go at us at half-time. They got us really wound up ready for the second half."

Harry got everything off his chest in quick time, and sent his players out for the restart five minutes early with his instructions echoing in their ears, "Press from the first whistle."

Tottenham, the club that brought us Push and Run, were now playing Press and Run. Watch out, Wigan, here they come! '

At top level in world football, there has rarely if ever been a second-half quite like this one. White Hart Lane – The Lane of Dreams – has been the stage for some remarkable spells of football down the years, but even the most veteran of supporters could not remember anything to match this. For the record, let me catalogue the goals:

- 51 minutes: Defoe smacks home Lennon's centre from close range with combination work that must make England manager Capello lick his lips with South Africa and the 2010 World Cup in mind. Spurs 2 Wigan 0.

- 54 minutes: Defoe nips in like an Artful Dodger pickpocket for his second goal, sweeping in a pass from Wilson Palacios after Wigan's bemused and confused Emmerson Boyce had missed his tackle. Spurs 3 Wigan 0.

- 57 minutes: Paul Scharner interrupts Defoe's stunning one-man show with a controversial goal that virtually everybody in the ground except the referee Peter Walton and his assistants know should have been disallowed. Wigan's Austrian midfielder blatantly controls the ball with his hand before steering it past Gomes. The Tottenham choir, in good humour, light up the Lane with chants of, 'Are you Henry in disguise?' Spurs 3 Wigan 1.

- 58 minutes: It is quickly back to the Defoe demolition work. The lethal Lennon is again the provider, collecting a fine pass from Vedran Corluka before sliding it into the path of Defoe, who shoots it home with the coldness of a wild west gunman for a hurricane hat-trick in just seven minutes of merciless mayhem (officially, six minutes 59 seconds). Statisticians dive for the record books to discover that it is the second-quickest Premier League hat-trick behind the whirlwind strike by Liverpool's Robbie Fowler against Arsenal in 1994. Spurs 4 Wigan 1.

- 64 minutes: Corluka and Crouch combine to create the opening for a well-deserved goal for the exceptional Lennon, a deliberately aimed drive into the bottom corner of the net that gives Kirkland no chance. The brave goalkeeper had stopped almost everything coming at him in the first half, but now he can only wave to the ball as it thumps into the net. Spurs 5 Wigan 1.

- 69 minutes: It's that man Defoe again back to haunt the Wigan defence, sprinting on to a beautifully weighted through ball from Corluka and smashing it in off the near post for his fourth goal. If this had been a boxing match the referee would now be stepping in to stop the fight. Spurs 6 Wigan 1.

- 87 minutes: Goal number five for Defoe, and this time it's all his own doing as he dispossesses the shell-shocked Erik Edman on the edge of the box and beats the oncoming Kirkland with a shot of exquisite accuracy. Spurs 7 Wigan 1.

- 88 minutes: David Bentley, on as a substitute for the splendid Aaron Lennon, joins the goal spree with a crashing free kick from 25 yards that hammers high against the goal frame with Kirkland beaten all ends up. The ball hits the goalkeeper on the back of the neck and rebounds into the net. Officially it goes down as an own goal, but all those who witness it know that by rights that goal belongs to Bentley. Spurs 8 Wigan 1.

- 90 minutes: With the Spurs fans hardly believing they are chanting, 'We want nine', Kranjcar – having his best game by a mile in a Tottenham shirt – obliges, hooking the ball into the top of the net after being allowed acres of space by Wigan defenders desperate for the final whistle. Spurs 9 Wigan 1.

We should not be greedy, but it would have been perfection if Tottenham could have become the first Premier team to hit double figures. It might easily have been. A close study of film of the match reveals that Tottenham would not have been flattered by a 14-1 scoreline, but Wigan would have been flattened. No wonder their humbled and humiliated players offered to refund the ticket money to their travelling fans. Harry Redknapp, meanwhile, called it a match in a million. Spurs 9, Wigan 1

After the shooting and shouting was over, Defoe said:

> Once the fifth goal went in, I started thinking about the double hat-trick. As I went to the

touchline, our coach Joe Jordan shouted, "Go for it, go for the sixth." I looked up and saw there were a few minutes left, so I knew it was on. That's how it is when you're a goalscorer. You always want the NEXT one. It was a like a dream, brilliant. I am so lucky to be playing with some fantastic footballers. There is always going to be a chance for me to score when surrounded by players of this quality. I've got the match ball and the five goals, but this was an all-round team effort. Just before the kick-off I got involved in some banter with Clive Allen, another of our coaches. My sponsors had given me a pair of green boots to wear, but Clive pulled a face and so I settled for a silvery, pink pair. I guess I will now look on them as my lucky boots. The goal I will remember most is the one that brought the hat-trick. Aaron gave me a perfect ball and I got across the defender, a move I practise all the time in training. It was so satisfying for it to come off at such a vital time. '

The Defoe blitz brought record books under close scrutiny:

- Defoe joined Alan Shearer and Andy Cole as the only players at the time to have netted five goals in a Premier League game.
- He is only the fourth Spurs player to notch five goals in a single game, following Ted Harper, Alfie Stokes and Les Allen.
- Willie Hall scored five goals in 30 minutes for England in a 1938 international against Northern Ireland.

- It was the biggest win in the Premier League since Manchester United beat Ipswich Town 9-0 in 1995, and Tottenham's biggest winning margin in a top-division match since joining the Football League in 1908.

- Debutant Colin Lee scored four goals and Ian Moores a hat-trick when Spurs last scored nine goals, in a Second Division match against Bristol Rovers in 1977.

- Tottenham have netted nine or more goals in five league matches, all at the 'old' Lane: 10-4 v Everton in 1958, First Division, Bill Nicholson's first match as manager; 9-0 v Bristol Rovers in 1977, Second Division; 9-1 v Wigan in 2009, Premier League; 9-2 v Nottingham Forest in 1962, First Division; 9-3 v Port Vale in 1931, Second Division.

- Spurs have scored nine or more goals in four major cup matches: 13-2 v Crewe in 1960, FA Cup fourth round replay; 9-0 v Worksop in 1923, FA Cup first round replay; 9-0 v Keflavik in 1971, UEFA Cup first round; 9-1 v Tranmere Rovers in 1953, FA Cup third round replay.

Tottenham's team that day was: Gomes; Corluka, Dawson, Woodgate, Assou-Ekotto (Bassong 82); Lennon (Bentley 79), Huddlestone, Palacios (Jenas 84), Kranjcar; Crouch, Defoe.

Defoe's career at Tottenham was, of course, about much more than one special match, but his performance that day against Wigan gave a perfect picture of his gift for poaching and turning a half-chance into a goal.

The 5ft 7in striker will always stand tall in N17 football folklore.

* * *

Tottenham's remarkable renaissance under Redknapp was recognised by his peers when he was voted the Premier

League Manager of the Year, only the second boss to collect the trophy when his side did not win the title. He was also rewarded with an extension of his contract until 2013, his 66th year.

The exciting and eventful 2010/11 season was played to a dramatic background of Tottenham trying to clinch a move from cramped White Hart Lane to the 2012 Olympic Stadium at Stratford. There was a huge backlash from supporters who did not want Tottenham to surrender their north London roots, but equally there were many who recognised that only a move to a bigger stadium would give Spurs the necessary income to be able to compete with the supposed 'big four' in the Premier League.

The stadium saga was an irritating distraction to Tottenham's rollercoaster adventure in both Europe and the Premier League. They ran all the way to the quarter-finals of the Champions League in a thrilling journey that promised so much but in the end provided only disappointment.

Along the way they eliminated both Milan giants, including an astonishing match in the San Siro when Spurs came back from 4-0 down against Inter to 4-3 after a remarkable solo performance from hat-trick hero Gareth Bale. It suddenly lifted the 21-year-old Welshman into the world-star category and he was eventually voted PFA Player of the Year despite a worrying spate of injuries.

The end of the first journey into the Champions League arena ended in anti-climax, and moments of madness from Peter Crouch, who had been a key man in getting Spurs to these heady heights. A dream quarter-final draw against Real Madrid whetted the appetite but brought only a bad taste. Hardly famous for his tackling, Crouch had a rush of blood and suddenly seemed to think he was Bites Yer Legs Hunter.

He made two reckless tackles in no-man's land at the Bernabeu that cost him first a yellow card and then a red. All this within the first 15 minutes.

Tottenham's team tactics went up in the air, and they were hammered 4-0. The 1-0 defeat in the second leg was a sad way for the great European adventure to end.

In the Premier League they produced a parade of Jekyll and Hyde performances, taming the top teams but continually dropping points to the basement sides battling for their lives. They eventually finished fifth, with the jeers of many of their hard-to-please fans assaulting their ears.

Some turned their frustration on Harry, and I found myself defending him on Facebook, Twitter and in a range of internet forums where he was being treated spitefully after giving Tottenham their best back-to-back seasons for years. An exciting team featuring Bale, Crouch and Lennon feeding off the passes of the hugely gifted imports Modric and van der Vaart produced football that was a reflection of the personality of their entertaining, chirpy, wise-cracking manager, but the demanding fans wanted more.

A dark cloud of gloom dropped over White Hart Lane in the summer of 2012 with the injury-forced retirement of the idolised Ledley King. He had been playing on wonky knees for years and finally had to give up the fight to keep battling the pain barrier. The highest praise I can give him is that whenever I select my all-time greatest Tottenham team, Ledley is always there at the heart of the defence. He was a magnificent defender, summed up by Harry Redknapp as 'the nearest I've seen to Bobby Moore as the perfect defender'.

The hope of Tottenham fans is that Ledley would sign off by lifting the FA Cup in his last season, but that dream died with a 5-1 thrashing by Chelsea in the FA Cup semi-final. More misery was piled on Tottenham when they were overtaken on the last day of the season by the Woolwich Nomads for third place in the Premier League. Then they lost their place in the Champions League qualifiers to a Chelsea team rewarded for their European Cup Final victory with bouncing out Spurs from the following season's tournament.

Happy Harry's reign as manager ended suddenly after three and three-quarter years during which he had restored Tottenham's pride and belief in themselves. His finishing places in his full seasons were fourth, fifth and fourth, which was remarkable considering the state he had found Spurs in when he took over from Juande Ramos.

He and the board could not agree whether he was sacked or had resigned, but Daniel Levy's official statement certainly made it sound as if he had been fired:

> This is not a decision the board and I have taken lightly. Harry arrived at the club at a time when his experience and approach was exactly what was needed. This decision in no way detracts from the excellent work Harry has done during his time with the club and I should like to thank him for his achievements and contribution. He will always be welcome at the Lane.

Harry's version of the parting was that he had wanted to negotiate an extension of his contract, but he and Levy could not agree terms. 'I've had a fantastic near-four years,' he said. 'I'm proud of the fact that some of our football was breathtaking. I'm not ready to put my feet up. I'll be back in the game, for sure.'

At 65 he still gave himself mountains to climb and he had spells with Queens Park Rangers, as the Jordan national team manager and, finally, with Birmingham City before becoming a national television favourite on *I'm A Celebrity, Get Me Out Of Here.* With his natural Cockney charm and charisma, he won the viewers' votes.

If you judge him on personality, Tottenham have never had another manager quite like him. What great fun he was, Harry Hotspur.

His old job went to a Portuguese. But it was not the Special One.

19

ANDRE VILLAS-BOAS
A Portuguese Man o' Peace

Born: Porto, Portugal, 17 October 1977
Appointed: 3 July 2012
Sacked: 16 December 2013
Games managed: 80
Won: 44
Drawn: 20
Lost: 16
Goals scored: 137
Goals conceded: 89
Win percentage: 55.00

THE CONTRAST between the outgoing Harry Redknapp and the incoming André Villas-Boas could not have been greater: the swashbuckling, wise-cracking, crafty Cockney – a veteran of a multitude of football battles both as player and manager – replaced by a serious, sophisticated 34-year-old Portuguese who had never played football beyond youth level and who Stamford Bridge fans gleefully reminded us was a Chelsea reject.

One thing's for sure, he spoke better English than Harry, taught to him in the cradle by his English grandmother (don't get the hump, Aitch, he also spoke more grammatical English than me and most people in the game).

While still in his 20s, he had been a startlingly successful manager with his local Porto club, digging deep into advice that had been given to him by two then Portugal-based mentors, Sir Bobby Robson and his countryman, José Mourinho.

But he had fallen flat on his face when given his first major challenge in the Premier League, paid off after just nine months in charge at Chelsea, where he alienated senior players who showed him little respect and on-pitch support. The attitude was, 'Why should we listen to a guy our own age who has never played the game professionally?'

He said all the right things when first filling the Redknapp boots, and showed good knowledge of Tottenham's traditions:

Tottenham have always been linked with great football over the years with a wonderful history back to Bill Nicholson. It's been football played in the right style. I've thought a lot about what happened to me at Chelsea, and I am very grateful for both the professional and personal experience I had. You can only learn by mistakes and by experience. I know I can do better and I will because I believe I am a better coach and person for it. Now we have to shorten the gap towards the top clubs. One thing is certain, there are responsibilities with my job. I can't expect to be in ninth or tenth and be in a comfortable position here. It is

demanded that we do better. This is obvious after
Harry left the club after finishing fourth. The
measure of success here is trophies. It's a
responsibility I have to take. If it fails, it fails. '

An engaging, likeable young man, highly intelligent, he
had us dancing on the table tops early in his career at the
Lane when he took Tottenham to the Old Trafford fortress
of Alex Ferguson and pulled off the first victory there over
Manchester United in 23 years. That was as good as it got.

The 'wunderkind' of football managers, who had pulled
off an extraordinary treble of both main domestic titles and
the Europa League trophy at Porto, became engulfed by the
Gareth Bale soap opera that caused huge disruption of the
playing squad.

While the Bale move to Real Madrid was being
conducted in Kremlin-like secrecy, Spurs bought seven
new players with the near-£100m they were collecting for
the Welsh wizard. On top of bringing in Icelander Gylfi
Sigurdsson and Ajax defender Jan Vertonghen, Villas-Boas
looked on like the rest of us as chairman Daniel Levy and
technical director Franco Baldini negotiated the arrivals of
the Bale replacements: Erik Lamela (Roma, £30m), Vlad
Chiriches (Steaua Bucharest, £8.5m), Etienne Capoue
(Toulouse, £8.6m), Roberto Soldado (Valencia, £26m),
Nacer Chadli (Twente, £6m), Christian Eriksen (Ajax,
£11.5m), Paulinho (Corinthians, £11.5m).

I think it fair to say that they were hardly the Magnificent
Seven, with Danish passing prince Eriksen and the injury-
prone 'Coco' Lamela the only ones who came close to giving
value for money. The biggest disappointment was Bobby
Soldado. We desperately wanted this whole-hearted player

to succeed but his confidence was so low he couldn't have, as they say, hit a barn door with a banjo. He could do everything but put the ball into the net.

All these players for Gareth Bale.

* * *

I am not one to blow my own trumpet (he said, blowing his own trumpet), but I was one of the first people to ring the alarms that Gareth Bale was 'on his bike' bound for Real Madrid. Most football reporters from Fleet Street were heavily defeated by Tottenham in the Bale saga, and they did not get within sniffing distance of one of the greatest transfer stories in history.

It was amusing and sometimes appalling to see how far out the newspapers were in their coverage of a tale that could have come from Ian Fleming's imagination.

I am not being wise after the event. I knew weeks before the transfer that Bale was destined for the Bernabéu and that the Real deal was about to be done.

Stupidly, I went on Facebook and Twitter sharing my knowledge and even gave the advance Bale quote, 'I have always dreamt of playing for Real Madrid since I was a boy.'

I had the advantage of a rosy-faced, 16-year-old Bale saying this in my hearing eight years earlier, when ex-Saints boss Lawrie McMenemy tipped me off that the Southampton Academy had unearthed two exceptionally talented kids in Bale and his then house-mate Theo Walcott.

All I got for my naivety in posting on the internet was shedloads of vile abuse from Spurs fans not wanting to face the truth. I could understand them not wishing to believe it, but seeing Fleet Street going down the same denial route made me wonder who on earth they have as their contacts these days.

I was astonished to see Lane legend Glenn Hoddle mouthing on television the mumbo jumbo that, 'Real Madrid have no money and cannot afford Bale.'

Anybody who knows their football history will confirm that Real have been doing business like this for years, going all the way back to when General Franco was virtually running his favourite club. They are a law unto themselves and have never failed to get their man – their *Galáctico* – despite being deep in debt.

Everybody was blinded by the smokescreen generated by Tottenham owners Joe Lewis and Daniel Levy. They cleverly put out the no-deal stories while buying in players. They splashed the cash like repentant misers while keeping Real Madrid dangling.

The facts are that Gareth wanted to go to Real. Real wanted Gareth. Jonathan Barnett, Bale's razor-sharp agent, wanted Gareth to go to Real. But billionaire Lewis and Cambridge Hons graduate Levy hung out for a phenomenal world record fee.

Real's interest went back a year, as later confirmed by their manager of the time, one José Mourinho.

It was a negotiating triumph for Levy and the mega-wealthy Lewis, who was born over a pub in Bow around the corner to me in the East End and to whose Hanover Grand nightclub I used to go in the 1970s when he was known as the Money Magnet. He is one of the most successful world businessmen ever. He and Levy masterminded the biggest transfer in football history and used the money in advance to build a brand new team: TTTTBB, The Tottenham Team That Bale Built.

Gareth had made out a case to be considered one of the greatest players ever to pull on the Lilywhite shirt in his near-six years at the old White Hart Lane. Real Madrid supported this assessment when they coughed up what was then a world record fee to take him to Spain in 2013.

He proceeded to establish himself as a dynamic power on the world stage, despite injuries that sidelined him for long spells.

Starting his career with Southampton, Gareth grew beyond recognition during the Harry Redknapp-management era. In his early days as a left-back, he got the reputation of being a 'jinx' player when Spurs failed to win one of his first 24 first-team matches. He switched to wing back and then the left wing and was transformed into a player with what seemed superman powers.

From being a player supporters mocked when his name was announced, he suddenly became the greatest Welsh wizard since the 1960s peak of Cliff 'The Whirlwind' Jones.

His devastating accuracy from dead-ball situations made him a free-kick specialist feared by all goalkeepers, and his jet pace, dribbling skill and shooting power lifted him into the land of legend with a series of scintillating performances for club and country. He grabbed international attention during the 2010/11 Champions League, and in 2011 and again in 2013 was named PFA Players' Player of the Year. The pros knew a great player when they chased one.

It got to the stage where Tottenham just could not hold him back any longer from his boyhood ambition of playing for Real Madrid, with whom he became prominent in their monopoly of the major prizes despite often taking a back seat to made-in-Madeira master, Cristiano Ronaldo.

It cut deep with Tottenham fans to see Bale dominant in a team that also later included his old White Hart Lane team-mate Luka Modric, and the 100-plus goals he scored in Spain could have gone into the Tottenham bank if they had been able to hold on to him. It was a privilege to watch him play in the Lilywhite shirt, and as I write we have welcomed him back into the Spurs fold. The Prodigal Son has returned.

* * *

It was left to Villas-Boas to pick up the jigsaw pieces and try to fit them together, a job I would not have envied the most experienced of managers. He had a nucleus of a decent team when finishing fifth in the Premier League in his first season, with Michael Dawson, Mousa Dembélé, Andros Townsend, Jermain Defoe and Aaron Lennon among the outstanding players. But all rhythm disappeared when he tried to bring in the 'Insignificant Seven' and it was clear that AVB, as he had become known, was on an uphill climb.

Just as the Portuguese man o' peace arrived at the Lane, chief playmaker Luka Modric followed Bale to Real Madrid (after months of speculation linking the classy Croatian with Chelsea). AVB had inherited the Redknapp team but with the two main cogs removed. You did not have to be Sherlock Holmes to determine that there were elementary things going wrong.

Modric acknowledges that his years at Tottenham were vital in establishing him as a world star:

> I spent four great years at Tottenham with a lot of emotions, with much love from the club and the

fans. I enjoyed every moment at the club. But in one moment you feel you need to take a step forward, to go to a higher level. I think it was the right time for me to go, but I will always be thankful to Spurs for everything they did for me. I became a better player there and they pushed me to this level where I am at the moment. '

AVB might have tasted success at the Lane if Modric had still been available to help put some pattern and passion to Tottenham's play. It was not long into the new 2012/13 season when I started getting whispers from Spurs contacts that André did not have the dressing room with him. After the relatively casual, play-it-off-the-cuff approach of Harry Redknapp, the players found themselves being lectured to and being shown baffling graphs and match stats that hurt the brain. AVB thought everybody was on the same intellectual planet as himself.

Soon we heard the familiar mantra that had leaked out of Stamford Bridge, 'What does he know? At what level did he play the game?'

I always remember Alan Mullery having the perfect riposte for those sort of arguments, 'Put your caps on the table.' He once challenged Malcolm Allison with that sabre-like thrust after getting a verbal roasting from TV pundit Big Mal during the 1970 World Cup finals. I wonder what Mullers would have said if Villas had tried telling him how to play the game.

I knew André was in trouble when first he started arguing with the press at after-match conferences, and then he committed the cardinal sin of criticising the Spurs supporters. 'They don't get behind us like they should,' he said. Ouch. Talk about biting the hand that feeds you. He was slaughtered on social media.

There were 11 reasons why he got sacked just before Christmas 2013 – six goals conceded at Manchester City and then before the bruises had healed five at home to Liverpool, each time with his leaden-footed forwards firing blanks in response.

Villas-Boas, who talked such a good game, had been booted out of a top job for the second time in two years, and his coaching team of Jose Mario Rocha, Luis Martins and Daniel Sousa went through the exit door with him.

He departed quietly, probably because of a contractual gagging order, but opened up three years later to Portuguese journalists while ploughing the football fields of Russia:

> The Chelsea experience was too much too soon. I wasn't flexible as a manager at that time. I was communicative, but I wasn't flexible in my approach. At Tottenham I learnt to be different. In professional football you have to live the day-to-day. The objective is the group performance, but every single individual requires a different response from a manager – you can't be the same person to each player. I made plenty of mistakes in England and maybe I was too aggressive with the press. I wanted to defend my players and the club and, at the end, I looked around me and saw that I didn't have anyone else with me. I was treated badly all the way through. Tim Sherwood, who took my job, was never one of my team and I reported to Mr Levy that he was detrimental to the club. Mr Levy is good at sacking managers.

> There is not time for long-terms projects in the
> Premier League. 」

Villas-Boas, who had the best win ratio to date (55 per
cent) of any Tottenham Premier League manager, was too
young to lay down and was soon back in work with Zenit St
Petersburg, and then took his computer brain to Shanghai
and on to Marseille. André – who drove rally cars as a form
of escapism from football – was still in his early 40s, when
most managers are just starting out. He now had loads of
experience in the bank, but you could imagine his players
still saying to him, 'What did *you* do as a player?'

Fleet Street showed they still did not have their fingers
on the Tottenham pulse. They were tossing names of the
possible new manager around like confetti: Fabio Capello,
Michael Laudrup, Jurgen Klinsmann, Frank De Boer and
even former bosses Glenn Hoddle and Harry Redknapp
were among the names being thrown about.

But I knew that somebody on the Tottenham staff
had the ear of Daniel Levy, and he talked himself into
landing the job. Enter Tim Sherwood. It was Tim Time
at Tottenham.

Clive Allen, with Voice of Spurs Paul Coyte, still talks a good game. The son of Double hero Les, he was on fire in the 1986/87 season, scoring a club record 49 goals.

A shot in a million from the one and only Paul Gascoigne. Just a split second later the ball was in the back of the Arsenal net, with David Seaman beaten all ends up in the 1991 FA Cup semi-final.

Gazza and Gary Lineker, who briefly lit up the Spurs skies with their double act for Tottenham.

The FA Cup comes home to Tottenham in 1991, carried high by goalkeeper Erik Thorstvedt. Skipper Gary Mabbutt (fourth left) is trusted with the lid.

Dimitar Berbatov and Robbie Keane, twin assassins who bulged the nets for Tottenham but often had their sights set on other hunting grounds.

The old and the new, Harry Redknapp managing Tottenham against Jose Mourinho's Real Madrid in the quarter-final of the Champions League in 2011.

Few could keep up with golden boots Gareth Bale before his record move to Real Madrid. But those boots seemed to have turned to lead on his return after seven trophy-drenched seasons in Spain. Then, too late for Mourinho, Gareth found his Midas touch again,

I have a special rapport with Eric Dier. His late grandfather Ted Croker was a good friend of mine when the Football Association supremo.

Mauricio Pochettino applauds the Tottenham fans, a manager who was admired – adored even – by most Lilywhite followers.

Christian Eriksen, Tottenham's Prince of Denmark, plots with Argentine dribbler Erik 'Coco' Lamela. Eriksen was in the Luka Modric class for passing. There can be no higher praise.

The Tottenham team that started the 2019 Champions League Final against Liverpool in Madrid. Back row, left to right: Toby Alderweireld, Moussa Sissoko, skipper Hugo Lloris, Jan Vertonghen, Dele Alli. Front: Danny Rose, Harry Winks, Harry Kane, Kieran Trippier, Christian Eriksen, Son Heung-min.

Harry Kane and Son, the most devastating Tottenham partnership since the G-Men, Greaves and Gilzean.

'One of Our Own' scoring a typical Harry Kane goal, and Dele wisely getting out of the way. The Goal King.

José Mourinho and Dele Alli caught in a rare moment of togetherness. Dele was later in danger of getting splinters from sitting on the bench … and Mourinho was soon being shown the exit door.

20

TIM SHERWOOD
Backed and then Sacked by Levy

Born: Borehamwood, Hertfordshire, 6 February 1969
Appointed: 23 December 2013
Sacked: 13 May 2014
Games managed: 28
Won: 14
Drawn: 4
Lost: 10
Goals scored: 47
Goals conceded: 41
Win percentage: 50

LIKE SOMETHING out of a Shakespeare tragedy, Tim Sherwood landed the manager's job at Tottenham by allegedly 'whispering' André Villas-Boas in the back. He got into chairman Daniel Levy's ear and convinced him that he could do a better job than the Portuguese, who had undoubtedly lost the dressing room.

Levy let Sherwood put action where his mouth was, but only allowed him until the end of the season following

AVB's December departure before giving him the exact same 'dagger thrust' treatment. Et tu, Brute?

Sherwood had a big advantage over Villas-Boas. He had played the game at the top level, including captaining Blackburn to the Premier League title in 1995, winning three England caps and playing many blinders for Tottenham until an earthquaking fall-out with the then manager Glenn Hoddle.

In all my 70 years on the Spurs watch, I had never seen a character quite like 'Intimidating Tim'. Something he will never let us forget – and why should he? – is that he was the one who had the vision to give Harry Kane his debut. For that alone, he is worth a place in the Tottenham annals.

Sherwood's brief time in the hotseat was overshadowed by four-goal defeats against Manchester City, Chelsea and Liverpool and their sixth place in the Premier League table had them trailing ten points behind Arsenal, the measurement that counts most to too many north London supporters.

But Tim, never one to be intimidated, is quick to remind everybody that Spurs were seventh when he took over and that at 59.09 per cent he had the best win ratio in league matches of any Tottenham manager in the Premier League era. 'My record here is second to none,' he stressed after the club's final home match of the season. It didn't save him from what Shakespeare might have called an 'exit, pursued by a howling mob'.

More than any previous manager at the Lane, Sherwood was brought down by the fans. They continually savaged him on the social network line and on the touchline. He turned the situation to farce when in his swansong match against Aston Villa he hauled a fan out of the crowd, threw his hugely publicised gilet at him and pointed him in the direction of his manager's seat.

It was a fingers-up gesture to all those supporters who thought they could do the job better. Irritatingly, during my 70-year march I have seen the emergence of a new type of opinionated fan who really does think he could do a better job in the hotseat, because they are so dominant in the managing games they play on computer.

Throughout most of his truncated reign, Tim had a faction of senior Tottenham players opposing him and his ideas, including Jan Vertonghen, Erik Lamela and Paulinho. He was more old-school and wanted to give youngsters their chance ahead of what he considered over-priced, over-paid prima donnas. He had worked as a coach with the young Academy players and knew there were golden nuggets among them who just needed polishing.

'I felt the young players deserved their opportunity and there really wasn't any reason for them to not have the same opportunities as the players that had been brought to the club for between £20m-40m,' he said, with an obvious dig at the expensive imports. 'I gave them a chance and, look, how the likes of Kane, Bentaleb, Rose and Walker were all integrated into the team.'

As I watched from the sidelines, I wondered if he would ever get the full support and encouragement he deserved from the internet lynch mob, who eventually got their way – exactly as they did with Harry Redknapp and AVB. The armchair sneerers and the snipers kept up up a continual barrage of criticism that was unfounded and unfair.

Let's look at the facts: Tim Sherwood inherited a team of passing strangers, not one of whom he brought into the club. Within hours of his appointment the couch coaches were out in force, complaining that he had no managerial experience and had achieved nothing to warrant him taking over from the hounded-out AVB. They roasted Daniel Levy for giving him the job.

These know-alls, most of them hiding behind the shield of anonymity, conveniently overlooked the fact that the two most successful managers in the club's history – Bill Nicholson and Keith Burkinshaw – were both coaches promoted from within.

Today's keyboard Rottweilers would have chased out both of them in their first seasons, when Bill's team finished 18th and Keith's side was relegated.

The social media assassins probably did not even know that Sherwood skippered the Premier League-winning Blackburn Rovers team, but many of them had deluded themselves into thinking they knew more about the game and tactics than this man who was steeped in football.

His critics thrashed around for evidence that he was the wrong man for the job, and stumbled on the fact he had supported Arsenal when he was a kid. Wow! Line him up against the wall and shoot him.

Did they think Bill Shankly supported Liverpool? Did they know that Matt Busby played for Manchester City? Did they think Bill Nick was supporting Spurs when growing up in Scarborough? Did Alex Ferguson even know Manchester United existed when he was growing up in Scotland? I made the point during many online arguments defending Sherwood that a good percentage of Tottenham fans did not start out with Spurs as their first love. My earliest matches were on the terraces at Millwall because that was the closest ground to my little, spindly six-year-old legs.

When Tim sensibly reinstated the enigmatic AVB nemesis Emmanuel Adebayor and Spurs went on a winning spree under him, his critics were forced to take a lower profile. They almost started to warm to him when he got a double act going with Adebayor, who would salute him like a soldier every time he scored or created a goal.

But thumping defeats by exceptional teams above them in the table again lit the touchpaper to their venomous attacks. 'Dim Tim' they started to call him, not giving a second's thought to the fact it just might be THEY who were dim by shooting at the man charged with trying to bring stability and success to the club.

What on earth, I wondered, happened to a thing called support? Why not leave it to the opposition fans to fire the criticism bullets?

Five months into Tim's tenure, the news/gossip leaked that he has been informed his services would not be required after the end of the season.

Never the most modest of men, Sherwood said after being told to pack his bags, 'I've got a 59 per cent win ratio in the Premier League and I think if I had started the season in charge we'd be in the Champions League.'

There was constant speculation over his future, and at one press conference he was challenged, 'You're keeping the seat warm for someone else.'

'Yeah, I am but the seat's getting quite hot,' Tim shot back. 'Every press conference I do it's "This manager's coming in, [Louis] van Gaal, then [Glenn] Hoddle, this one and that one". Some of these managers are actually touting themselves for my job. I don't think that's right. It's something that doesn't sit well with me. I've got the job and I'll continue to do it to the best of my ability.'

The old enmity between Sherwood and Glenn Hoddle came bubbling to the surface following Tim's linking of him with his manager's seat. He rushed on line to respond:

> I read yesterday that Tim Sherwood is having a go at managers "touting" themselves for his Tottenham job and has decided to include me as one, along with Louis van Gaal. How wrong can you be? The truth of the matter is vastly different, and I can imagine by naming me he is deflecting attention from himself, which is fair enough – managers do it all the time.
>
> However, I have stated many times in numerous interviews that I have been a Spurs supporter from the age of eight, played for the club from the age of 11, have played for Tottenham, managed Tottenham and would never turn my back on Tottenham. If they asked me, I would help them.
>
> And they did ask me: The club asked my opinions. And I spoke with them when André Villas-Boas was sacked, and again they asked my opinion.
>
> What is at the crux of Tim Sherwood's annoyance with me is crystal clear: I made an observation, which I am perfectly entitled to do, about the body language of the Spurs players, one in particular, in the tunnel prior to the Liverpool match.
>
> I would say I was proven 100 per cent right by what happened on the pitch after I made that observation. The team didn't look focused on their way to defeat, but Tim should know that I also made it clear that the management shouldn't be

blamed for that. It was the wrong attitude of the players, but that sort of attitude prevails at times in the modern game. '

Things got worse for Tim. After a 4-0 defeat by José Mourinho's Chelsea, he went angrily after his players with the sort of vicious verbal attack that I had rarely heard fall from the lips of any of his Tottenham predecessors. 'You can't legislate for a capitulation – you can't have that,' he said in a cold fury. 'Lack of characters, too many of them too nice to each other. You need to show a bit more guts and not want to be someone's mate all the time. There are a few I can count on in this team, others I can't. The fans were fantastic today, but they've been let down big time. People at the club keep talking about finishing top four. They should wake up. It's not going to happen.'

I sensed from Sherwood's body language that he knew his days as manager at Tottenham were numbered, and what hurt him – and me, as a biased observer – was that too many players were not giving spirit and soul for the Spurs shirt. They were taking their money but not running.

The Sherwood show came to an end less than six months after it had started. I just wonder how different it might have been had he managed to get the supporters on his side, or – as he pondered – he had spoken with a foreign accent.

He later briefly managed at Aston Villa and advised at Swindon before following a new career as a biting television pundit, dishing out the sort of vicious criticism that dogged him throughout his 'Tim Time' at Tottenham. Yes, it's a funny old game.

His successor took us back into the tangoland of Ossie and Ricky. Bienvenido, Mauricio Pochettino.

21

MAURICIO POCHETTINO
A European Cup Final Ends in Tears

Born: Murphy, Argentina, 2 March 1972
Appointed: 27 May 2014
Sacked: 19 November 2019
Games managed: 290
Won: 159
Drawn: 62
Lost: 69
Goals scored: 549
Goals conceded: 306
Win percentage: 54.83

WHEN MAURICIO Pochettino walked through the gates of the old White Hart Lane in the summer of 2014 he could barely speak a word of English. By the time he left Tottenham five and a half years later, he was fluent in our language and had lifted us Spurs disciples into new, unexplored territory. They were mostly wonderful times in whichever tongue you talked. As I headed towards my 70th year as a Spurs watcher, this is the chapter that I have enjoyed the most since the Glory-Glory days of my dear old friend and Spurs legend Bill Nicholson. And it was all down to one man: take a curtain call, Mauricio Pochettino, the farm labourer's son from Argentina, who has ploughed the fields of football success after a playing career when he delivered a different game to that which he now preaches.

Mauricio was a hard-as-nails defender, prowling as a long-haired warrior who took no prisoners. He will be remembered by England fans for conceding the penalty from which David Beckham virtually knocked Argentina out of the World Cup in 2002 (to this day he argues with mock outrage that his tackle on Michael Owen that led to the vital spot-kick was fair and that the England striker dived!).

His peak performance as Tottenham manager before the sun suddenly set on his reign was the astonishing feat of guiding Spurs to the 2019 Champions League Final against Liverpool. He fell at the top of the mountain but never let us forget that he had taken us to that glorious peak.

The dream of winning the top trophy fragmented from the first minute of the match, when Moussa Sissoko was adjudged to have handled as the ball rolled down his arm. It was a penalty, confirmed by the recently introduced VAR method of retrospective judgement.

Those Spurs fans who vehemently cussed VAR seemed to have forgotten that it was this same system that got them into the semi-final thanks to a ruled-out goal in the last minute, which lifted Tottenham to an unforgettable, heart-stopping victory over Manchester City at the Etihad Stadium.

That led to galloping on-field celebrations, and Pochettino had later gone on his knees to the ground crying tears of joy after the dramatic victory over Ajax in the semi-final, no doubt in disbelief that he had got Spurs into the most prestigious of all finals ahead of schedule. Every one of us who witnessed the match in which Lucas Moura scored a dramatic second-half hat-trick will always be warmed by the memory of that magical night in Amsterdam.

When Poch arrived at Tottenham from Southampton – with just a smattering of English – he made it clear that he wanted all the players to buy into his philosophy, an ideology that demanded super fitness and putting teamwork ahead of individual glory. For those of us who have followed the fortunes of Spurs for decades, we witnessed push-and-run being upgraded to press-and-run. It was electrifying to watch, much of it on away grounds – including the adopted 'home' of Wembley – as White Hart Lane was demolished to make way for a super new stadium suited to the stylish, ahead-of-its-time Pochettino football.

Mauricio gives credit for his modern methods to his first coach, the eccentric Marcelo Bielsa, who happily goes along with his nickname in Argentina of 'El Loco' – The Madman. Pochettino came under his intoxicating influence at the age of 14 when he joined Newell's Old Boys, the club formed in Sante Fe in 1903 by English footballing pioneer Isaac Newell.

It was Bielsa's coaching and gung-ho tactical theories (later seen at Leeds) that motivated the young Pochettino, to such an extent that he refers to him as 'my second father, I owe so much to him. He has always inspired me to not only play the game but to think about it.'

Bielsa encouraged an intense, fast-tempo and high-pressing game, suffocating the opposition, the style we became accustomed to under Pochettino's baton at Tottenham.

From several generations of farm labourers, Mauricio was not frightened of hard work and expected – or rather, demanded – this ethic from his players. Anybody not prepared to sweat for success was unwelcome in the Pochettino camp.

He became a have-boots-will-travel mercenary after establishing himself as a tough and reliable defender with Newell's, and won 20 Argentine international caps while tackling for Espanyol in Spain, Paris Saint-Germain and Bordeaux in France and then back to Espanyol for the wind-down days of his playing career.

Throughout his playing days, Pochettino was a student of the game and was renowned for continually analysing matches with more the eye of a manager than a player. In 2007, he started coaching the Espanyol ladies team while taking coaching and sports management courses and was appointed men's club coach after earning his UEFA Pro Licence.

When he took over as the virtual manager in January 2009, the club were stuck deep in the relegation zone. Espanyol were due to move to an expensive new stadium (sound familiar?) and it was vital they stayed up. He steered them to a crucial 2-1 win over bitter rivals Barcelona at the Nou Camp to trigger a run of victories that kept them at the top table.

After three years he became embroiled in club politics, and – following a stuttering start to the 2012/13 season– he was sacked, much to the chagrin of the Espanyol supporters, with whom he had a great rapport. He was admired for always giving chances to young local youth team players, and believed in the old football adage that if you're good enough, you're old enough.

He did not get the warmest of welcomes when he arrived at Southampton in January 2013 in place of Nigel Adkins, who had won back-to-back promotions from League One to the Premier League. Former Saints and Spurs midfielder Jamie Redknapp, whose dad had managed at Southampton, described the Saints chairman as 'deluded'.

To Southampton fans, in place of the popular Adkins they had got an 'unknown' who arrived with an interpreter because he could not speak English.

These same supporters who were lukewarm about his appointment were up in arms when he was poached by Spurs. Pochettino took over with Saints third from bottom in the Premier League and left in May 2014 after they had finished eighth. Spurs chairman Daniel Levy, who changed managers like other people changed socks, quickly realised that here was a coach with special motivational powers and an ability to think and act outside the box.

Southampton midfielder Jack Cork gave a fascinating insight into Pochettino's off-beat approach to coaching:

> There is no question that he improved the play and performances of any players willing to listen to him. It was always his way or no way, but we were a young team and he gave us confidence – and his message was always to enjoy our football. I don't think he did an interview in English the whole time he was at the club but he always managed to get his message across to the players. He was quite calm most of the time. I remember one game at Wigan when we had come from behind to take the lead

with five minutes to go. We conceded in the last minute and I thought he was going to be really angry. Instead, he had a few minutes to himself in the shower and came out and shook every player's hand. It made each one of us feel seven foot tall.

He was full of ideas. We went on a pre-season tour to Spain and he had organised a team-building exercise which involved an arrow. Each player had to place the point of the arrow into the soft tissue area of their throat while a team-mate held the other end. You then had to push against the arrow until it bent or snapped. It was plastic and there was no chance of injuring yourself. It was all to do with building up trust in your team-mates. We also had to walk across hot coals. The players all embraced it.

There was always lots of running and a lot of training with Mauricio. At times it was very tough. You needed two hearts to play the Pochettino way. Goalkeeper Kelvin Davis once brought the clock out of the dressing room to remind him how long the session had been.

But his methods worked. There was a lot of despondency in the dressing room when he left for Tottenham. 〕

Let's be honest, Spurs supporters regarded Pochettino with some suspicion when he arrived at the old Lane. He was the tenth manager over a 12-year span and there was a lynch mob on social media ready to string up Levy if he had got it wrong. But Mauricio quickly won everybody over with his charm and charisma, and – most of all – the sudden improvement in the performances of the team. He was shown the Spurs way of doing things by his charming countryman, one Osvaldo Ardiles.

Poch has spoken emotionally about the bond he built with Ardiles on arrival at Tottenham. Ossie was able to 'mentor' Mauricio into the 'Tottenham way' in a style that only another Argentinian could understand, which helps explain the manner in which Poch (just like Ossie) was able to forge such a special rapport with Lilywhite diehards. The only problem that Ossie says he had with Mauricio is when Ricky Villa dropped in, 'They are two farm boys and soon started speaking about a number of things [cattle and corn] that I, as a city boy, did not understand.'

At one of his always intriguing news conferences with his rapidly improving English, Poch gave us a sneak, intimate peep into his philosophy. 'I believe in energía universal,' he explained. 'Universal energy, the idea that people, places and things are charged with a hidden energy, positive or negative.'

Fanned by his guru Bielsa and trusted right-hand man Jesus Perez, the philosophy has shaped Pochettino's approach to life and it was at the heart of his psychological and physical transformation of Spurs.

To Mauricio, everything – in football, in life – is related to energy and it not only drove Tottenham's high-octane style during his reign, but also the spirit and camaraderie of his players. He insisted that his players run themselves to the edge of exhaustion – most vitally, during his demanding pre-season training sessions – but, also, that they be prepared to battle until the last breath of every game. Those of us brought up on Tottenham teams that too often folded under pressure knew that Pochettino's players never gave up until the final whistle and continually created crucial late goals.

He did not concentrate on the narrow, myopic view of measuring the season by how Tottenham did compared with Arsenal, and he was a visionary suited to build a team fit for the new billion-pound stadium that is widely acknowledged as one of the most impressive grounds in the world of football.

It is eye-opening to study Pochettino's first and last selections as Tottenham manager to reveal how the team evolved during his tenure. He kicked off with a 1-0 win at West Ham on 16 August 2014, the crucial goal scored in the 90th minute by debutant Eric Dier from a pass by substitute Harry Kane. The team in a 4-2-3-1 formation was:

Lloris

Naughton   Kaboul (captain)   Dier   Rose

Capoue   Bentaleb

Lamela (Holtby 61)   Eriksen   Lennon (Townsend 61)

Adebayor (Kane 83)

Lloris, a French intellectual from a family of lawyers, became his skipper and trusted confidant. He gave the Tottenham defence a strong foundation throughout the Pochettino reign and said after being awarded the captaincy, 'Our relationship transcends football. Mauricio matters a lot to me. One day I believe he will prove himself the best manager in the world.'

Pochettino stood by his goalkeeper following a drink-driving scandal after leading France to their World Cup triumph in Russia in 2018. 'Hugo the Boss' rewarded his loyalty with a series of match-saving performances that had Spurs supporters mentioning him in the same breath as all-time Lane legend Pat Jennings.

Lloris was injured and missed what was to prove to be Pochettino's final match, a 1-1 draw with Sheffield United on 9 November 2019. The team in a 4-2-3-1 formation was:

Gazzaniga
Aurier (Lucas Moura 86)   Sanchez   Dier   Davies
Ndombele (Winks 46)   Sissoko
Lo Celso   Dele (Foyth 72)   Son
Kane (captain)

Eric Dier was the only player who appeared in every minute of both matches. He had been a relatively unknown boy from Lisbon via Cheltenham when he played his first match for Spurs under the wing of 'mother hen' Pochettino.

I have a special bond with Eric, whose granddad Ted Croker was a good companion in the days when he was a fire-fighting Football Association supremo.

Ted was a real man's man, a war hero who won a gallantry medal after crawling a half mile from a crashed bomber with broken ankles to get help for his injured crew-mates. He recovered to continue his football career after the war at Charlton with his brother Peter, and later became a hugely successful businessman when starting an earthmoving equipment company in Gloucestershire. He was head-hunted to become the voice of the FA at a difficult time in the 1980s, and almost certainly cost himself a knighthood when he had the guts to tell Prime Minister Margaret Thatcher to her face, 'Don't blame hooliganism on football. It's your society you need to get sorted out.'

Eric – son of former professional tennis player and later high-powered sports agent Jeremy Dier – was born a year after his grandad died, and I have been able to tell him to his face that Ted would be enormously proud of what he is achieving in the game.

He and his four siblings moved to Portugal when he was seven after his mother, Louise – Ted's daughter – landed the job of helping organise the hospitality for the 2004 European Championship, and as well as becoming bi-lingual he developed as a utility defender with Sporting CP in Lisbon.

With every Sporting team from youth through to the seniors, he eventually became captain. He admits the club he supported as a kid was Manchester United, and he had loan spell experience with Everton as an Academy player, but Spurs claimed his heart.

Eric can do it all: ride shotgun in midfield, shore up in the middle of the back line, or play in one of the full-back roles. Watch the way he barks orders to team-mates when the pressure is on; it's reminiscent of Captain Marvel Dave Mackay. Yes, a born leader just like his granddad.

How lucky was Gareth Southgate to inherit so many Tottenham youngsters, who have developed through the system, where the fitness-first-do-the-simple-things-well philosophy of Professor Pochettino prepared them for international honours.

But everything turned sour for Poch and his body language at the end of the match against Sheffield United sent warning signals that all was not well. Soon after came the bombshell news that he had been sacked, just five months after leading the team to the Champions League Final.

That masked, however, an alarming slump on the domestic front that saw Spurs win just six of their previous 24 Premier League games.

At the time of his dismissal, the Argentine had been in command for 293 games in all competitions, making him fourth in the club's all-time list. Only Bill Nicholson (832), Peter McWilliam (505), and Keith Burkinshaw (431) had been in the hotseat longer. And only Nicholson (55) led them in more European games than Pochettino (53).

At 47, he had taken charge of more Premier League matches than any other Spurs manager (202) and, before his final season, boasted the best points-per-game ratio of any Tottenham boss in Premier League history. When he made his exit, he was in second place behind Tim Sherwood, 1.89 to 1.91, but this needs to be weighed alongside the fact that Sherwood was involved in far fewer games.

It remains a mystery as to what went wrong for Pochettino, and we will have to wait for the inevitable memoirs to discover why he suddenly seemed to lose his powers to lift and inspire his players. Mauricio had run out of universal energy.

He was still king of the castle when Tottenham at last opened their new showpiece stadium on 3 April 2019 after two years of renting out Wembley. I was a privileged guest of Tottenham in their state-of-the-art media centre at the 'New White Hart Lane' for the opening match at the new home. They allowed me to compare the facilities with the old Spurs press box from where I had first reported 60 years earlier. This is what I reported at the time:

'My debut match as a reporter at the original Lane was on Boxing Day 1958. West Ham were the visitors, 24 hours after taking both points against Spurs in a Christmas Day First Division match at Upton Park. Can you imagine a back-to-back fixture like that today?

'These were in the days when footballers were on a maximum £20 a week, Wolves (the Cullis Cubs) and Manchester United (the Busby Babes) were the dominant clubs and kick-offs were traditionally at three o'clock on a Saturday afternoon.

'Move forward 60 years and I had entered another planet. There I was, honoured to be sitting in the Tottenham media centre and ready to watch the first Premier League match at a stately, state-of-the-art stadium that just takes the breath away. For anybody from my silver-top generation of Tottenham supporters, it was a hugely emotional trip back to the future.

'The first league match was against Crystal Palace and ushered in a new golden age for Tottenham Hotspur, the biggest leap forward since that late summer's night in 1882 when a group of local schoolboy cricketers – including future club director Bobby Buckle – met under a gaslit lamppost in Tottenham High Road and elected to launch a football club to take them through the winter months.

'The well-educated pupils chose to name their team after 14th-century nobleman and warrior Harry Hotspur, whose descendants owned huge swathes of land in the Tottenham area. This included the marshes on which the first matches were played, with home-made goalposts carried to and from the pitch by the Hotspur boys.

'Now that same land is overwhelmingly dominated by the billion-pound stadium in which I was now sitting, in awe of the grandeur and towering splendour of what Spurs can boast is one of the finest football grounds in the world. It truly is magnificent. Take a bow, club chairman Daniel Levy, Bahamas-based owner Joe Lewis and ENIC, the company that gets terrible stick from some keyboard warriors while taking the club into tomorrow's world. Many of the armchair critics smashing Levy and ENIC week in and week out could not organise a loft conversion.

'When I reported from the old, Victorian-built Lane for the first time back in 1958, the press box was tucked away at the back of the main stand behind the directors' seats. There were no telephone points and copy boys had to race downstairs to dictate running match reports back to newspaper telephonists sitting at typewriters in their Fleet Street offices. These were the now defunct copy takers.

'Reporters from those hot-metal newspapers that did not have a budget for copyboys had to choose the moment to dash downstairs and dictate their own copy, hoping that nothing significant happened on the pitch while they could only judge events by the roar of the crowd.

'I wrote on an Olivetti portable typewriter, with carbon paper for back-up. Now I was sitting with my ageing fingers dancing on my Apple MacBook keyboard, connected directly to the internet and in a seat as comfortable as in a plush cinema. I had been transported to another planet.

'More than 150 journalists from around the world had a seat and a wifi-friendly desk allocated to them, and each had a ten-inch monitor on which to watch live action of the match that was just 25 yards away on the immaculate pitch that can, at the push of a button, be spun to give an alternative gridiron surface for the planned NFL matches. Yes, another planet.

'There were critics sneering on line that Spurs were breaking with their past by introducing American sport, not having an inkling of the fact that their first major owner – Charles Roberts – was a baseball fanatic who introduced the game to White Hart Lane in the 1920s.

'Earlier I had sat eating succulent roast chicken in the impressive media restaurant area with queen of sportswriters, "Dame" Julie Welch, who broke all sorts of glass ceilings when becoming the first female football reporter in our man's world more than 40 years ago. She is Tottenham's official biographer, and was collecting material for a re-print of her history book to take in an opening ceremony of fireworks, fanfares and, finally, a football match.

'Many of today's top football reporters were there to chronicle this historic match, and a string of them – Henry Winter, Martin Samuel, Darren Lewis, Neil Ashton, Gerry Cox and Paul Hayward – came and paid homage to Julie and to prod this old dinosaur to see if I was still alive. The jury is out.

'Julie and I were chasing headlines and deadlines when they were in nappies and we wondered how they would have fared "in our day" when we were begrudgingly given a half-time cup of tea and had to chase around in the car park for a hoped-for quote or snatch of team news.

'Now in the "auditorium" the reporters sit in leather armchairs questioning manager Mauricio Pochettino at an after-match conference that is conducted by the hugely efficient Tottenham PR staff like a presidential address.

'Today's journalists are spoon-fed background information and match details, but the challenge is just the same as "in our day" to find the right words at the right time when that first whistle blows.

'But because they send their words into the ether they do not have to clear the hurdles that faced us, with copy takers asking, "Are you staff?"; "How d'you spell your name?"; "Is there much more of this?"; "I can't hear you because of the crowd in the background."; "I'm changing my typewriter ribbon, you'll have to wait."

'Happy days, and neither Julie nor I would change our memories for the world. But I do envy the reporters who will be filing their copy from Planet Tottenham in the years ahead. They will be witnessing and chronicling footballing history from the new Lane of Dreams, home of the 2019 Champions League runners-up to Liverpool.

'And all under the baton of Generalissimo Pochettino.'

* * *

Tim Sherwood is never shy to point out that it was he who laid the foundation for Pochettino's success, and there can be no denying that it was his bold promotion of Harry Kane to the first team that gave Spurs striking power that had been missing for too long. How to give 'Our Harry' the projection he merits as I approach the final lap of my 70-year Tottenham journey? I never thought I would live to see the day when anybody matched the fantastic feats of my old mate (and hero) Jimmy Greaves, but 'Hurrikane' Harry is not only keeping pace with the 1960s master; he could one day even overtake him.

He is barely out of the foothills of his career yet already in his Essex manor house has a trophy cabinet crammed with awards. Pride of place goes to the Golden Boot he collected as leading marksman in the 2018 World Cup finals.

As I have established earlier in this odyssey, in a previous life I was a member of the *This Is Your Life* scriptwriting team for 14 years, and I am going to tell the extraordinary Harry Kane story with the sort of words I would have scripted for Eamonn Andrews and then Michael Aspel (with thanks to my old BBC friends for help with the research).

THIS IS YOUR LIFE HARRY KANE

Harry Edward Kane, you were born in Whipps Cross Hospital in Leytonstone on 28 July 1993, the same maternity wing where David Beckham came into the world 18 years earlier. You are the son of Kim and Patrick Kane, an Irishman from Galway, and you have an older brother, Charlie. You spend your early days at the family home in Walthamstow, three and a half miles from the Tottenham Hotspur ground at White Hart Lane.

HARRY: 'We often talk as to where I got my sporting genes. Dad likes to think it's from the Irish side, but my grandad Eric – Mum's dad – was a good footballer and Mum says I take after him. Sorry, Dad!'

You move with your family to Chingford where you attend Larkswood Primary Academy. It's with local football club Ridgeway Rovers that you have your first football trial at the age of six. This is how coach Dave Bricknell – a scout for Tottenham – remembers it:

'We staged our trials at Loughton rugby club, and I remember six-year-old Harry volunteering to go in goal. He was full of enthusiasm and a daredevil with his diving. Just as I was thinking we'd found ourselves a natural goalkeeper I was informed he'd come for a trial as a forward. So I stuck him upfield and he was even better than when he was in goal, passing the ball with intelligence and with an eye for goal. I could not believe his maturity and the great belief he had in himself. When he missed a chance he didn't let his head drop and just worked harder for the next chance. Even at that age you could see he had something special.'

From a family of Tottenham supporters, you cause consternation among your relatives when you accept an offer to join Arsenal at the age of eight. You even go as far as having your hair dyed red! After one season with 'the other' north London club, they decide you do not have what it takes and let you go. Former Arsenal youth academy director Liam Brady:

'It was considered that young Harry was "a bit chubby" and "not very athletic". Arsène Wenger didn't know whether to laugh or cry when he was told we'd had him on our books. But he was hardly a boy wonder, and it's easy in hindsight to see we made a mistake. I am delighted for him and the way he has developed into a world-class striker. It shows what you can achieve with the right attitude and application.'

HARRY: 'I was choked when Arsenal let me go. I did not feel as if I'd been given a proper chance to show what I could do. It made me very determined to prove that I could make it. My dad believed in me and told me not to give up. There was no chance of that. Looking back on it now, being released by Arsenal was probably the best thing that ever happened to me because it gave me a drive that wasn't there before. I was always trying to prove them wrong.'

You have trials with both Tottenham and Watford but they decline to sign you and you return to Ridgeway Rovers. At 11, you switch to Chingford Foundation School, where David Beckham used to study, and you meet your idol at the David Beckham Academy in 2005. You are photographed with Becks along with your 12-year-old friend Kate Goodland, who becomes your childhood sweetheart. Ten years later you become engaged and have two children together. In the summer of 2019, you marry in a romantic beach-side ceremony, and then you announce you are about to become a foursome with a baby boy on the way. Louis Harry Kane arrives in the winter of 2020.

HARRY: 'I am the luckiest man in the world to have found Kate. The fact that we've known each other so long means she knew me before I made it in football, and we deeply love each other. She went to university and worked hard to make something of herself, and is a great mum to our three children. Kate keeps me grounded and she and my close family have worked just as hard as me to get me where I am today.'

Both you and Kate go to the same Chingford school, where you show exceptional talent as a cricketer, but it is football that remains your first love. You are a sports fanatic, and take a close interest in American football, idolising New England Patriots quarterback Tom Brady. Your PE teacher Mark Leadon recalls:

'Harry was obsessed with sport, with football number one on his agenda. Even at 11, he was technically gifted. He had a great first touch, and could shoot with either foot. He was possibly an even better cricketer, and used to open the bowling and was a powerful batsman at number four. But it was football that took most of his concentration, and he was an outstanding team player. I have never seen a youngster so driven. There was nothing of the prima-donna about him. He was just determined to make his mark and gave everything for the team.'

You shine in a match for Watford boys against Tottenham boys and Spurs have second thoughts and invite you to become a registered schoolboy player with them. This pleases your Spurs-supporting family after that early experience with the red side of north London. You are at first tried as a midfield holding player, then as an attacking schemer before you at last settle into the striking role for which you have become world-famous.

HARRY: 'It was scoring goals that gave me the biggest buzz. I wanted to be like my idol of the time, Ronaldo of Brazil. The English player who took my eye was Teddy Sheringham. I was excited by the way he would come through to score brilliant goals. That's what I wanted to do.'

But despite your enthusiasm it was touch and go whether Spurs would sign you on scholarship terms on your 16th birthday. Alex Inglethorpe, then head youth coach at Tottenham and now in the same role at Liverpool, reveals:

'I got my first look at Harry when I was working with the Spurs Under-14s. He was a hard grafter, full of enthusiasm but he was far from the finished product. There were several players ahead of him in potential. He was not impressive in the air and not particularly strong on his left side. But he listened and he learned and became his own coach, pushing himself to improve his weaknesses. I'd be lying if I said we thought he was the best of our young talent. He was not even in the top half-dozen. What eventually persuaded us to sign him was his high energy and clear intention to improve. In fact he was obsessed with making himself a better player, which is the sort of reaction we coaches love. We almost had to drag him off the training ground.'

Spurs are overcrowded with squad players, and it is decided to send you out on loan when you are 17. Your first port of call is League One Leyton Orient in east London. This is considered a make-or-break opportunity for you to learn your trade. On 15 January 2011 you make your league debut away at Rochdale in front of a crowd of under 3,000, coming on as a 73rd-minute substitute for veteran striker Scott McGleish, approaching the end of his career after scoring more than 200 goals in nearly 600 league games. He recalls:

'We all liked Harry. He was not one of those know-it-alls who thought he was superior 'cos he was on the books of a Premier League club. From his first day he was willing to learn from more experienced players, and was prepared to fight for his place in the team. He quickly learned where the goal is because it's all about the markings on the pitch. He instinctively knew where he was because of the white lines. That's important for any striker, to know exactly where you are. He worked really hard in training to know what sort of shot suited what position you are in. Harry was a natural.'

You score the first league goal of your career on 22 January 2011 when making your full debut against Sheffield Wednesday at Brisbane Road, steering a Dean Cox free kick into the net from close range. Orient win 4-0 and by the end of the season you have found the net five times in 18 matches. Your brief stay at the club makes a deep impression and later on you repay their role in helping to lay a foundation to your career by sponsoring their club shirts to support three charities.

HARRY: 'It gives me a platform to say a big thank you not only to Orient but to the many frontline heroes and charities who provide care and support during challenging times. A percentage from every shirt sold goes to good causes.'

Recalled to White Hart Lane, you make your Tottenham debut in the second leg of their Europa League qualification tie against Hearts on 25 August 2011. It's a goalless draw and you miss from the penalty spot. It's the first of six appearances in the Europa League that season, and you score your first senior goal in a Tottenham shirt in the 4-0 away win at Shamrock Rovers on 15 December 2011. You come on as substitute for Jermain Defoe and net that historic goal a minute into injury time.

The following week after the Shamrock victory you and club-mate Ryan Mason join Championship club Millwall on loan. You are named Millwall's Young Player of the Year for 2011/12 when your seven goals in the final 14 matches steer Millwall away from the threat of relegation. A goal that you score during a training match impresses notorious Millwall hard-man defender, Alan Dunne:

'It was the greatest and most unbelievable goal I ever saw. This was in training, and it was out of nothing. The ball was thrown long by the keeper, and Harry's caught it on the volley at an angle where it didn't look possible that he could score. Our jaws all just dropped. We couldn't believe it, a goal in a million. If there's one word to describe his finishing, it was immaculate. The most accurate finisher I've ever witnessed. Millwall was the making of him. There's no tougher crowd in the league, and instead of going into his shell and being intimidated by them he set out to win the fans over with his extraordinary energy. It was obvious he was going places.'

You return to Tottenham and make your Premier League debut when coming on as an 86th-minute substitute for Sandro against Newcastle United on 10 August 2012. The Geordies win 2-1. A brief loan spell at Norwich City is interrupted when you break a metatarsal bone, an injury that is to come back to haunt you later in your career. Then you are loaned out to Leicester City, and share the substitutes' bench with a young striker called Jamie Vardy:

'There are pictures of Harry and me together on the bench when he was on loan to Leicester. Three years later we were playing for England against Germany. We both came through together and have a lot of respect for each other. He's a smashing lad.'

In all, you make 13 appearances for Leicester and mark your home debut with a goal in a 3-0 victory over Blackburn Rovers on 26 February 2013. Back at Tottenham for the start of the 2013/14 season you score the extra-time equaliser in a League Cup tie against Hull and put away your penalty in an 8-7 shoot-out victory.

It is on 7 April 2014, that you are given your first Premier League start for Tottenham, in a 5-1 win against Sunderland, and you score your first Premier League goal in the 59th minute. It is the first of three goals in successive matches and suddenly the Tottenham fans realise your talent and start chanting that you are 'one of our own'. Tim Sherwood is the manager who hands you your first-team debut:

'It was not a gamble giving Harry his chance. I knew all about him from the days when I was coaching him as a youth player and saw his potential. My only problem with him was stopping him training! He always wanted to do extra time to sharpen his skills. He was a coach's dream because he only needed to be told once and it would sink in and he'd do what you asked of him out on the pitch. Harry was quite slight but has worked hard in the gymnasium to give himself a fine physique. Roberto Soldado was considered our number one striker, but every day in training Harry was outperforming him. He forced me to choose him ahead of Bobby and he never ever let me or himself down. For me, he was a mix between my former team-mates Teddy Sheringham and Alan Shearer, and I became his biggest fan. I am proud of the fact that I gave him his start. He is continually proving me a good judge.'

England come calling at every level and you play for the Under-17s, Under-19s, Under-20s and Under-21s. In 24 international appearances before your senior debut you score 17 goals. Peter Taylor, a former Tottenham player and England Under-20s coach:

'What struck me most about Harry apart from his talent was his attitude. I knew from day one of working with him that here was a likeable, well-grounded lad who was not going to have any regrets at the end of his career because he was going to give it everything he had. He was intelligent and was always asking questions to improve his understanding of the game. An absolute joy to coach.'

On the arrival of Mauricio Pochettino as Spurs manager, you move up a notch with your tactical knowledge and goals output. Your all-round game improves to the point where you are not just a goal-scorer with either foot and head but also a goal-maker with prodigious passes of which any schemer would be proud. In Pochettino's first full season at Tottenham, you net 31 goals across all competitions, and finish as the Premier League's second-highest scorer, winning the PFA Young Player of the Year award.

Over the next two seasons, despite recurring foot problems, you win and then retain the Golden Boot as top Premier League marksman. Goals pour from you in the 2017/18 season when you register a remarkable 41 goals in 48 games. You equal the six-time record held by Steven Gerrard for most Premier League Player of the Month awards and become a regular selection by your peers for the Team of the Year. Mauricio Pochettino:

'Harry is a killer, an assassin. He's always in practice and he wants to kill the goalkeeper in a football sense. You need to stop him from training because he always wants to train. He is so obsessed with scoring that sometimes, when it is against him, he needs more freedom – not to be obsessed. But he is going to learn and he is starting to be really mature. Harry is English and sometimes the media push him to the sky and paradise and then you put him on the outside. For me, this treatment is very confusing and not easy to understand.

'If Harry was Italian and playing for Italy, he would be a bit more protected because the Italian people are more protective of their players. It's difficult to push them but when they are there, they try to keep them up there. It's similar in Spain. Here, it is more up and down. I see parallels between Kane and my excellent former Argentine team-mate Gabriel Batistuta. His mentality is similar.

'Maybe Harry is going to improve even on Batistuta's stats. I know Batistuta very well and I know Harry. They are of a similar mind, focus and determination. I cannot give him higher praise. Tottenham are very lucky to have him on their books.'

The Republic of Ireland invite you to become an Irish international because of your father's Galway birthplace, but you prefer to try to break into the England team. Your patience and belief pays off when Roy Hodgson selects you for the squad to play Lithuania in a Euro 2016 qualifying group match on 19 March 2015. You come on as a second-half substitute for Wayne Rooney and score just 80 seconds later, heading in a Raheem Sterling cross. Your international career is up and running.

HARRY: 'It was the start I had always dreamed of, easily the best moment of my career so far. To represent your country at senior level is the top, and then to score a goal almost as soon as I got on the pitch! It doesn't get better than that. Hopefully I can keep doing it and it's the first of many.'

After the disappointment of defeat by Iceland in the Euro finals, Roy Hodgson is replaced as England manager by Gareth Southgate, and following the retirement of Wayne Rooney he selects you as captain in the 2018 World Cup qualifier against Scotland at Hampden Park. You score an injury-time equaliser to force a 2-2 draw. On 5 October, you net an added-time winner against Slovenia which clinches England's qualification for the World Cup finals in Russia. Gareth Southgate joins your army of admirers:

'I named Harry as my captain because he sets standards that I know will motivate and inspire his team-mates. He knows only one way to play the game, and that is with 100 per cent energy, concentration and determination. He is one of the greatest goalscorers in the world, and adds to this gift by being an unselfish team player.'

With you as a driving captain, England exceed all expectations by reaching the semi-finals of the World Cup, and you win the coveted Golden Boot by finishing as the tournament's top scorer, including a hat-trick against Panama. This makes you only the third England player to score a hat-trick in a World Cup finals match, after Geoff Hurst against West Germany in the 1966 final and Gary Lineker against Poland in 1986. Gareth Southgate is rewarded with an OBE and you receive the MBE.

HARRY: 'I am busting with pride. It has all been quite surreal, really. What a great year it's been for club and country. It's hard to put into words the way I am feeling. I'm very passionate about our country, very patriotic and I'm extremely proud that what we achieved in Russia brought everyone together. I'm thankful to all my team-mates, all the coaches at Tottenham and England, Mauricio, Gareth, all the staff, the guys as well – without them I wouldn't be scoring the goals and getting these accolades.'

Yet another foot injury keeps you sidelined but you fight back to get fit for the Champions League final against Liverpool in 2019. After collecting a runners-up medal you come into the new season banging in goals galore until a hamstring injury requires an operation that sidelines you for four months. But you are quickly back on the scoring trail on your return and you pass 200 goals for Spurs and you now have Jimmy Greaves's all-time record club collection of 266 goals in your sights. You form a striking partnership with a player who establishes himself as one of the greatest footballers ever to come out of Asia, South Korean Son Heung-min:

'I am honoured to play with Harry. He is remarkable, not only at scoring but at feeding team-mates with fantastic passes. We know how to instinctively find each other on the pitch, and I owe many of my goals to his wonderful service. It is quite understandable that the Tottenham supporters love him so much. I love "Haitch", too.'

This is your life, Harry Kane, but it is still in its early days. You have so much more to give and it is a pleasure and a privilege for all Spurs fans to watch your progress and productivity. Long may you reign, King Harry. One of our own.

* * *

When Mauricio Pochettino took over in 2014, the club had managed only two top-four finishes in 22 Premier League seasons, both of them in Harry Redknapp's reign. Under the cool Argentine they achieved that feat in four of his five seasons in charge and reached a Champions League Final, the first in the club's history.

His tally of 382 Premier League points then ranked behind only Manchester City (446), Liverpool (404) and Chelsea (398) during that same period. But suddenly at the start of the 2019/20 season the magnificent Mauricio lost his powers to motivate, and with Spurs sluggish and stifled in 14th place in the Premier League he was – 'reluctantly' – shown the door by Daniel Levy. One theory about Poch's dismissal is that he had not only burned out his players but also himself with his demands for high-octane energy. My favourite time under his stewardship was when he had Christian Eriksen and Moussa Dembélé operating together in midfield, the Prince of Denmark with his precise passing and Dembélé's slalom running with the ball the like of which I have never seen before.

At his peak with Tottenham, Mauricio's greatest skill was man-management and he was never afraid to put his faith at the feet of untried youngsters. At Espanyol, he launched the careers of Jordi Amat, Alvaro Vásquez and Javi Márquez; at Southampton he gave James Ward-Prowse, Callum Chambers and Luke Shaw their starts, and at Tottenham he boosted young players such as Harry Winks, Eric Dier and, of course, Harry Kane.

It was as if reaching the top of the mountain with the Champions League Final had exhausted not only Pochettino but his players. The following season he just did not seem to have his heart in the job, and there was a school of thought that he was engineering his exit. The most exciting Tottenham team for years suddenly went into decline and won just three of their opening 12 matches, and they were humiliated in the League Cup by the minnows of Colchester United.

An embarrassing 7-2 collapse to eventual European champions Bayern Munich signalled that his taxi would soon be summoned.

But before those final months of misery, Pochettino had been the most popular and successful Tottenham manager since the launch of the Premier League and there was genuine sadness that he was leaving. We all felt we were losing a friend. Harry Kane posted his sincere thoughts online:

> Gaffer. I will be forever thankful to you for helping me achieve my dreams. We have had some amazing moments over the last five and a half years that I will never forget. You were not just my manager but my friend as well and I thank you for that relationship. Good luck with your next chapter.

When the Tottenham players reported to the stunning club training HQ at Enfield the day after his departure, they found this message, accompanied by a huge, drawn heart, in Poch's handwriting chalked on the team tactics blackboard:

> Big thanks to you all. Sorry we can't be here to say goodbye. You will always be in our heart.

Mauricio Pochettino, a class act from first day to last. He took a year off to recharge his batteries, much of his time spent farming in Argentina before being lured back to his first love of football as manager at the crack European club for which he used to play, Paris Saint-Germain. He carried the best wishes of all the Tottenham players and supporters he had charmed, excited and entertained.

Now I wondered what was in store for Our Harry and Spurs as the baton passed to the 21st manager for what was the final lap of my 70-year journey with Spurs. Here comes the Special One.

22

JOSÉ MOURINHO
Not So Special After All

Born: Setubal, Portugal, 26 January 1963
Appointed: 19 November 2019
Sacked: 19 April 2021
Games managed: 86
Won: 44
Drawn: 19
Lost: 23
Goals scored: 162
Goals conceded: 100
Win percentage: 51.16

SO WE reach the last lap of my 70-year journey. Thank you for sticking with me (and Spurs). I am writing much of this chapter almost in real time, so let's see what develops as José Mourinho fills Mauricio Pochettino's shoes with almost indecent haste. His instant appointment confirmed rumours that the takeover had been planned and plotted weeks before by scheming Spurs chairman Daniel Levy. Few of us could believe that Tottenham were suddenly under the mesmerising management of the Marmite Man of football, lauded and loathed in equal measure.

My instant reaction in my Spurs Odyssey blog was that it would end in tears. I just could not see how José would be a good fit, but I was prepared to give him my full support and, if necessary, sympathy as he took over from the admired – adored even – Pochettino.

It was less than 12 hours after Pochettino's sudden departure that José was being unveiled on 19 November 2019, following two spells at Chelsea and one at Manchester United. His uncomfortable Old Trafford ride had ended with him being sacked by United in December 2018 after two and a half years in charge. He spent much of his 'wilderness year' as a television pundit, always with interesting and often controversial things to say. All the time he was on our screens you could not help but see him as a shadow over any top manager who dropped his standards, and it was Tottenham's Pochettino who suddenly came off the rails.

Announcing his capture, Levy admitted that the vast experience of the Portuguese – impressively including three Premier League titles for Chelsea and two Champions Leagues, with Porto and Inter Milan – had been a major factor in the appointment.

Levy, a long-time suitor of Mourinho, trumpeted, 'In José we have one of the most successful managers in football. He has a wealth of experience, can inspire teams and is a great tactician. He has won honours at every club he has coached. We believe he will bring energy and belief to the dressing room.'

From being the self-styled 'Special One' at Chelsea, Mourinho – a chameleon of a character – now cleverly presented himself as the ''Umble One'. He was suitably modest, showering praise on all but himself, 'I am excited to be joining a club with such a great heritage and such passionate supporters. The quality in both the squad and the academy excites me. Working with these players is what has attracted me.'

Nothing, of course, to do with his reported salary of £13m a year.

Mourinho had an impeccable pedigree with 25 trophies, including a domestic title in a record four different countries. That was in stark contrast to Pochettino, who had yet to win a trophy in his managerial career despite navigating Tottenham to the Champions League for each of his four full seasons in charge, including that astonishing run to the final in 2019.

Tottenham fans were torn between licking their lips at the prospect of at last ending the silverware drought and welcoming the appointment of a manager many had openly castigated for his arrogance during his days of supremacy at Stamford Bridge. It was easy to recall he had once said he would never ever consider managing Spurs, as if it was something beneath him. And there were few supporters who were admirers of his safety-first football, but it had won him trophies by the bucketload. The jury was out on Senhor Mourinho.

It was only the second time that he had taken charge of a club midway through a season, and he got off to a promising start that lifted spirits after the doldrums caused by the Pochettino exit. Tottenham dominated throughout most of their 3-2 win at West Ham in his first game, though a worrying defensive meltdown in the closing minutes scarred an otherwise impressive display. It was Tottenham's first away win for almost a year and underscored why Pochettino had been asked to pack his bags.

Mourinho's first team selection was:

Gazzaniga

Aurier; Sanchez; Alderweireld; Davies

Dier; Winks

Moura; Dele; Son

Kane

* * *

The online chatter switched from cynical criticism to glowing praise for Mourinho as Spurs won four of his opening five Premier League games, with his first defeat coming at Manchester United – a setback he would avenge a year later in spectacular style. He also made an impact in the Champions League, Spurs coming from two goals down to beat Olympiakos 4-2. We realised he meant business as a tactician when he hauled off Eric Dier inside half an hour to make way for Christian Eriksen. This was the action of a man in command and with full confidence in his ability to make the right calls.

A resounding 5-0 victory over Burnley followed, including a crashing long-range shot from 'Our Harry' Kane and then a wonder goal from Son Heung-min. The careering Korean raced with the ball at his flying feet from the edge of his own penalty area ahead of a pack of chasing Burnley defenders before depositing it into the net with his pursuers breathless and beaten. No wonder it was voted goal of the season.

José used this match to blood 17-year-old Troy Parrott, an exciting prospect, and the preening manager was able to boast at the after-match press conference that he was 'ready to give youth a chance'. But it was Sonny who stole the headlines with his gem of a goal, which helped further cement him into the land of Tottenham legend. He had illuminated Spurs with his style and smile since arriving from Bayer Leverkusen for £22m in 2015. Able to play wide as a conventional winger or attacking through the middle, his explosive acceleration, ability to finish with either foot and his deft ball control turned him into one of the most feared strikers in the Premier League. And when paired with Harry Kane, they looked the greatest Tottenham double act since the G-Men, Greavsie and Gilzean. This is the pinnacle of praise.

Sonny laid the foundation to his career at SV Hamburg from the age of 18 after following his father as a professional footballer, and he has become a huge sporting idol at home in South Korea, where he has a thousands-strong fan club tracking his every move and murmur.

Skipper of the South Korean international team, he is widely recognised as one of the most accomplished players ever to come out of Asia. He has continually taken on the role of main Tottenham striker during Kane's injury lay-offs, and is an equal partner when they play together as a two-pronged striking force. Their combinations of scoring and scheming has broken all Premier League records for goals and assists between two team-mates.

Son is among the wealthiest footballers in the UK, because Asian sponsors and advertisers queue for his endorsement. In 2018 he led South Korea to the Asian Games gold medal, which earned him and his team-mates exemption from mandatory military service.

He guaranteed himself a place of honour in the Spurs history books by scoring the very first Premier League goal at the new Tottenham Hotspur Stadium against Crystal Palace on 3 April 2019. Then he created another famous milestone when netting the first in European competition at the stadium in a 1–0 win against Manchester City in the quarter-finals of the 2018/19 Champions League. In the monumental return leg at the Etihad, Son scored twice to earn Spurs a triumph on the away goals rule after a 4-4 aggregate draw and helped the club reach the semi-final of the competition for the first time since 1962, when it was known as the European Cup. His golden pair made him the highest-scoring Asian player in the history of the tournament with 12 goals. He also became the first overseas player to score 100 goals for Tottenham: a true legend. Everybody loves Sonny.

* * *

The Mourinho magic started to wear off as his old Chelsea team, briefly under the management of his former star player Frank Lampard, took all three points at the new Lane, and he lost his main strike force when Kane (hamstring surgery) and then Son (fractured arm) were both sidelined at a critical time in his first season. Goalkeeper and skipper Hugo Lloris was among another four key players injured in what was a crisis that demanded action in the 2020 January transfer window. Steven Bergwijn arrived from Holland and scored a memorable winner in his Premier League debut against mighty Manchester City.

We were able to watch the ups-and-downs of life at Tottenham in Amazon Prime's revealing fly-on-the-wall *All Or Nothing* series – aka The José Mourinho Show – which revealed just how well the club is run from top to bottom. All the many critics of Daniel Levy, Joe Lewis and

ENIC had to eat their words when it came across loud and clear that Tottenham have become one of the best run and organised clubs in the world of football. All they needed to top it off and to silence the social media sneerers and snipers was silverware.

The many critics online destroying Levy and Lewis rarely came up with an alternative. Blood-on-their-hands Arabs? The Glazers? A Russian dictator? A Trump-style American? A conniving Chinese overlord? My stubborn stance was 'better the devil you know' and I fell out with many keyboard warriors who continually called for Lewis and Levy to sell up and get out.

The fascinating documentary spotlighted Mourinho welcoming his backroom staff to the sumptuous training headquarters at Enfield, with João Sacramento and Nuno Santos joining from Lille. Sacramento was installed as assistant manager, while Santos became the new goalkeeping coach. Carlos Lalin – who worked with Mourinho at United and Real Madrid – was confirmed as fitness coach, with Ricardo Formosinho and Giovanni Cerra taking roles as match and player analysts. Chris Powell and Ryan Mason continued in charge of the vital academy wing. Then the legendary Ledley King was promoted to assistant coach, with special responsibilities for defensive tactics. The Pochettino era was well and truly over. I recalled my early meetings with Bill Nicholson in the 1950s when his skeleton backroom staff could be counted on the fingers of Tottenham ticket tout One Arm Lou. Yes, another planet.

Two contradicting things I learned from the series are how multi-tongued linguist José leans on Anglo-Saxon expletives of the most crude kind, and that in stark contrast he is dedicated to having God on his side. There were several cutaway shots of him crossing himself and even on his knees praying. Cussing and crossing are strange bedfellows.

I have not heard so many swear words fall from the lips of a member of the Tottenham management team since the days of Eddie Baily, who could rarely get through a sentence without dropping the f-bomb. It made me wonder how José controls his tongue when this devout Roman Catholic, so he told us, talks to his God every day.

He was soon up to his old mind-game tricks, notably with £56m club record signing Tanguy Ndombele and the idolised Dele Alli. He publicly criticised the high-price Frenchman's performances and attitude and suddenly shut Alli out in the cold. Under Pochettino, Dele had been hailed as the Golden Boy, but now he was in danger of getting splinters sitting on the bench.

A home FA Cup defeat on penalties by Norwich poisoned the atmosphere at Tottenham Hotspur Stadium, which was still awaiting a naming rights deal. We looked on in horror as the usually controlled Eric Dier angrily climbed into the stands to confront a Spurs supporter who had verbally abused his brother. It was a loss of temper that brought a suspension and yet more selection problems for Mourinho. Even worse, Chelsea's black German centre-half Antonio Rüdiger complained that he had been racially abused by a Spurs fan during the 2-0 Premier League defeat of Tottenham, but nobody could find a culprit. It helped hurry along the Black Lives Matter movement and the sobering sight of all players taking the knee before matches.

More gloom and doom followed with a Champions League exit against RB Leipzig, managed by 32-year-old Julian Nagelsmann, who was being hailed as the 'wunderkind' of coaches just as Mourinho had been 20 years earlier. Injury-hit Spurs – runners-up the previous season – looked out of their depth on a stage where they sparkled under Pochettino.

Giovani Lo Celso had arrived at Tottenham three months ahead of Mourinho, and with Christian Eriksen making it clear he wanted to join Inter Milan, the Argentinian playmaker emerged as Spurs' most influential midfielder, often winning the ball eagerly and driving forward with his impressive dribbling skills and accurate passing. When he linked with fellow Argentinian ball artist Erik Lamela, those of us of a certain age warmed with memories of the Ardiles-Villa tango partnership of the 1970s and 1980s.

Just as we sensed that Mourinho was getting his act (and team) together, my 70 years of watching Spurs was interrupted in a bizarre and frightening way with the invasion of the COVID-19 pandemic that impacted and affected all our lives. There was a school of thought that the 2019/20 season should be abandoned, but after a three-month hiatus Project Restart was launched and somehow they managed to get all ends tied up, including Liverpool proudly and properly being declared champions for the first time in 30 years.

With a late surge Tottenham finished sixth, clinching Europa League football by taking 14 points from the final six games behind closed doors, beating Everton, Arsenal, Newcastle and Leicester and drawing in frenetic matches at Bournemouth and Crystal Palace.

Some Tottenham purists nodded quietly in agreement when Dele Alli was caught saying in an episode of *All or Nothing*, 'We're just smashing it long and f***ing defending.' Perhaps it was then that Mourinho decided to give him the deep freeze treatment.

His strange handling of Alli made little sense to those of us who had watched the midfielder grow into one of the most exciting and skilful midfield players of his generation. The son of a Nigerian father and English mother, Dele – as he prefers to be known – was brought up by foster parents, and elected to play for the country of his birth rather than Nigeria.

He was discovered playing for his hometown club Milton Keynes by the omniscient David Pleat while on a scouting mission. 'His potential was obvious and I knew Spurs was the right club for him,' David told me, continuing to loyally serve Tottenham the club he loves.

After signing for Spurs in 2015 for an initial fee of £5m, Dele quickly developed into a player of immense talent, whether as a support striker or creative midfielder. In his first two full seasons with Spurs he was voted PFA Young Player of the Year, and after early problems with a touchpaper temperament he matured into a very confident if occasionally cocky competitor. Dele admits to having been a Liverpool fan when growing up, and names Steven Gerrard as the hero who did most to inspire him. He is less forceful yet more subtle than the ex-Anfield skipper, and can turn a game with a flash of individual genius. 'Too many flicks and tricks,' Mourinho was overheard saying, not appreciating that was exactly why so many Tottenham fans loved him.

His goals were often of the classic variety, and he had the skill and the vision to bring team-mates – particularly Kane – on to his radar screen. He came through the England Under-17, Under-18 and Under-19 teams to establish himself on the international stage, and was a prominent member of the Gareth Southgate squad that reached the semi-finals of the 2018 World Cup.

In his first two seasons in the Premier League he got a reputation for diving, and defenders played on this suicidal tendency, but the maturing Dele of the 2018/19 season was generally controlled and living up to his promise as one of the world's outstanding young footballers. Then José Mourinho came into his life.

Mauricio Pochettino had a huge influence on the way Dele carries and conducts himself on the pitch and describes him as 'an extraordinary all-rounder who – in the box – looks like a striker, and outside the box plays like a midfielder'. If Mauricio had got his way, he would have signed Dele on loan for PSG in the 2021 January transfer window, but the proposed deal fell through. It was then all eyes on Mourinho to see if he could mend bridges and rediscover the 'old' Dele.

* * *

Tottenham followers had got used to being frustrated by summer transfer windows producing little but draughts, but this time around Daniel Levy – José no doubt breathing down his neck – splashed the cash as in came combative midfielder Pierre-Emile Højbjerg from Southampton, solid right-back Matt Doherty from Wolves, experienced ex-England goalkeeper Joe Hart on a free, Benfica's goal-grabbing Brazilian striker Carlos Vinicius on loan, and most exciting of all a double whammy from Real Madrid in stylish left-back Sergio Reguilon and 'prodigal son' Gareth Bale, returning after seven years in Spain gathering medals and mountains of money. Spurs were reported to be splitting his £600,000 a week wages with Real. I wonder what the likes of Len Duquemin, Les Bennett and Bobby Smith would have made of that. On-loan Bale was picking up in a week – yes, in just seven days – more than the three of them had earned together throughout their entire careers.

The promising Kyle Walker-Peters was allowed to go to Southampton, while the admirable but ageing Jan Vertonghen elected to join Benfica for the final tackles of his illustrious career. His partnership with countryman Toby Alderweireld had been a joy to behold.

Mourinho had inherited Pochettino's team, but now in 2020/21 this was definitely his squad.

Everything was looking rosy. The Kane & Son firm were back in business – goals delivered to order. The England skipper set up the South Korean captain for a four-goal salvo at Southampton before bulging the Saints' net himself. A 3-1 victory over Chelsea in the League Cup quarter-final was followed by a comfortable win over Brentford in the semi-final to clinch a Wembley date in April with Manchester City. In October there had been one of the more astonishing performances in Tottenham's Premier League history when they mangled Manchester United 6-1 at Old Trafford. We just could not believe our eyes.

But José was soon frightened back into his defensive shell after Spurs had somehow surrendered a 3-0 lead to West Ham with 15 minutes to go and finished up with just one point. Suddenly he was back to his cautious contain and counter tactics, which do not sit comfortably with Tottenham fans fed for many years on a diet of front-foot football, and the famous Danny Blanchflower doctrine, 'The great fallacy is that the game is first and last about winning. It is nothing of the kind. The game is about glory, it is about doing things in style and with a flourish, about going out and beating the other lot, not waiting for them to die of boredom.'

* * *

From briefly being top of the Premier League in November 2020, Spurs found themselves down in ninth place after three successive defeats in eight depressing days. They had been hit by injuries to key players, but worse, the spirit of the club was bruised, and there were growing calls for Mourinho's head by supporters who had never laid out the welcome mat when he arrived as successor to the popular Pochettino. The fans were as divided as the team, some seeing Mourinho as disruptive while others claimed it was the players being rebellious that was causing the sudden fracture of faith in the club.

The calls for José to be axed became a cacophony when Spurs lost an extraordinary FA Cup fifth round tie 5-4 at Everton, followed by a Premier League defeat by runaway leaders Manchester City at the Etihad and then a 2-1 loss at West Ham.

The lynch mob seemed ready to march on the new Lane but put down the rope when Wolfsburg were swept out of the way in the Europa League and Burnley got crushed 4-0 and Crystal Palace 4-1 to stop the slide in the Premier League.

A deflating 2-1 defeat in the north London derby at the Emirates was memorable for a stunning 'rabona' goal from Erik Lamela, who then went and undid the inventive work by getting himself red-carded for a reckless hand-off that triggered a ban. The #MourinhoOut hashtag spread again like a bad rash as the keyboard assassins got him back in their sights, and just four days later the demands for his head hit the Richter scale.

Spurs ran around like headless cockerels and managed to lose their 2-0 first-leg lead and exited the Europa

League after an extra-time downfall in Zagreb. I struggled to remember a more depressing defeat in all my 70 years watching the club.

Mourinho had given us the belief that he had the key to the Europa League trophy, but suddenly our faith in him and his 'special' status crumbled in Croatia. Skipper Hugo Lloris summed up the performance perfectly when he said with searing honesty, 'We were a disgrace.'

The usually discreet and dignified Frenchman then revealed in front of the TV cameras the hidden depths of the problems behind the scenes at Spurs. He told the nation in his Maurice Chevalier accent, 'I hope everyone in the changing room feels responsible. The taste of defeat is more than painful. We are a club full of ambition, but I just think at the moment it is a reflection of what is going on in the club. We have a lack of basics, fundamentals, our performances are just in relation of that. Mentally we should be stronger, more competitive. When you are not ready at this level, you pay. There is quality everywhere and if you don't respect the opponent they can punish you, that's what happened.

'The way we play is just not enough, not enough. It's one thing to come in front of the camera to say we're ambitious, the other is to show it every day in training sessions, to show it every time on the pitch. You cannot put it down to if you play or don't play. To behave as a team is the most difficult thing in football, whatever is the decision of the manager you have to follow the way of the team. If you follow the team only when you are in the starting 11, that causes big problems.'

* * *

It was like a scene from *Les Misérables* to hear Lloris digging into his soul and questioning the commitment of his teammates. I have never known a Spurs club captain need to be so outspoken for public consumption. It was completely out of character for the philosophical Frenchman, and his remarks were translated by many to mean that Hugo was sending an 'act now' message to Mourinho. The 'Special One' being held to account. José talked of several players 'hiding' on the pitch, and it now became painfully clear that he was in charge of a split camp.

In my opinion, much of the disharmony in the Tottenham dressing room was being caused by stirring, avaricious agents who were feeding the press with poisonous gossip and disinformation. The arrival of self-interested agents has been one of the worst developments in the game in my 70-year vigil, and their emergence out of the woodwork like vermin was a major reason why, for example, Bill Nicholson quit the manager's chair at Tottenham back in 1974. Most of them take, take, take without putting anything back. Many are just parasites, feeding off the beautiful game and interested only in making a packet for their own pocket.

As I am writing this final chapter virtually in real time to make the press day deadline, I feel as if I am ageing with every sentence and every match. Time for a break here while I regain my composure after being pushed into a dungeon of despair by those back-to-back defeats at the Emirates and in Zagreb.

* * *

Just before lockdown, I was privileged to play an anchor role in a filmed tribute to The Master, Jimmy Greaves.

Called simply *Greavsie*, it was a work of art by young producer/director Tom Boswell and his BT crew. It gave me the opportunity in my weekly Spurs Odyssey blog to wax lyrically (and a little hysterically) about three 'proper' Tottenham footballers. I give you Cliff 'Welsh Wizard' Jones, Steve 'Skip' Perryman and Glenn 'God' Hoddle.

They were among the guests at the sky-scraping BT Tower on Thursday, 6 February 2020 – note the date, 6 February, on which one of English football's biggest tragedies is remembered each year – for the premier of the film. I invite you to drop in on the conversations I had with this trio of Tottenham titans as I recorded them in my blog.

Let's kick off with Cliff Jones, who was hugely emotional on what was the eve of his 85th birthday. He was accompanied by his son Stephen, who looked after his dad like a precious Ming vase, and quite rightly as he is a Tottenham (and Wales) treasure. Cliff told me he had recently been diagnosed in the early stages of dementia, but he looked the picture of good health and fit enough to still play the game at which he was, yes, a wizard. Simply one of the greatest wingers the world has ever seen.

It was 62 years ago almost to the day that Cliff scored in a 2-0 victory for Wales against Israel in Cardiff on 5 February 1958 when he was a Swansea player. At the same time, Manchester United were drawing 3-3 with Red Star in Belgrade in a European Cup quarter-final.

The next day Cliff travelled to London to sign for Tottenham Hotspur for what was then a record £35,000. This was on 6 February 1958. It was nothing new to the Jones family. Twenty years earlier his uncle Bryn had moved from Wolves to Arsenal for a world record £14,000, a fee that brought comments that football had gone mad.

Cliff was met at White Hart Lane by coach Bill Nicholson, standing in for unwell manager Jimmy Anderson. 'Bill had tears in his eyes,' Cliff recalled. 'The news had just that moment broken that the Manchester United plane had crashed on take-off after refuelling at Munich. I started to cry, too, when I realised one of my best mates in the Army was on board, Duncan Edwards. He, along with John Charles, was the greatest footballer I ever played with. Fantastic player and lovely bloke.'

His memory now in full flow, Cliff said, 'The Welsh team manager at the time was Jimmy Murphy, one of the most knowledgeable football people I ever knew. He was also Matt Busby's right-hand man at Manchester United, and he would have been on board that plane but for the game against Israel.

'I made my debut for Spurs against the Arsenal at Highbury on 22 February, and it was the start of a love affair with the club and its supporters that continues to this day. It was my honour to score 19 goals in our Double year, and the team became even better when Greavsie signed for us the following season.'

It was, of course, Jimmy who had brought us all together at the stunning BT Tower, and I asked Cliff how he rated Spurs' record scorer. 'Simply the greatest British goalscorer there has ever been,' he said without hesitation. 'As good as Messi, and could he have done it on the mud heap pitches on which we played – with defenders like Chopper [Chelsea's Ron Harris] and Bites-Yer-Legs [Norman Hunter of Leeds] allowed to kick you from behind? Jimmy took all the tackles in his stride and just got on with playing the game like the artist that he was. It was a privilege to be on the same pitch.'

Cliff started to well up, 'It's not only as a footballer that I love Jimmy Greaves. He is a wonderful man, and he saved my life. But for him, I'd have been dead years ago. I was losing out to the bottle and it was his advice to turn to Alcoholics Anonymous that stopped me drinking myself to an early grave. Yes, I owe him my life.'

Next, I was reunited with my dear old mate Stevie Perryman, and was delighted to see him looking ridiculously well after his health scares of a few years back. I put his recovery down to the love and support of his beautiful wife, Kim, who was at the premier along with Steve's ghostwriter Adam Powley.

Between them they have produced one of the sports books of the year: *Steve Perryman, A Spur Forever!* Highly recommended.

I asked Steve, looking younger than springtime, for his assessment of Greaves. 'If there has been a better goalscorer in British football I've not seen him,' he said. 'He was getting to the end of his Spurs career when I got into the team, and I was in awe. But he treated me as an equal and his next boast will be his first. He and Gilly [Alan Gilzean] were magical together.

'We became good mates when he started his roadshows, and he was as funny a stand-up speaker as any of those professional comedians. It's sad what's happened to him with the stroke, but let's remember the good times. What a life he's had. Unbelievable.'

Steve Perryman, a prince among men.

Third of my conversations was with 'Hod the God'. If I had to name the finest footballers ever produced on the playing fields of England, two high on my list would be Jimmy Greaves and Glenn Hoddle. Both were world-class and Glenn matched even Push and Run conductor Eddie Baily for long-range accuracy with his passes.

I am glad to report that Glenn looked in excellent health, which is quite remarkable when you think he was close to death after a vicious heart attack on his 61st birthday on 27 October 2018.

How did he rate Greavsie? 'I grew up watching him and have never altered my opinion that he was a footballing genius,' he said. 'There was always a buzz when he collected the ball and the whole crowd suddenly came alive. I unashamedly copied his positioning and awareness, always looking over my shoulder Greavsie-style to make sure I knew exactly where any opponent was positioned. I had seen Jimmy doing that from the Tottenham terraces as a kid and I made a mental note that was how it should be done. Always know where you are on the pitch and who's around you. It's an honour to be one of those paying homage in a terrific film.'

As a mate of Jimmy's for more than 60 years, I was also proud to play a part in the BT tribute to mark the great man's upcoming 80th birthday on 20 February 2020. It is an emotional rollercoaster and includes many of his greatest goals and footage that will make you laugh, cry, cheer and groan.

If you have not caught up with the *Greavsie* film yet, I can strongly commend it as the best close-up you will ever see of one of Tottenham's favourite sons. Look out for the pitches on which he played. They were invariably mud-heaps, but he glided across the surfaces as smoothly as a gazelle. Greavsie the Gazelle. A bit late to start giving him a new nickname!

While all this was going on, I was trying to reinvent myself as a crime novelist, nothing I know to do with this

Spurs journey but a welcome distraction from the stresses of the season and the COVID crisis.

I was once interviewed by the notorious Kray twins, Reggie and Ronnie, for the job of part-time publicist for the charitable wing of their organisation. I have used this as the launching pad for the creation of a private eye/public hack called J.C. Campbell, a former Fleet Street crime reporter turned detective. He teams up with a covert MI5 agent called Terry Conway, whose cover is that he drives a black London cab. There is a series of four novels to date set in the 1970s, and featuring these two characters as a crime-busting duo.

It was a writing exercise that took my mind off the travails of Tottenham, and I had fun by making J.C. a close friend of both Bobby Moore and Jimmy Greaves, a mirror of my own life. It was a release to lose myself in the composing of the books and I temporarily escaped the Spurs saga in my 70th year of following the fortunes of Tottenham.

But, meantime, back at the ranch.

* * *

Tottenham started to repair the ground after their disastrous departure from the Europa League with a battling 2-0 victory over Aston Villa at Villa Park, when they showed the commitment and character strangely absent at the Emirates and in Zagreb. The win lifted them into sixth place in the table and suddenly the polluting pessimism was overtaken by a mood of optimism. The talk was of a late run for a fourth place and a return to the Champions League, and there was always the Carabao Cup. No wonder a new word had entered the vocabulary, 'Spursy'.

Our intense interest in club matters was interrupted by the international break that brought Gareth Bale back into the spotlight, and his Spurs legend was dented by his widely reported remarks about using his return to the club to get fit for skippering Wales in their European and World Cup campaigns. Social media almost went into meltdown with blistering criticism of the Welshman's comments and priorities, which his exasperated agent Jonathan Barnett claimed had been taken out of context.

It was noted that Bale failed to make an impact when coming on as a substitute in a depressing 2-2 draw at relegation-threatened Newcastle. This provided yet another example of Spurs frittering away valuable points, and the mathematicians among the fans worked out that 15 had now been dropped from winning positions without a whimper. Both Tottenham goals were plundered by Harry Kane, which added more fuel to the fire of the hottest topic in British football, 'Should Kane look for pastures new?'

In the previous few weeks I'd seen Harry sold online to either of the two Manchesters, Real Madrid, Barcelona and – the favourite – set up for a reunion with his old commander Mauricio Pochettino at Paris Saint-Germain. Television pundits, particularly straight-talking Roy Keane, ex-Gunner Ian Wright and once-a-Spur Graeme Souness, insisted the time was right for Harry to move on. They, of course, could not care less what Tottenham fans thought. Their job is to say it as they see it. Those of us who follow the fortunes of Spurs were weighed down with vested interest and, in many cases, one-eyed bias.

My view was that at the age of 27 – turning 28 on 28 July 2021 – Harry was at the peak of his power as a player and as an earner. If he was ever going to cash in, this was the moment, when he was again the leading scorer in the Premier League and in net-busting form for club and country.

There is no tougher negotiator than Spurs chairman Daniel Levy, who was unlikely to let Tottenham's star man go for a penny less than a world record £175m. There would be several clubs thinking, 'We can raise much of that by selling three or four of our all-star squad.'

My thoughts as I approached the final stretch of this 70-year journey is that you could bet your boots that Dan the Man – if he was unable to talk Harry into staying a Spur – would do all he could to ship him abroad, rather than have him scoring goals for a rival Premier League club. I wondered if he could soon be having some interesting chats with his former employee, 'Professor' Pochettino in Paris.

If I were Harry's father – and his career is managed by his dad, Patrick, and older brother, Charlie – I would have been advising him to move on if Spurs did not clinch a place in the Champions League for the 2021/22 season.

I personally wanted him to stay at Spurs and take over from Jimmy Greaves as the club's all-time record goalscorer. But rising above my devotion to the Lilywhites, I could recognise the sense of Harry moving on to one of the world's major clubs as soon as the European Championship had been decided.

He would immediately treble his earnings and bolster his chances of collecting medals as a tangible sign that he is one of the most devastating goalscorers of all time.

I can almost hear you saying, 'Why does he need more money?'

Let me tell you, there is never enough money to do the things you want to to do. For instance, I have four grandchildren and twin great grandsons. I would love to be able to leave them each a million pounds when I kick the bucket (with Harry Kane accuracy and power).

But, sadly, they will be getting peanuts, unless my books start selling in their millions rather than in ones and twos.

Our Harry would be able to look after his childhood sweetheart wife, Kate, her family, their three children, his parents, Charlie, nephews and nieces and favourite people, and have a lot left over to dish out to deserving causes. Just imagine being able to help your loved ones get started with a house and the best education that money can buy. I promise you can never have enough money if you have any imagination and a desire – a duty, even – to help others. Harry has always been community-minded and will know how best to handle and share his fortune.

But all that was pure speculation as Spurs approached their next challenge, a home match against Manchester United, one of their main rivals for that precious top four place in the Premier League – and that was when the drama became a crisis. A 3-1 defeat in a bad-tempered match set social media on fire, and there were literally thousands of online posts screaming for the heads of Daniel Levy, Joe Lewis and, loudest of all, of José Mourinho. The chances of a top-four finish were suddenly remote, and the likelihood of losing Harry Kane and possibly even Son Heung-min came sharply into focus.

You will know how it all turns out soon after this book is published, and at this moment I am writing blind as a press deadline that waits for no man rushes forward. My publisher gave me a stay of execution until the day after the League Cup Final – now in the guise of the Carabao Cup

– against a Manchester City team recognised as one of the strongest in world football.

I was quietly tipped off by a German newspaper contact that the now 33-year-old Julian Nagelsmann was being lined up to take over from Mourinho in the summer, and it will have amused (and aged) the Portuguese that the young German had been described as 'the new' Mourinho. Mighty Bayern were also interested in Nagelsmann, so Jose thought he could relax a little. But the wolves were at the door.

* * *

While awaiting the crucial Carabao Cup Final I allowed my mind to wander to random thoughts about the way the game has changed since I first stood on the terraces watching Spurs going through their Push and Run gears back in the 1950s. Looking through the eyes of the players, I would have to say the biggest difference between then and now is the financial side of the game. Tottenham's first-team squad wage bill for 2020 was in excess of £133m. In the championship-winning season of 1950/51, it was less than £20,000.

The second major change has been to the pitches. The surfaces were invariably mud-heaps in the good old, bad old days right up until the Premier League clubs, using modern grass-growing technology, set new standards in the early 1990s. Supporters of a certain age will recall the old White Hart Lane pitch when sections of it had a mud mixed with shale top and players used to come off at the end with their Lilywhite shirts covered in a mix of pink and black muck. It would have broken the heart of the original groundsman of the Lane, John Over, who had the honour of laying the first Test pitch at The Oval in 1880 and during his time as

Tottenham groundsman for more than 40 years was always proud of his 'green and pleasant' pitch.

The laundry bill was one of the biggest items on Tottenham's balance sheet in the glorious muddy days. I remember being with the two great Bills – Nicholson and Shankly – when the pitch just about survived an inspection by the referee before Spurs faced Liverpool in the early 1970s. 'Och, Bill,' growled Shanks in his bagpipes accent, 'you should come up and see our pitch at Anfield. We've got professional grass.'

The balls have changed, of course. They were leather, laced and panelled until the introduction of what the old-time pros call beach balls. But the weight at kick-off remains the same (one lb 16oz, or 0.453kg) as in the old days, the difference being today's footballs are water-resistant. The old leather balls used to weigh twice as much by the end of a game in the mud, which explains why so many of our veteran heroes – particularly centre-halves and centre-forwards – finished up with the footballer's curse of Alzheimer's. It's one of the reasons I am sharing profits from this book with the Tottenham Tribute Trust, which helps our old idols, so thanks for your donation.

Another huge difference is in the boots. Back in the day, they were just the one drab colour and like clodhoppers, heavy enough to withstand the kicks, trips, ankle taps and tackles that were an accepted part of the game. Now they come in all colours of the rainbow and are, in the words of Cliff Jones, 'Like carpet slippers.'

On the playing side of things, the biggest change is that football has become less and less a game of physical contact. The beautiful game used to be the brutal game. When the tackle from behind (without getting the ball) was outlawed in the 1990s football started to lose its bite, which was good for the attacking players but not so good for the spectators. There was no greater sight than a flying winger trying to evade a full-blooded tackle from a determined full-back. Then Tottenham-educated Alf Ramsey decided to play without wingers in the 1960s. His tactics won for him the championship at Ipswich and the World Cup for England in 1966. Great as it was for Sir Alf, it has to be said that from then on the game was a less exciting spectacle as teams copied his idea of playing without traditional wingers, and ferocious, take-no-prisoners tackling was all but extinguished from the game.

I wonder how many goals our old hero Greavsie would have scored without defenders trying to kick him up in the air every few minutes?

The one change that has improved the game and rarely gets a mention is the enforcement of the ten-yard rule at free kicks by the referees using vanishing foam as a marker, invented by a Brazilian in 2000 and instantly stopping the arguments that often raged over the positioning of wall defences.

There is, of course, one rule change on which the jury is still out, the introduction of VAR. I had always campaigned for TV evidence to be used to settle contentious decisions, but having now seen it in practice I feel it has robbed football of spontaneity and often kills the flow of a game. I fear it is here to stay; if so the video assistant referees must get their decisions right, or we will have to bring in VAR-VAR, a video assistant referee to judge the video assistant referee. Yes, I am joking but the way the system is holding up many matches is robbing football of fluency and atmosphere.

The biggest change off the pitch is how millions of spectators worldwide can watch Tottenham play, most of them without ever having set foot in the old White Hart Lane or the dazzling new Tottenham Hotspur Stadium. They all have an opinion online, where debates are driven by people who have never kicked a ball at a serious level. I rarely come across a fan who can watch both teams in a match with a balanced view. Disciplined by many years of press box neutrality, I can control my bias, but so many supporters are as one-eyed as Cyclops. Blinkered keyboard warriors are the curse of the modern game. As Bill Nicholson told me all those years ago, 'Worst part of my job is being told how to do it by people who cannot trap a bag of cement.' Bill, if you can hear me up there, it's a million times worse now.

A development that Bill would not recognise is the fast-growing promotion of women's football. Tottenham, along with all the major clubs, have a professional team that regularly draws attendances of more than 20,000. The top players earn more in a week than the Push and Run heroes picked up in a year. This is a wing of the Beautiful Game that is going to become huge over the coming decades.

* * *

I continually find myself being pulled into debates as to who has been the greatest Tottenham player of my 70 years watching the team. Everybody expects me to say (with some justification) my dear friend Jimmy Greaves, who is in all our thoughts as he battles with his health crisis. He is unquestionably the greatest British goalscorer of any time. But I am looking past Jimbo, and even modern masters like Glenn Hoddle, Gareth Bale and Harry Kane.

Coming joint top in the cavalcade of great players queuing on my memory screen are two maestros who wore the Lilywhite number six shirt with pride, power and super proficiency. I give you Welsh dragon Ron Burgess and Scottish braveheart Dave Mackay.

Burgess was the driving force behind the magnificent Push and Run Spurs that won the Second Division and First Division titles in successive seasons from 1949 to 1951. Don't just take my word for it. Let me call an expert eyewitness.

Master manager 'Sir' Bill Nicholson was something like George Washington in that he could not tell a lie. He was one of the most honest men ever to cross my path, so when I once trapped him into naming Tottenham's greatest player of his lifetime you had to sit up and take notice. The player he selected was Burgess, a goliath from the Welsh valleys.

As I revealed in the Bill Nicholson chapter, I used to sit at his feet listening to his tales of football days past in my time as chief football reporter for the *Daily Express* in the 1960s through to the 1970s. One day I challenged an uncommonly relaxed Bill, 'Who would you select as the number one player for Spurs in your era as player and manager?'

Fence-sitting Bill would usually have ducked the question, but I had caught him in reflective mood. 'Of the early 1960s side it would be a toss-up between Danny [Blanchflower] and Dave [Mackay],' he said, 'and without question the number one forward Jimmy [Greaves]. But I would pick one player ahead of all of them – Ron Burgess, skipper of our Push and Run team.'

'What made him so special?' I asked, having only seen him play through schoolboy eyes.

'He had it all,' Bill said, looking off into the mid-distance as if transporting himself back in time. 'Strength, skill, a lion in defence, a motivator in attack, a cool head, a precise passer of the ball, able to read the game to perfection and, above all, a colossal heart. He was an inspiring captain, and carried out manager Arthur Rowe's instructions, yet not being afraid to make tactical changes if situations on the pitch demanded it. And don't forget, like a lot of us, he lost his peak years to the war.'

Then there's the great Mackay. Dave mixed brain and brawn into a perfect cocktail, and it was his opponents who were shaken and his team-mates who were stirred. Jimmy Greaves, his Tottenham pal and partner on the pitch and at the bar, told me long ago, 'Dave made us try twice as hard to keep up with him. He was only just over 5ft 7in tall, but with that barrel chest of his he had the impact of a giant. Because of his reputation for being hard, people tend to forget that he had exceptional technique. He used to win all the skill competitions in the gym and he could be delicate as well as powerful with that left foot of his. Many's the time I've put my hands together and offered a prayer of thanks that he was on our side and not against us! Definitely the most inspiring skipper I ever played with, just ahead of the more cerebral Danny.'

So that's the verdict of this old hack – in joint first place, Ronnie Burgess and Dave Mackay. How Tottenham would have liked to have had them both at the peak of their powers for the 2021 Carabao Cup Final.

* * *

Approaching the final at Wembley, it took two opportunistic rifled goals from Our Harry to salvage a point in a 2-2 draw at Everton before he hobbled off in the last minute with yet another ankle injury.

This was the big talking point for us Spurs disciples until two headline-grabbing events in 24 crazy hours almost literally took the breath away.

First of all, Tottenham revealed they were one of 12 clubs – quickly nicknamed the Dirty Dozen – who planned to form a breakaway European Super League. Their 'companions in crime' were Arsenal, Chelsea, Liverpool, Manchester City, Manchester United, AC Milan, Atlético Madrid, Barcelona, Inter Milan, Juventus and Real Madrid.

Here I was, celebrating 70 years of loving – yes, loving – the beautiful game and suddenly being betrayed by my mistress through all that time, Tottenham Hotspur. I felt as if the gorgeous woman I have flirted with since I was a football virgin had suddenly proved to be a tart who will give her body to anybody for money. Big, big, big money. Yes, the root of all evil.

Sorry to boil this down to such a selfish observation, but the news of the breakaway league torpedoed the little matter of my 81st birthday celebrations. I needed all my breath to blow out the candles on my cake, but had no puff left because of the stupefying tidings from Tottenham.

I found myself spitting blood, and was ready to aim much of it at two men I had constantly defended over the previous few months when Spurs followers were screaming for their heads. In the stocks, ENIC owners Joe Lewis and Daniel Levy.

Remember when dear Keith Burkinshaw, The General, walked out on Spurs with the parting shot, 'There used to be a football club there'? As far as I was concerned they were now preparing to sell the club to the devil, and my immediate reaction was that Lewis and Levy could go to 'ell unless they performed an about-turn and walked away from this appalling project.

Sure enough, within 48 hours – driven by a mass reaction of outrage from supporters – they followed Chelsea and Manchester City in announcing they had decided that the 'super' league was a bad idea after all. Anybody with an ounce of common sense could have told them that there was no way it would work. But by the time they pulled the plug the damage had been done, and it was my view that Daniel Levy's position had become untenable. Even Prime Minister Boris Johnson climbed aboard the 'banned' wagon and had promised legislative action to prevent the project.

The esteemed Tottenham Hotspur Supporters' Trust had a remarkable 90 per cent support for a statement which read, 'We call for the immediate resignation of the executive board of Tottenham Hotspur Football Club, and for the owners to work with us to appoint a new board that has elected and accountable fan representation on it. That representation must make key decisions about the running of the club dependent upon fan approval, and we would expect to see that made a legal requirement across the game.'

* * *

I was astonished and astounded that men as bright and worldly as Lewis and Levy could not see the ESL plan was unworkable in the form in which it was presented and tossed towards an unsuspecting football world like a hand grenade. To me, it showed a mixture of arrogance and ignorance. It was arrogant of the 'Dirty Dozen' to even begin to think they could set up their elitist league without all the other clubs in Europe protesting, and it was ignorant that they did not think their project through.

There is, in my opinion, a way to get an international super league off the launching pad, starting with having the supporters and players on board and making it a pyramid from which the bottom clubs at least have a hope of one day emerging at the top. But the selfish, pompous ESL project was still-born because it was so poorly conceived by some of the wealthiest men in the world.

They were not going to allow relegation and I wonder how long it would have taken for the powerful Yanks in the covert cabal to have pressed for an end to drawn matches. Daniel Levy quite rightly took heavy criticism. An intelligent, Cambridge-educated man with an honours degree in land management, he parted company with his judgement and lost everybody's confidence over the way he took our beloved Tottenham Hotspur to the cliff edge of a catastrophe. It was even worse than that idea he once had of doing a Woolwich Arsenal in reverse and moving the club to Stratford.

What sickened me down to the sole of my boots and the soul of my Spurs addiction is that during the COVID pandemic – the most dangerously worrying time since the Second World War – Lewis and Levy had been among a small cartel of billionaires plotting to bring down the game of football as we know and love it. All so they could further fleece the fans who already pay way over the odds for their football fix, so that players can be paid obscene amounts of money.

While we were being lockdown-isolated from the deadly disease, the Dirty Dozen were carving up the game with little or no care or concern for those clubs not involved in their morally corrupt plan. Oh, how I wish I could have hacked into their Zoom calls as Lewis and Levy discussed the taking over of our beautiful game with oil-rich Arabs, dollar-doped American moguls, Spanish and Italian bosses, and a rich-beyond-belief Russian oligarch. I would have put in my pennyworth by speaking up for the supporters who are the true owners of the game. To try to get it past them without the tiniest input was blinkered and brainless.

As if all this was not enough to test my sanity in the final furlong of my 70-year adventure, Spurs chose this confusing time to announce they were parting company with the suddenly not-so-Special One, José Mourinho.

We were still digesting news of the breakaway league when the always preening Portuguese was given the golden boot (including a bundle of compensation money), just six days before the Carabao Cup Final. A statement read, 'The club can today announce that Jose Mourinho and his coaching staff Joao Sacramento, Nuno Santos, Carlos Lalin and Giovanni Cerra have been relieved of their duties.'

Chairman Levy, acting as if the proposed European Super League had little or no significance, said, 'Jose and his coaching staff have been with us through some of our most challenging times as a Club. He is a true professional who showed enormous resilience during the pandemic. On a personal level I have enjoyed working with him and regret that things have not worked out as we both had envisaged. He will always be welcome here and we should like to thank him and his coaching staff for their contribution.'

The haste with which Levy delivered the coup de grâce triggered the conjecture that he saved millions in compensation, blocking any chance of José collecting huge bonuses by finishing in the top four or winning the League Cup. We will have to wait for the inevitable memoirs to get to the truth, because it was obvious there was a gagging clause on Mourinho. Levy was not going to say anything outside his statement because he was too busy dodging bullets over his foolhardy plan to join the ill-fated ESL.

I had always been a Levy admirer and supporter, taking on legions of his detractors online, but now he and billionaire owner Joe Lewis had gone too far. ENIC had never hidden the fact they were in the game for the profit, but to treat their fans with such utter contempt was unacceptable. My 70-year trip was ending in tears. My tears.

* * *

Young Ryan Mason, a Tottenham favourite as a player and now on the backroom coaching staff, was appointed interim caretaker manager, and in his debut match was rewarded with a 2-1 home victory over Southampton, coming back from a goal down with a second half full of the character that Mourinho had been unable to coax from the Spurs players in his swansong days. And, glory be, we saw glimpses of the real deal Gareth Bale.

It has to be said there were few tears shed for José, who found Pochettino's boots too big to fill. I said early in this chapter that the jury was out on Senhor Mourinho. The verdict has to be that he was guilty of suffocating himself by losing his way in a maze of his own making. He played unwise and unnecessary mind games with too many of his players and lost their trust and commitment. His cautious tactics were completely out of step with the adventurous play with which Pochettino had entertained us over the previous four and a half years and we were just not going to accept it.

We Spurs supporters – yes, arrogantly – like to think we specialise in superior, easy-on-the-eye football at Tottenham. It's in our DNA. To dare is to do. But José too often had his foot on the brake, and paid the price with an avalanche of losing points from winning positions. He would then go to press conferences and make coded attacks on his players, blaming them for the run of sub-standard performances rather than admitting that it was he who too often got it wrong with what can now be described as outdated tactics and over-cautious team selections. Slowly, like the drip, drip drip of a ruptured water pipe, he lost his old ability to inspire and – most serious of all – lost the dressing room. You don't win matches unless you have the players on your side.

Now Enfield-born Mason faced the challenge of leading Spurs out for the Carabao Cup Final to which José would remind us he had steered the team. What a *Boys' Own* story. Just four years previously, Ryan had been near death's door after fracturing his skull in a frightening collision with Chelsea's Gary Cahill. He was playing for Hull City after proving a popular player for Tottenham in the Harry Redknapp/Mauricio Pochettino era.

The injury was so serious that he was forced to retire from playing at the age of just 26. Big-hearted Pochettino welcomed him back to Tottenham as a development coach at the academy, where he impressed everybody with his enthusiasm, knowledge and energy.

It was to Mason that Daniel Levy turned after his merciless axing of Mourinho, offering him the role of interim manager for the final seven games of the season.

At 29, he became the youngest manager in Premier League history, and three of the players he sent into the League Cup Final against scorching favourites Manchester City were older than him – substitute Gareth Bale, Toby Alderweireld and skipper Hugo Lloris.

A little bit of Spurs trivia for you: John Cameron was also 29 when he led Tottenham to the 1901 FA Cup Final triumph as the first player-manager to capture the trophy. Spurs were the only Southern League side to win what was then the biggest prize in football. Ryan Mason was following in good footsteps.

There could rarely have been a final chapter of a football book to compete with this one for drama and tales of the unexpected. The appointment and sacking of Mourinho, the coronavirus pandemic and games behind closed doors, the birth and death of the crazy European Super League idea and now here we were at Wembley for the Carabao Cup Final in front of 8,000 COVID-tested spectators. The 2,000 representatives of Tottenham managed to make themselves heard with defiant and telling chants of 'Levy out, Levy out'. And this was before a ball had been kicked.

Sadly for the Spurs supporters and temporary manager Mason, the game proved a huge anti-climax. Tottenham simply did not turn up and the wonder was that City won by only the one goal, headed in from a set-piece in the 82nd minute after a shoal of missed chances. The one talking point was that the winning goal was scored by Aymeric Laporte, who should have received two bookings adding up to a red card in the first half. But it was a weak and pathetic argument to put up on behalf of a team that had simply been outclassed. You could almost feel the ghost of

Mourinho haunting the Wembley pitch as disjointed Spurs went down without a fight.

I wondered what Harry Kane was thinking as he watched his former Spurs team-mate Kyle Walker climb the Wembley steps to collect his seventh major award since leaving Tottenham in 2017. How many goals would Harry have scored had he been playing for the City slickers?

Sonny was inconsolable as he knelt on the unforgiving Wembley turf crying his eyes out. It's a cruel old game.

So there was to be no fairytale for Ryan Mason, and no silver-lined finish to my journey, just a feeling of frustration that the 2021 Spurs were not a patch on the Push and Run team I came in with back in 1950/51.

That's the brutal truth, not my ancient memory playing tricks.

* * *

As I approach the final sentences of my 70-year trip down White Hart Memory Lane let me make a pertinent and important point. Economically, legally and logistically, ENIC own Tottenham Hotspur lock, stock and both barrels. For example, before putting my memories down on paper for publication I had to confirm acceptance that all historic facts about Spurs are the intellectual property of the club. But let me make it clear that they are only temporary owners, holding the baton until the next handover.

Regardless of the harebrained decision to go along with the short-lived idea of a breakaway European Super League, the heart and soul of Tottenham Hotspur will always permanently belong to its supporters: to Bible-bashing John Ripsher who went door to door collecting twopenny club subscriptions to keep Tottenham Hotspur alive in its infancy; Bobby Buckle and the pioneer boys who used to carry the homemade goalposts to and from Tottenham marshes; every fan who stood on The Shelf, cheered from the stands, travelled to support in all weathers, sang the 'McNamara's Band' song in the Push and Run days, marched to the Glory Glory Hallelujah choruses of the Double season, went all trembly at Wembley with Chas & Dave and Ossie and Ricky; Harry Redknapp's Blue and White Army; Pochettino's disciples who followed him all the way to a Champions League Final; the diehards who have supported Spurs with spirit and passion through a surreal season of lockdown and bitter disappointment.

Joe Lewis and Daniel Levy had the vision and the financial muscle to build a tomorrow's world stadium, for which anybody with an open mind would give them credit. Among their loudest critics are those who could not organise a loft conversion. But this still did not buy them Tottenham Hotspur Football Club. Oh, no.

Spurs will always be the property of the supporters. 'Audere est Facere' is the club motto. To dare is to do. Whether you say it in English, Latin, Yiddish or any other tongue, Tottenham Hotspur belongs to the fans.

That's it, friends. My 70 years of Spurs, over in the blink of an eye. Hope you enjoy your journey as much as I have mine. And it all started with that Superman save by Ted Ditchburn in 1950/51. Yes, love at first flight.

Thank you for your company. Keep daring. Keep doing. COYS!

THE 70-YEAR DREAM TEAMS

THERE IS a selector lurking and no doubt smirking in every one of us, and after 70 years of watching Spurs I cannot resist picking a Tottenham dream team from the parade of players who have (literally) passed before my eyes.

I have broken my choices down to a before and after the Premier League, and then following much deliberation and arguments with myself I come up with my combined choice for a Dream Team.

This is the line-up of my pre-Premier League side, aching with agony as I ignore so many of my old heroes. The team lines up with a 3-1-3-3 formation:

Pat Jennings
Alf Ramsey; Mike England; Ron Burgess
Dave Mackay
Danny Blanchflower (Capt); Glenn Hoddle; Ossie Ardiles
Cliff Jones; Alan Gilzean; Jimmy Greaves

I have gone for three at the back in front of the unbeatable Pat Jennings, with the intimidating Dave Mackay patrolling like a mine sweeper, supporting either in defence or attack. England's reliable right-back Alf Ramsey and Welsh walls

Mike England and Ron Burgess would be a considerable barrier to any forward line.

My front six is as good as it gets, with the measured passes from Danny Blanchflower, Glenn Hoddle and Ossie Ardiles prompting the flying wizard Cliff Jones, and with the G-Men providing the best possible finishing touch. What would you pay to see this team in action?

I am allowing myself five substitutes: Ted Ditchburn, John White, Bobby Smith, Eddie Baily, Steve Perryman.

Facing them, a team of modern giants who have all featured for Tottenham in the Premier League, which kicked off in 1992. The formation is 4-3-3:

Hugo Lloris
Kyle Walker; Toby Alderweireld; Ledley. King; Jan Vertonghen
Mousa Dembele; Teddy Sheringham; Luka Modric
Son Heung-min; Harry Kane (Captain); Gareth Bale

The substitutes would be: Paul Robinson, Jermain Defoe, Dimitar Berbatov, Christian Eriksen, Gary Mabbutt

The easiest choice was the front three of Son, Kane and Bale, with the Welshman selected on his superman performances in his first spell at Spurs before hunting gold and goals in Spain. Son, Kane and Bale together at peak form would have been unstoppable.

In midfield, I have gone for the combined skill and subtlety of Dembele, Sheringham and Modric, who got the nod just ahead of his successor as schemer, the Great Dane Christian Eriksen. I selected Dembele rather than the talented Rafael Van der Vaart because of his gift for doing the unexpected. Modric was simply a master of the midfield. What a pity he seemed to spend much of his time at Tottenham trying to get to other clubs, first Chelsea and then Real Madrid.

I did not consider Jurgen Klinsmann because in his two impressive stints in the Lilywhite shirt he managed only 68 competitive games. Gary Lineker arrived after his peak years, and Gazza was just a passing magician. I admit to having found it hard to omit, in particular, Chris Waddle and – from the old-timers team – the two Martins, Chivers and Peters.

My back four for the Premier League squad of Walker, King and Belgian buddies Alderweireld and Vertonghen picked themselves. I considered Sol Campbell, the Rolls-Royce of a central defender, but gave the shirt to Toby to pacify all those supporters who have never forgiven Campbell for switching his allegiance to that other team in north London. Campbell and King together were very special at the Everest peak of their partnership. Just how good would Ledley have been with two reliable knees?

And so the combined team that covers my 70 years of watching Spurs. Let the arguments begin:

Pat Jennings
Kyle Walker; Mike England; Ledley King; Gareth Bale
Glenn Hoddle; Luka Modric; Dave Mackay (Captain)
Son Heung-min; Harry Kane; Jimmy Greaves

Only one manager, of course: 'Sir' Bill Nicholson, with Mauricio Pochettino as his coach.

That's it, friends. My 70 years of Spurs. Over in the blink of a Greavsie goal.

Come on you Spurs.

THE CAST

My thanks to the 235 footballers who paraded their talent for Tottenham during my 70 years of watching them. This table shows those who have played in the Lilywhite shirt, the span of their service to Spurs, their total games and their goals.

Player	Years	Apps	Goals
Vic Buckingham	1935–1949	230	1
Freddie Cox	1938–1949	105	18
Bill Nicholson	1938–1954	341	6
Les Medley	1939–1953	164	46
Ron Burgess	1939–1954	324	16
Sid Tickridge	1946–1951	101	0
Les Bennett	1946–1954	294	117
Arthur Willis	1946–1954	160	1
Ted Ditchburn	1946–1958	452	0
Ernie Jones	1947–1949	57	14
Eddie Baily	1947–1955	325	69
Len Duquemin	1947–1957	307	134

THE CAST

Player	Years	Apps	Goals
Sonny Walters	1947–1957	234	71
Charlie Withers	1948–1956	164	2
Alf Ramsey	1949–1955	250	25
Harry Clarke	1949–1956	322	4
Tony Marchi	1949–1957/1959–1965	232	7
Ron Reynolds	1950–1960	86	0
Johnny Hills	1950–1961	29	0
Tommy Harmer	1951–1960	222	51
George Robb	1952–1958	200	58
Johnny Hollowbread	1952–1964	67	0
Mel Hopkins	1952–1964	240	0
Johnny Brooks	1953–1959	170	51
John White	1959–1964	183	40
Peter Baker	1953–1965	342	3
Alfie Stokes	1953–1958	69	42
Dave Dunmore	1953–1959	75	23
John Ryden	1955–1959	63	2
Eddie Clayton	1954–1967	102	20
Danny Blanchflower	1954–1963	382	21
Bobby Smith	1955–1964	317	208
Terry Dyson	1955–1965	209	55
Ron Henry	1955–1965	287	1
Maurice Norman	1955–1965	411	19
Terry Medwin	1956–1963	215	72

Player	Years	Apps	Goals
Bill Dodge	1957–1962	10	0
Jim Iley	1957–1959	53	1
Cliff Jones	1958–1968	378	159
Len Worley	1959–1960	1	0
Les Allen	1959–1965	137	61
Bill Brown	1959–1966	262	0
Dave Mackay	1959–1968	318	51
Ron Piper	1961–1963	1	0
Ken Barton	1960–1964	4	0
Frank Saul	1960–1967	129	44
John Smith	1959–1964	23	1
Roy Low	1961–1967	8	1
Jimmy Greaves	1961–1970	379	266
Phil Beal	1963–1975	420	1
Laurie Brown	1964–1966	62	3
Jimmy Robertson	1964–1968	181	31
Alan Mullery	1964–1972	374	30
Alan Gilzean	1964–1974	439	133
Cyril Knowles	1964–1975	506	17
Pat Jennings	1964–1977	590	1
Terry Venables	1966–1969	141	9
Mike England	1966–1975	397	19
Joe Kinnear	1966–1975	258	2
Dennis Bond	1967–1970	23	1

THE CAST

Player	Years	Apps	Goals
Peter Collins	1968–1972	101	5
David Jenkins	1968–1972	14	2
Jimmy Pearce	1968–1973	193	35
Martin Chivers	1968–1976	367	174
Phil Holder	1969–1974	13	1
Ray Evans	1969–1975	181	4
John Pratt	1969–1980	415	49
Steve Perryman	1969–1986	854	39
Martin Peters	1970–1975	260	76
Jimmy Neighbour	1970–1976	156	11
Terry Naylor	1970–1980	301	4
Ralph Coates	1971–1977	248	23
Barry Daines	1971–1981	173	0
John Duncan	1974–1978	120	62
Keith Osgood	1974–1978	127	14
Chris Jones	1974–1982	185	42
Don McAllister	1975–1981	202	10
Glenn Hoddle	1975–1987	490	110
Gerry Armstrong	1976–1980	98	16
Peter Taylor	1976–1980	140	33
Jimmy Holmes	1977–1981	92	2
Garry Brooke	1978–1985	73	15
Ricardo Villa	1978–1983	179	25
John Lacy	1978–1983	152	3

Player	Years	Apps	Goals
Osvaldo Ardiles	1978–1982/1983–1988	311	25
Terry Yorath	1979–1981	62	1
Milija Aleksic	1979–1982	25	0
Mark Falco	1979–1986	236	89
Tony Galvin	1979–1987	73	31
Paul Miller	1979–1987	285	10
Chris Hughton	1979–1990	398	19
Steve Archibald	1980–1984	189	77
Garth Crooks	1980–1985	182	75
Graham Roberts	1980–1986	287	35
Tony Parks	1980–1988	37	0
Micky Hazard	1980–1985/1993–1995	170	25
Paul Price	1981–1984	62	0
Ally Dick	1981–1986	17	2
Ray Clemence	1981–1987	330	0
Gary Mabbutt	1982–1998	611	38
Gary Stevens	1983–1987	200	8
Danny Thomas	1983–1987	116	1
John Chiedozie	1984–1986	75	14
Clive Allen	1984–1988	135	84
Chris Waddle	1985–1989	173	42
Paul Allen	1985–1993	370	28
Richard Gough	1986–1987	65	2
Nico Claesen	1986–1988	63	23

THE CAST

Player	Years	Apps	Goals
Steve Hodge	1986–1988	54	9
Mitchell Thomas	1986–1991	157	6
Vinny Samways	1987–1994	247	17
Paul Gascoigne	1988–1991	112	33
Paul Stewart	1988–1992	171	37
Paul Walsh	1988–1992	156	21
Terry Fenwick	1988–1993	118	10
Guðni Bergsson	1988–1994	86	2
Erik Thorstvedt	1988–1996	218	0
David Howells	1988–1998	335	27
Gary Lineker	1989–1992	106	67
Pat Van Den Hauwe	1989–1993	145	0
Nayim	1989–1993	144	18
Steve Sedgley	1989–1994	211	11
Justin Edinburgh	1990–2000	276	1
Gordon Durie	1991–1993	78	17
Ian Walker	1991–2001	313	0
Nicky Barmby	1992–1995	108	27
Dean Austin	1992–1997	150	0
Sol Campbell	1992–2001	315	15
Teddy Sheringham	1992–1997/2001–2003	277	125
Darren Anderton	1992–2004	358	48
Colin Calderwood	1993–1999	199	7
Stephen Carr	1993–2004	270	8

Player	Years	Apps	Goals
Ronnie Rosenthal	1994–1997	100	11
Jürgen Klinsmann	1994–1995/1997–1998	68	38
Ruel Fox	1995–2000	129	15
Chris Armstrong	1995–2002	173	62
Andy Sinton	1996–1999	100	7
Allan Nielsen	1996–2000	115	18
Steffen Iversen	1996–2003	176	47
David Ginola	1997–2000	127	22
Ramon Vega	1997–2001	64	7
Stephen Clemence	1997–2003	109	3
Les Ferdinand	1997–2003	149	39
Øyvind Leonhardsen	1999–2002	72	11
Steffen Freund	1999–2003	131	0
Chris Perry	1999–2003	146	4
Tim Sherwood	1999–2003	118	16
Mauricio Taricco	1999–2004	156	2
Ledley King	1999–2012	318	12
Neil Sullivan	2000–2003	81	0
Gary Doherty	2000–2004	77	8
Sergei Rebrov	2000–2004	76	13
Simon Davies	2000–2005	146	18
Anthony Gardner	2000–2008	144	3
Gus Poyet	2001–2004	98	23
Christian Ziege	2001–2004	55	10

THE CAST

Player	Years	Apps	Goals
Kasey Keller	2001–2005	85	0
Jamie Redknapp	2002–2005	49	4
Robbie Keane	2002–2008/2009–2011	306	122
Frédéric Kanouté	2003–2005	73	21
Michael Carrick	2004–2006	75	2
Paul Robinson	2004–2008	175	1
Jermain Defoe	2004–2008/2009–2014	363	143
Jamie O'Hara	2005–2011	34	2
Mido	2005–2007	63	20
Teemu Tainio	2005–2008	83	3
Lee Young–pyo	2005–2008	93	0
Tom Huddlestone	2005–2013	209	15
Jermaine Jenas	2005–2013	202	26
Michael Dawson	2005–2014	324	10
Aaron Lennon	2005–2015	364	30
Danny Murphy	2006–2007	22	2
Steed Malbranque	2006–2008	62	6
Dimitar Berbatov	2006–2008	102	46
Pascal Chimbonda	2006–2008/2009–2009	103	4
Didier Zokora	2006–2009	134	0
Benoît Assou–Ekotto	2006–2015	200	4
Darren Bent	2007–2009	79	25
Gareth Bale	2007–2013/2020–present	214	59

Player	Years	Apps	Goals
Younès Kaboul	2007–2008/2010–2015	153	8
Alan Hutton	2008–2011	66	2
Jonathan Woodgate	2008–2011	65	3
Vedran Ćorluka	2008–2012	109	1
Niko Kranjčar	2008–2012	71	11
Luka Modrić	2008–2012	159	17
Roman Pavlyuchenko	2008–2012	113	42
David Bentley	2008–2013	62	5
Heurelho Gomes	2008–2014	130	0
Andros Townsend	2008–2016	93	11
Ryan Mason	2008–2016	70	4
Peter Crouch	2009–2011	93	24
Wilson Palacios	2009–2011	86	1
Sébastien Bassong	2009–2012	71	3
Kyle Walker	2010–2017	228	4
Rafael van der Vaart	2010–2012	78	28
Sandro	2010–2014	96	3
Danny Rose	2010–present	214	10
Scott Parker	2011–2013	63	0
Emmanuel Adebayor	2011–2015	113	42
Harry Kane	2011–present	312	205
Gylfi Sigurðsson	2012–2014	83	13
Mousa Dembélé	2012–2018	249	10
Hugo Lloris	2012–present	347	0

Player	Years	Apps	Goals
Jan Vertonghen	2012–2020	315	14
Harry Winks	2013–present	159	3
Paulinho	2013–2015	67	10
Christian Eriksen	2013–2020	304	69
Nabil Bentaleb	2013–2016	66	1
Nacer Chadli	2013–2016	119	25
Roberto Soldado	2013–2015	76	16
Erik Lamela	2013–present	235	35
Eric Dier	2014–present	261	11
Ben Davies	2014–present	213	5
Michel Vorm	2014–2020	13	0
Toby Alderweireld	2015–present	217	9
Dele Alli	2015–present	234	64
Son Heung–min	2015–present	255	101
Kieran Trippier	2015–2019	114	2
Moussa Sissoko	2016–present	183	5
Victor Wanyama	2016–2020	97	7
Davinson Sánchez	2017–present	132	1
Serge Aurier	2017–present	97	7
Juan Foyth	2017–present	5	0
Paulo Gazzaniga	2017–present	22	0
Lucas Moura	2018–present	133	28
Oliver Skipp	2018–present	15	0
Giovani Lo Celso	2019–present	57	7

Player	Years	Apps	Goals
Tanguy Ndombele	2019–present	22	0
Steven Bergwijn	2020–present	14	0
Pierre–Emile Højbjerg	2020–present	34	1
Japhet Tanganga	2020	6	0
Matt Doherty	2020–present	15	0
Sergio Reguilon	2020–present	23	0
Joe Hart	2020–present	5	0
Joe Rodon	2020–present	14	0
Ryan Sessegnon	2019–present	6	0
Carlos Vinicius	2020–present	9	1
Troy Parrot	2020–present	2	0
Dane Scarlett	2020–present	1	0

(Figures correct at time of going to print)

Other Books by Norman Giller

(www.normangillerbooks.com)

Headlines Deadlines All My Life (an autobiography)
Banks of England (with Gordon Banks)
Bobby Moore, The Master
Footballing Fifties, When the Game Was in Black and White
The Glory and the Grief (with George Graham)
Banks v Pelé (with Terry Baker, Pelé and Gordon Banks)
Spurs '67, the First all-London FA Cup Final (introduced by
   Pat Jennings and Ron 'Chopper' Harris)
Lane of Dreams (History of White Hart Lane)
Tottenham: The Managing Game
Bill Nicholson Revisited (40 years of conversation
   with 'Mr Spurs')
Danny Blanchflower This WAS His Life (the story Eamonn
   Andrews could not tell)

The Golden Double (all you need to know about the historic 1960/61 season)

Football And All That (an irreverent history of the game, introduced by Jimmy Greaves)

The Seventies Revisited (with Kevin Keegan)

The Final Score (with the 'Voice of Football', Brian Moore)

ABC of Soccer Sense (Tommy Docherty on football tactics)

Billy Wright, A Hero for All Seasons (official biography)

Billy Wright, My Dad (with his daughter Vicky Wright)

The Rat Race (with Tommy Docherty, managing with the gloves off)

Denis Compton (the untold stories)

McFootball, the Scottish Heroes of the English Game

Chopper's Chelsea (with Ron Harris)

Hammers '80 (introduced by Trevor Brooking and featuring the 1980 FA Cup final triumph)

The Book of Rugby Lists (with Gareth Edwards)

The Book of Tennis Lists (with John Newcombe)

The Book of Golf Lists (majoring on Jack Nicklaus)

Book of Cricket Lists (with Tom Graveney)

Top Ten Cricket Book (with Tom Graveney)

Books in collaboration with Jimmy Greaves:

This One's On Me (Jimmy's story of how he beat the bottle)

Novels:

The Final

The Ball Game

The Boss

The Second Half

Let's Be Honest (with Reg Gutteridge)

Greavsie's Heroes and Entertainers

World Cup History (from Uruguay 1930)

GOALS! (100 major players selecting their finest goal)

Stop the Game, I Want to Get On (crazy and unbelievable moments on and off the pitch)

The Book of Football Lists

Taking Sides (matching the greatest teams against each other)

Funny Old Games (with Ian St John)

Sports Quiz Challenge

Sports Quiz Challenge 2

It's A Funny Old Life (the switch from footballer to television celebrity)

Saint & Greavsie's 1990 World Cup Special (every match, every goal, every team in Italia '90)

Greavsie At Seventy (a celebration, with Terry Baker and Michael Giller)

The Sixties Revisited

Don't Shoot the Manager (the adventures and records of England football managers)

Boxing books:

The Ali Files (his fights, his foes, his feats, his fees, his fate)

My Most Memorable Fights (with Henry Cooper)

How to Box (with Henry Cooper)

Henry Cooper's 100 Greatest Boxers

Henry Cooper, A Hero for All Time (official biography)

Know What I Mean (with Frank Bruno)

Eye of the Tiger (with Frank Bruno)

From Zero to Hero (with Frank Bruno)

Watt's My Name (with Jim Watt)

Mike Tyson Biography (with Reg Gutteridge)

Mike Tyson, the Release of Power (with Reg Gutteridge)

Crown of Thorns, the World Heavyweight Championship (with Neil Duncanson)

Fighting for Peace (Barry McGuigan biography, with Peter Batt)

The Real Rocky (Dial M for Marciano) Big Fight Quiz Book

Other sports books:

World's Greatest Cricket Matches

World's Greatest Football Matches

Golden Heroes (history of the FWA Footballer of the Year, with Dennis Signy)

The Judge (1,001 arguments settled)

The Great Football IQ Quiz Book ('The Judge' from *The Sun*)

The Judge Book of Sports Answers

The Concorde Club (The first 50 years, with Col Mathieson)

Timeframed: Great Moments in British History (Partwork)

How to Self Publish (trust me, I'm an author)

The Marathon Kings

The Golden Milers (with Sir Roger Bannister)

Olympic Heroes (with Brendan Foster)

Olympics Handbook 1980

Olympics Handbook 1984

TV Quiz Trivia

Sports Quiz Trivia

TVIQ Puzzle Book

Gloria Hunniford's TV Challenge

Cricket Heroes (with Eric Morecambe)

Lucky the Fox (with Barbara Wright)

July 30 1966, Football's Longest Day

World Cup 2010 (with Michael Giller)

The Glory-Glory Game (Spurs Writers' Club)

Comedy novels:
Carry On Doctor
Carry On England
Carry On Loving
Carry On Up the Khyber
Carry On Abroad
Carry On Henry
What A Carry On

Novels:
A Stolen Life
Mike Baldwin: Mr Heartbreak (with Johnny Briggs)
Hitler's Final Victim
Keys to Paradise (with Jenny Robbins)
The Glory and the Greed
A Blaze of Lives
The Contenders
One of the King's Horses
The Bung

Books in collaboration with Ricky Tomlinson:
Football My Arse
Celebrities My Arse
Cheers My Arse
Reading My Arse (the search for the Rock Island Line)

Crime novels featuring J.C. Campbell:
Beyond the Krays
The Henley Murders
The Fleet Street Murders
The Football Murders

Children's books:
Tales of Uncle Rhymo
Rhyming Stories from Nicely-Spicely Land
Duncan the Talking Football

Author's note: If you wish to correspond with me, I am always happy to field your email comments at author@ normangillerbooks.com

Keep alive the spirit of Bill Nicholson, Father of Spurs.

COYS!